Shojo Beat

VAMPIRE KNIGHT MEMORIES

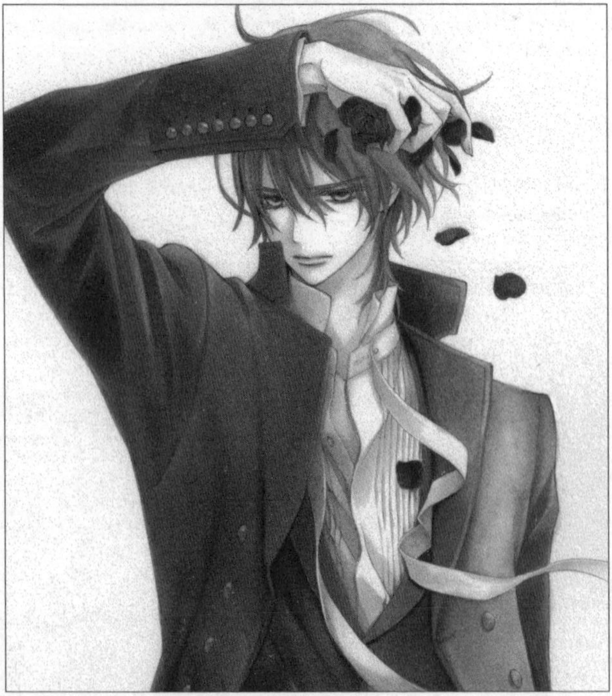

VOLUME

7

STORY & ART BY

Matsuri Hino

The Story of VAMPIRE KNIGHT

Previously...

———— At the End of *Vampire Knight* ————

◆ Kaname had been planning to kill all purebloods in order to protect Yuki, but he chose to entrust the future to Yuki and Zero instead. He threw his heart into the furnace, and that became the ancestor metal used to create weapons capable of killing vampires. He then slept in a coffin of ice.

◆ A thousand years later, Yuki gave her life to revive Kaname as a human being. Ren and Ai deliver the words Yuki left to Kaname...

———— *Vampire Knight: Memories* Begins ————

◆ Kaname has lost his memory after being revived after a thousand years. Kaname desires to know what happened with the woman he can't quite remember, so his daughters begin to tell him stories from the past thousand years.

◆ During the time Kaname was in the coffin of ice, the split between humans and vampires widened. In order to prevent the worst possible outcome—a massacre of the humans by the vampires—Yuki took on the role of a "traitor" and disappeared. Zero followed her, and the two began their journey. Ai, who was entrusted with the rest, lead the vampires to isolate themselves from the outside world...

CHARACTERS

YUKI KURAN (CROSS)

The adopted daughter of the headmaster of Cross Academy. She is a pureblood vampire and the princess of the noble Kuran family. She has always adored Kaname, even when she did not have her memory.

KANAME KURAN

A pureblood vampire and the progenitor of the Kurans. He is Yuki's fiancé and was raised as her sibling. He threw his heart into the furnace to become the ancestor metal for weapons that would kill vampires.

ZERO KIRYU

He was born into a family of vampire hunters and later was turned into a vampire. He had a strong hatred toward vampires, but he decided to live his life with Yuki.

REN AND AI

Yuki's children

HANABUSA AIDO

He was an upperclassman in the Night Class. He is working to create a medicine that will turn vampires into humans...

VAMPIRE KNIGHT

MEMORIES

CONTENTS

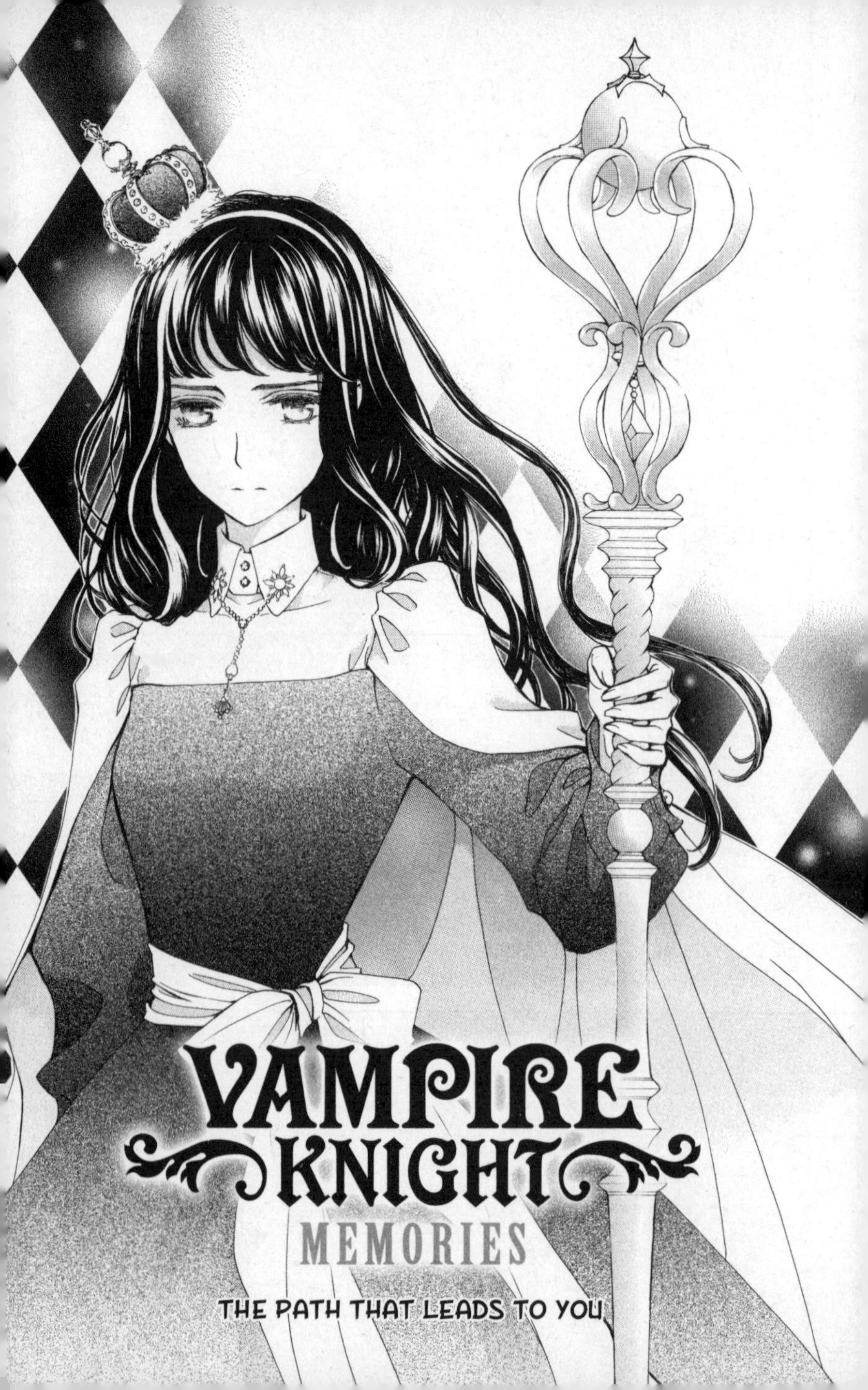
VAMPIRE KNIGHT
MEMORIES
THE PATH THAT LEADS TO YOU

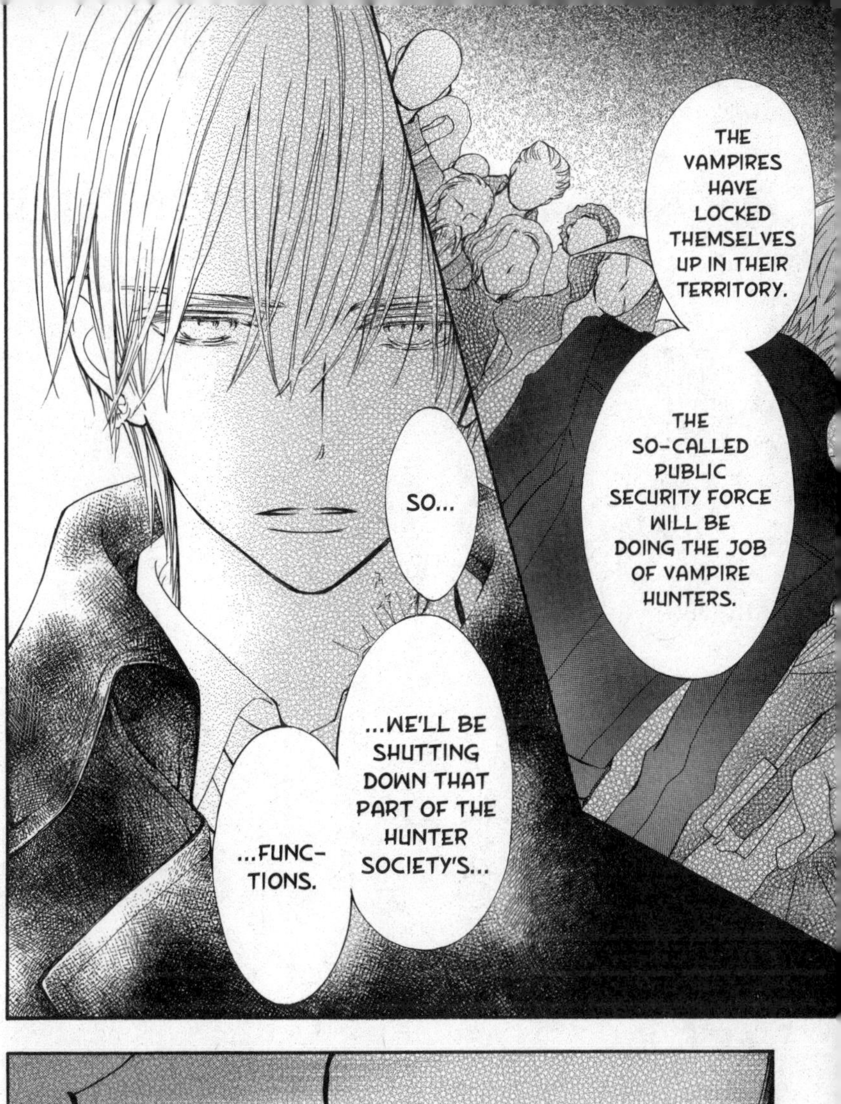
THE VAMPIRES HAVE LOCKED THEMSELVES UP IN THEIR TERRITORY.
THE SO-CALLED PUBLIC SECURITY FORCE WILL BE DOING THE JOB OF VAMPIRE HUNTERS.
SO...
...WE'LL BE SHUTTING DOWN THAT PART OF THE HUNTER SOCIETY'S...
...FUNC-TIONS.
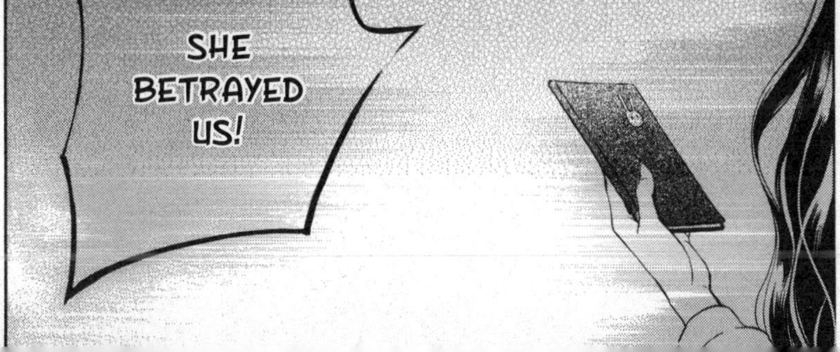
SHE BETRAYED US!

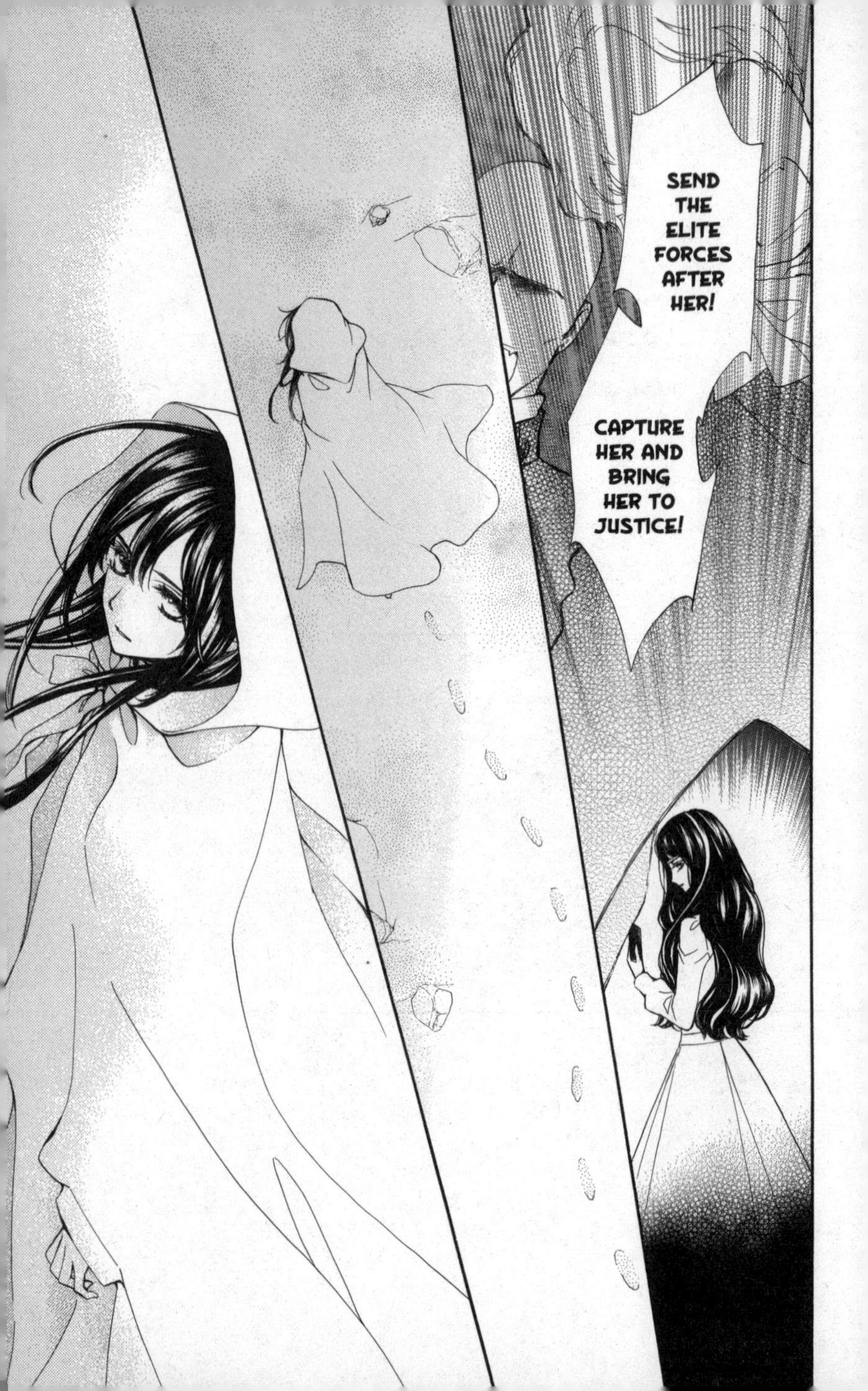
SEND THE ELITE FORCES AFTER HER!
CAPTURE HER AND BRING HER TO JUSTICE!

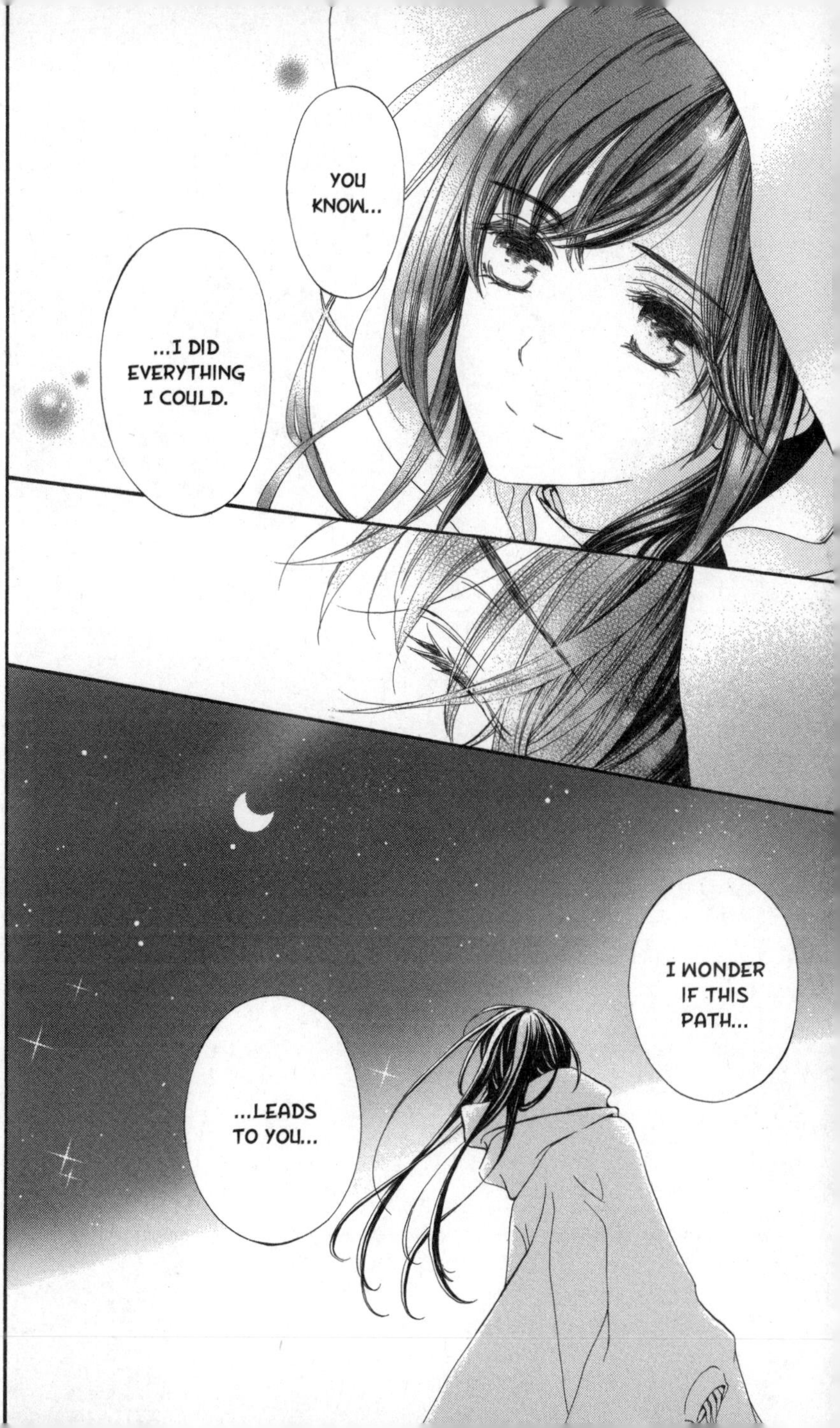
YOU KNOW...
...I DID EVERYTHING I COULD.
I WONDER IF THIS PATH...
...LEADS TO YOU...

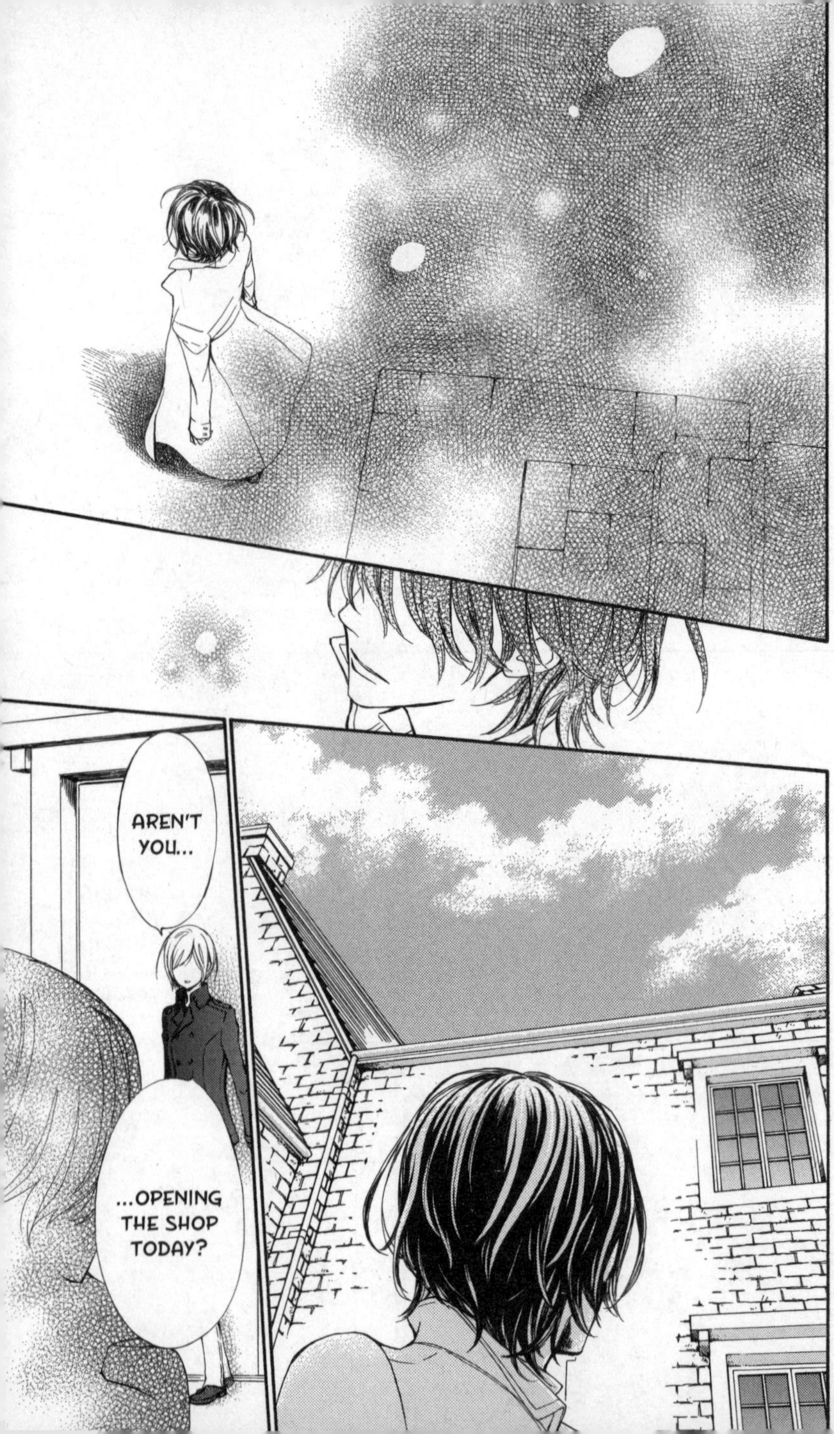
AREN'T YOU...
...OPENING THE SHOP TODAY?

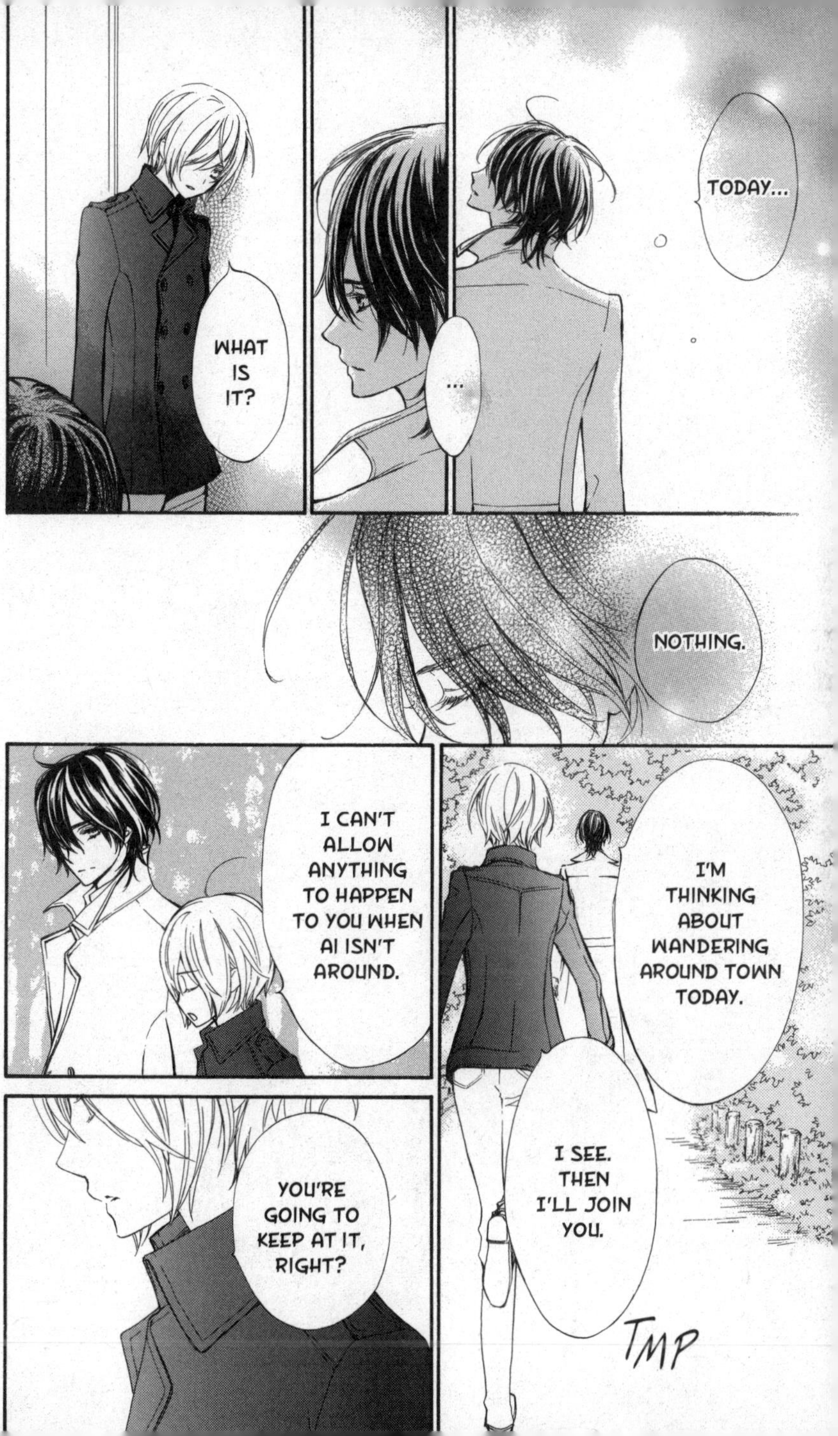
TODAY...
...
WHAT IS IT?
NOTHING.
I'M THINKING ABOUT WANDERING AROUND TOWN TODAY.
I SEE. THEN I'LL JOIN YOU.
TMP
I CAN'T ALLOW ANYTHING TO HAPPEN TO YOU WHEN AI ISN'T AROUND.
YOU'RE GOING TO KEEP AT IT, RIGHT?

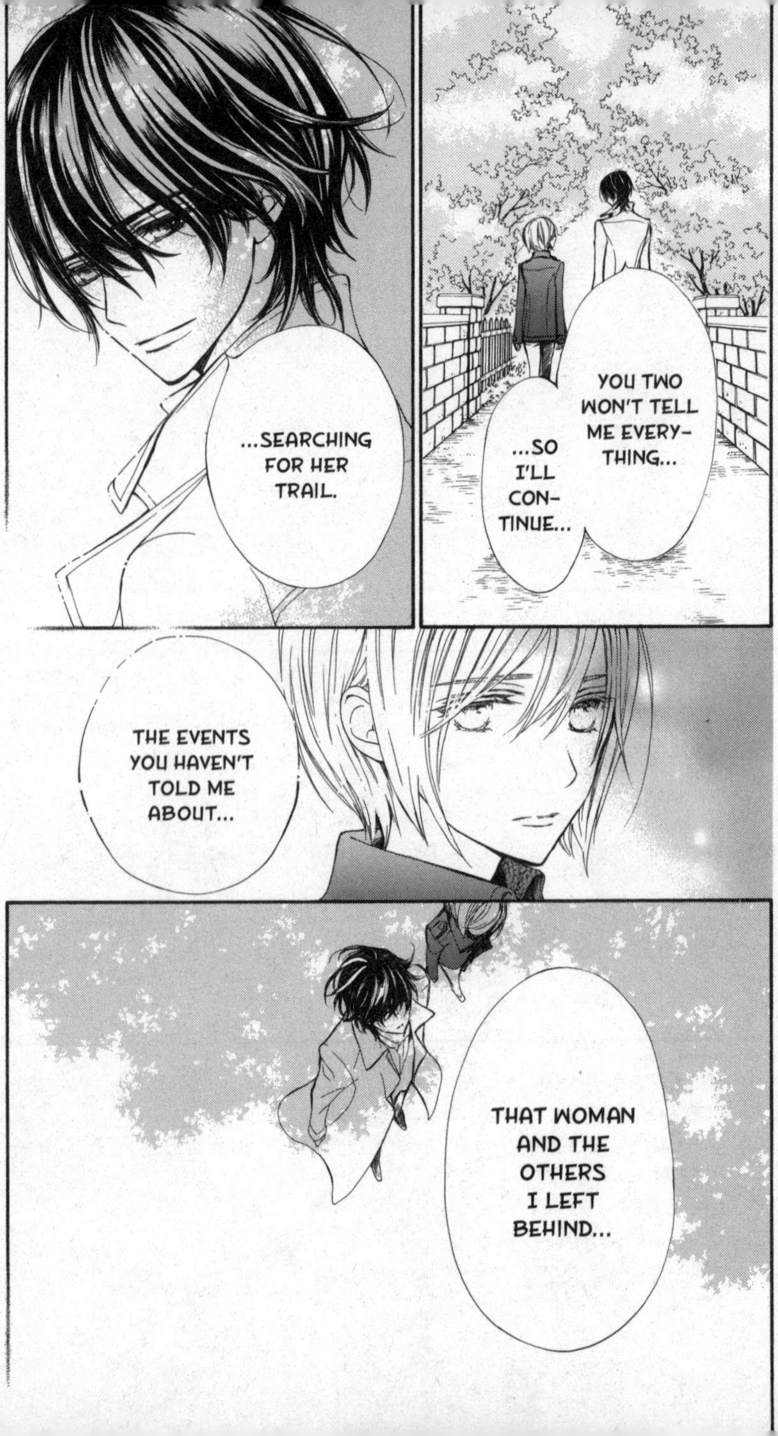
YOU TWO WON'T TELL ME EVERY-THING...
...SO I'LL CON-TINUE...
...SEARCHING FOR HER TRAIL.
THE EVENTS YOU HAVEN'T TOLD ME ABOUT...
THAT WOMAN AND THE OTHERS I LEFT BEHIND...

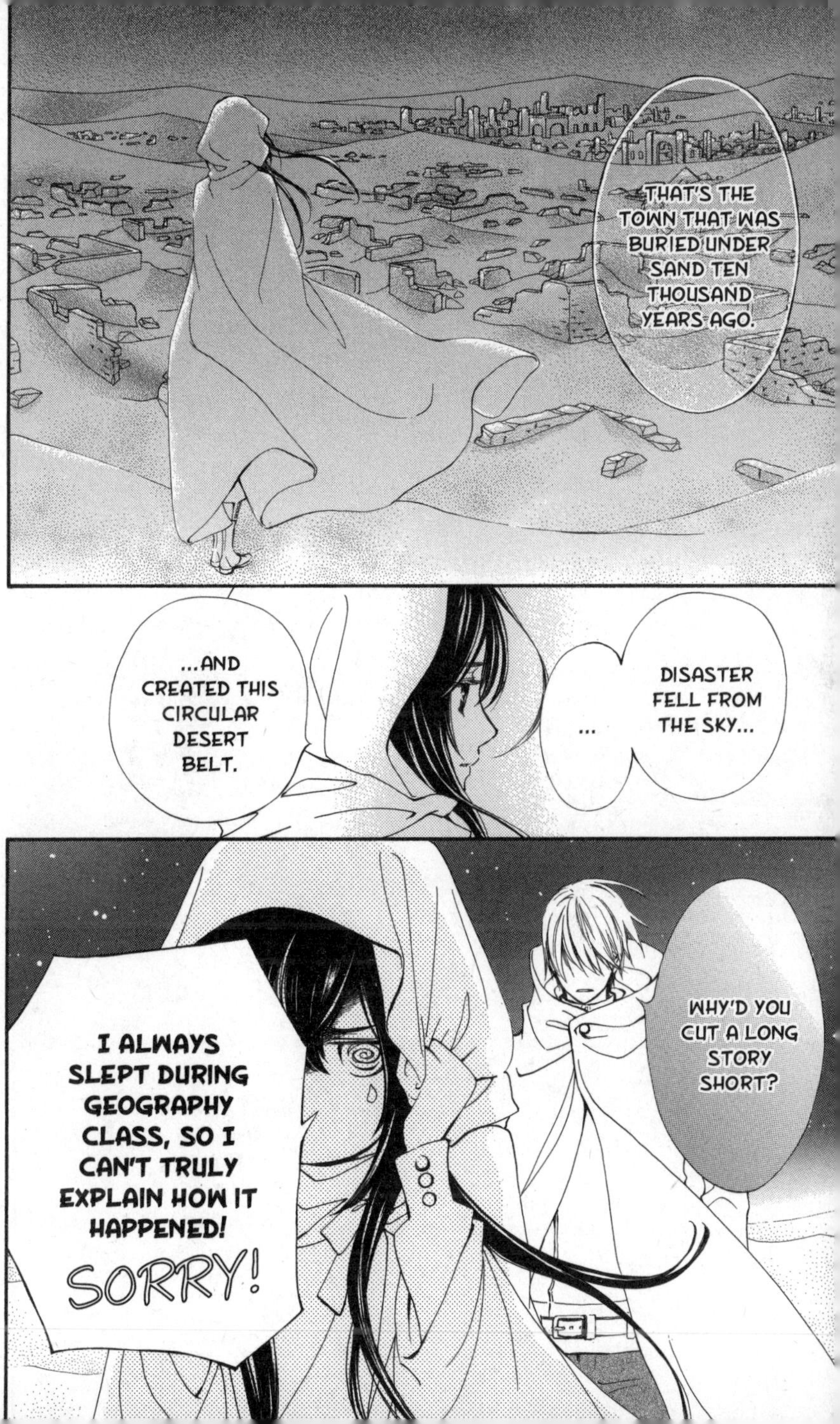
THAT'S THE TOWN THAT WAS BURIED UNDER SAND TEN THOUSAND YEARS AGO.
... DISASTER FELL FROM THE SKY...
...AND CREATED THIS CIRCULAR DESERT BELT.
WHY'D YOU CUT A LONG STORY SHORT?
I ALWAYS SLEPT DURING GEOGRAPHY CLASS, SO I CAN'T TRULY EXPLAIN HOW IT HAPPENED!
SORRY!

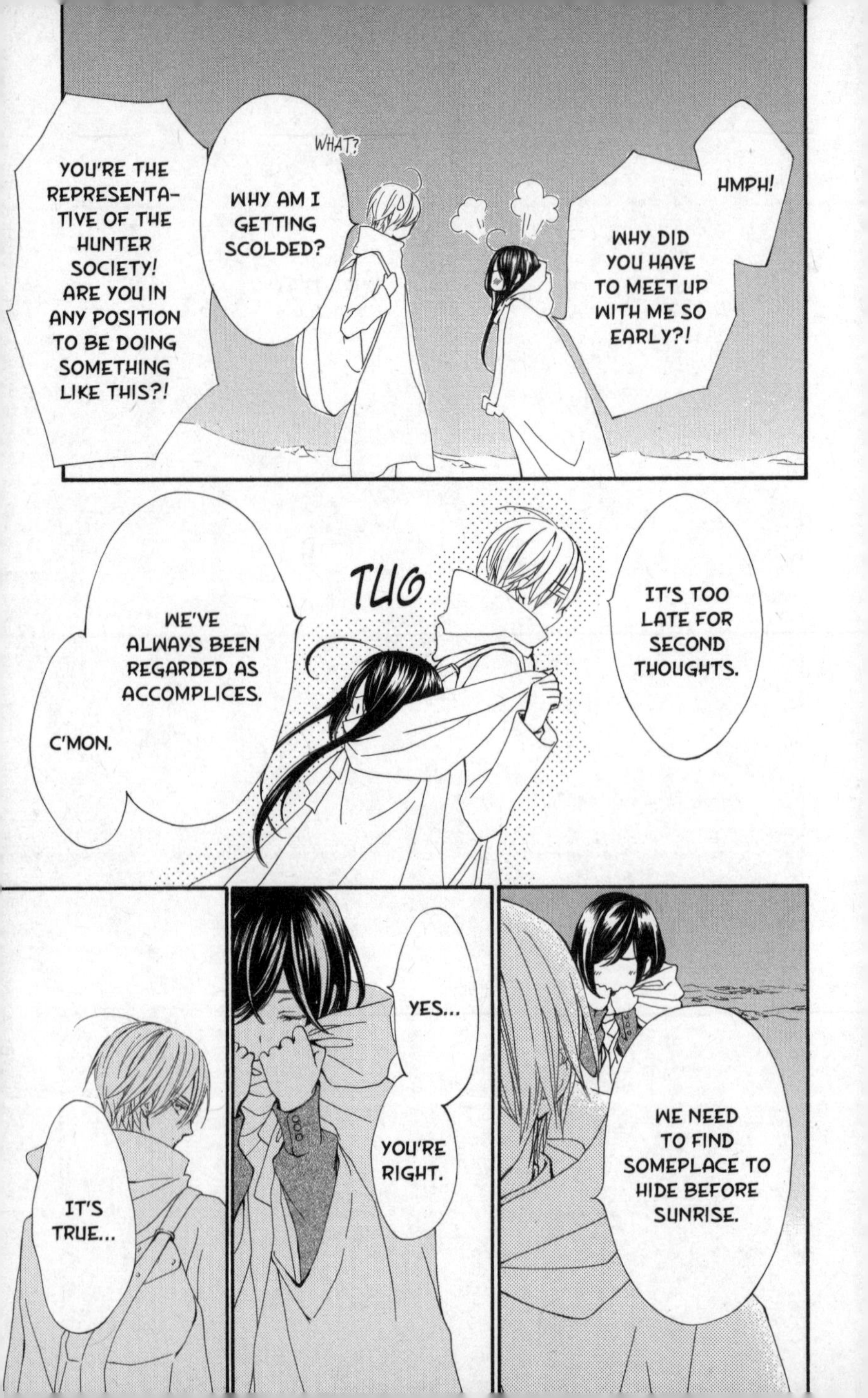
HMPH!
WHY DID YOU HAVE TO MEET UP WITH ME SO EARLY?!
WHAT?
WHY AM I GETTING SCOLDED?
YOU'RE THE REPRESENTA-TIVE OF THE HUNTER SOCIETY! ARE YOU IN ANY POSITION TO BE DOING SOMETHING LIKE THIS?!
IT'S TOO LATE FOR SECOND THOUGHTS.
TUG
WE'VE ALWAYS BEEN REGARDED AS ACCOMPLICES.
C'MON.
WE NEED TO FIND SOMEPLACE TO HIDE BEFORE SUNRISE.
YES...
YOU'RE RIGHT.
IT'S TRUE...

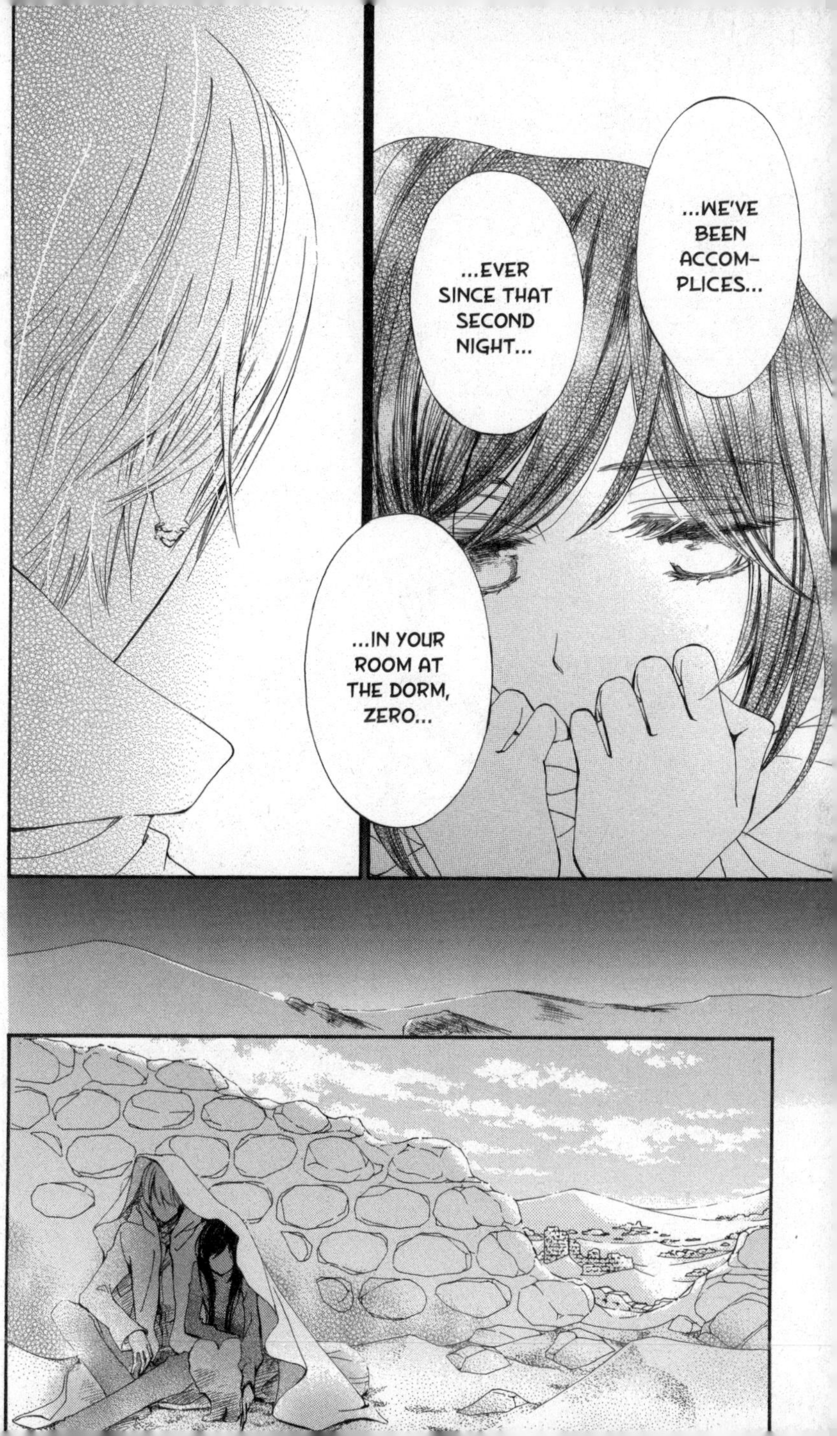
...WE'VE BEEN ACCOM-PLICES...
...EVER SINCE THAT SECOND NIGHT...
...IN YOUR ROOM AT THE DORM, ZERO...

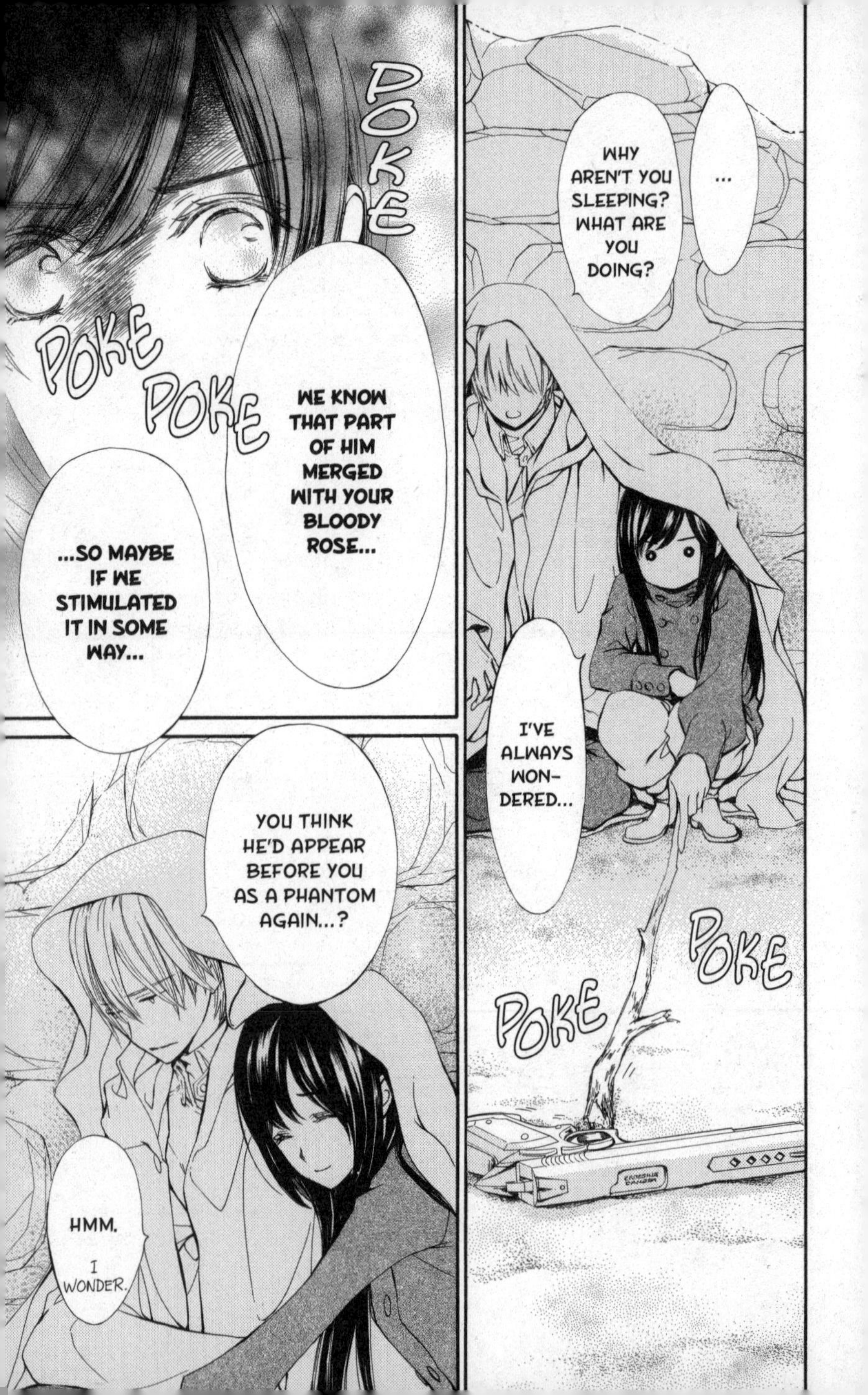
...
WHY AREN'T YOU SLEEPING? WHAT ARE YOU DOING?
I'VE ALWAYS WONDERED...
POKE
POKE
POKE
POKE
POKE
WE KNOW THAT PART OF HIM MERGED WITH YOUR BLOODY ROSE...
...SO MAYBE IF WE STIMULATED IT IN SOME WAY...
YOU THINK HE'D APPEAR BEFORE YOU AS A PHANTOM AGAIN...?
HMM. I WONDER.

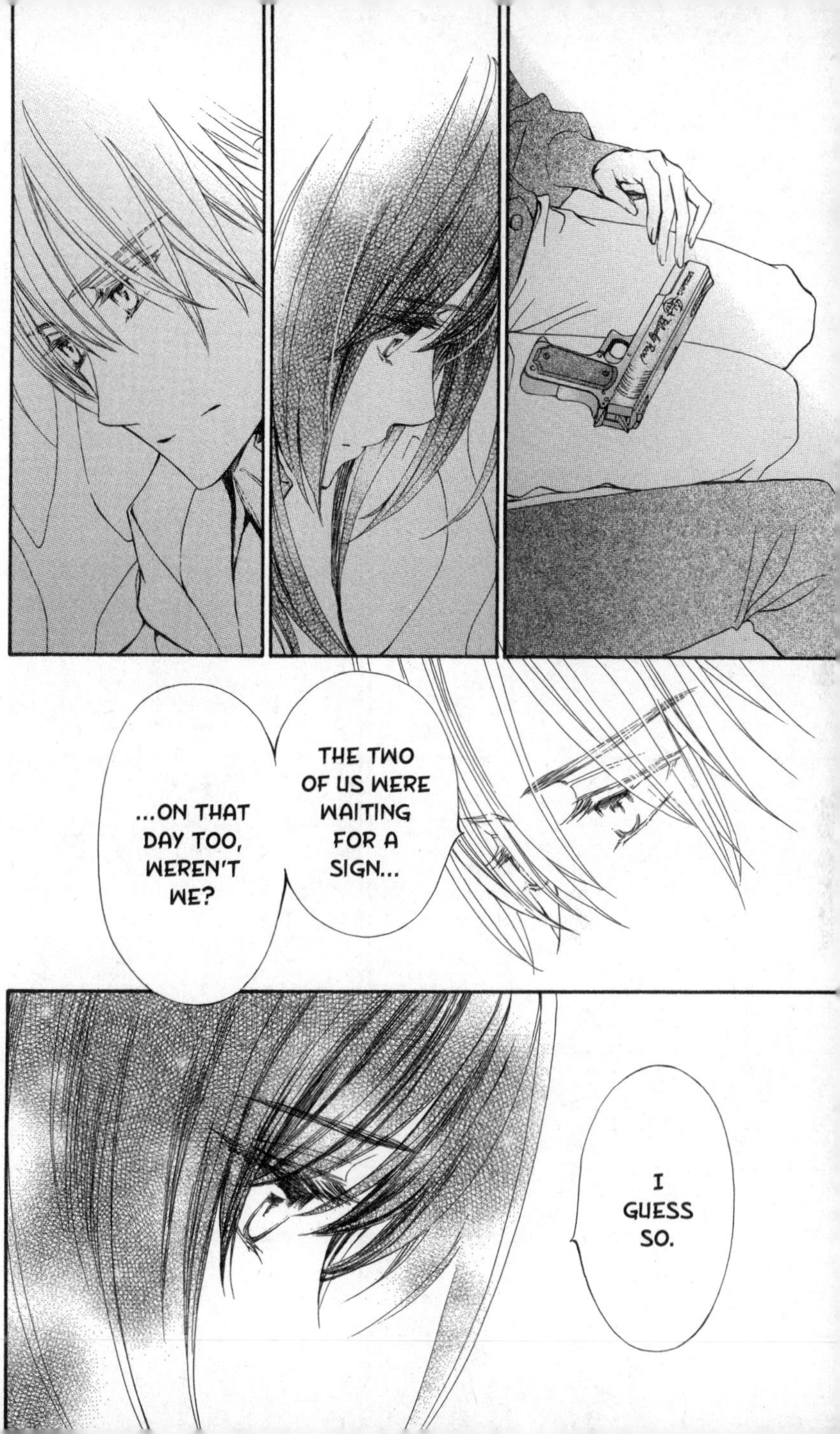
THE TWO OF US WERE WAITING FOR A SIGN...
...ON THAT DAY TOO, WEREN'T WE?
I GUESS SO.

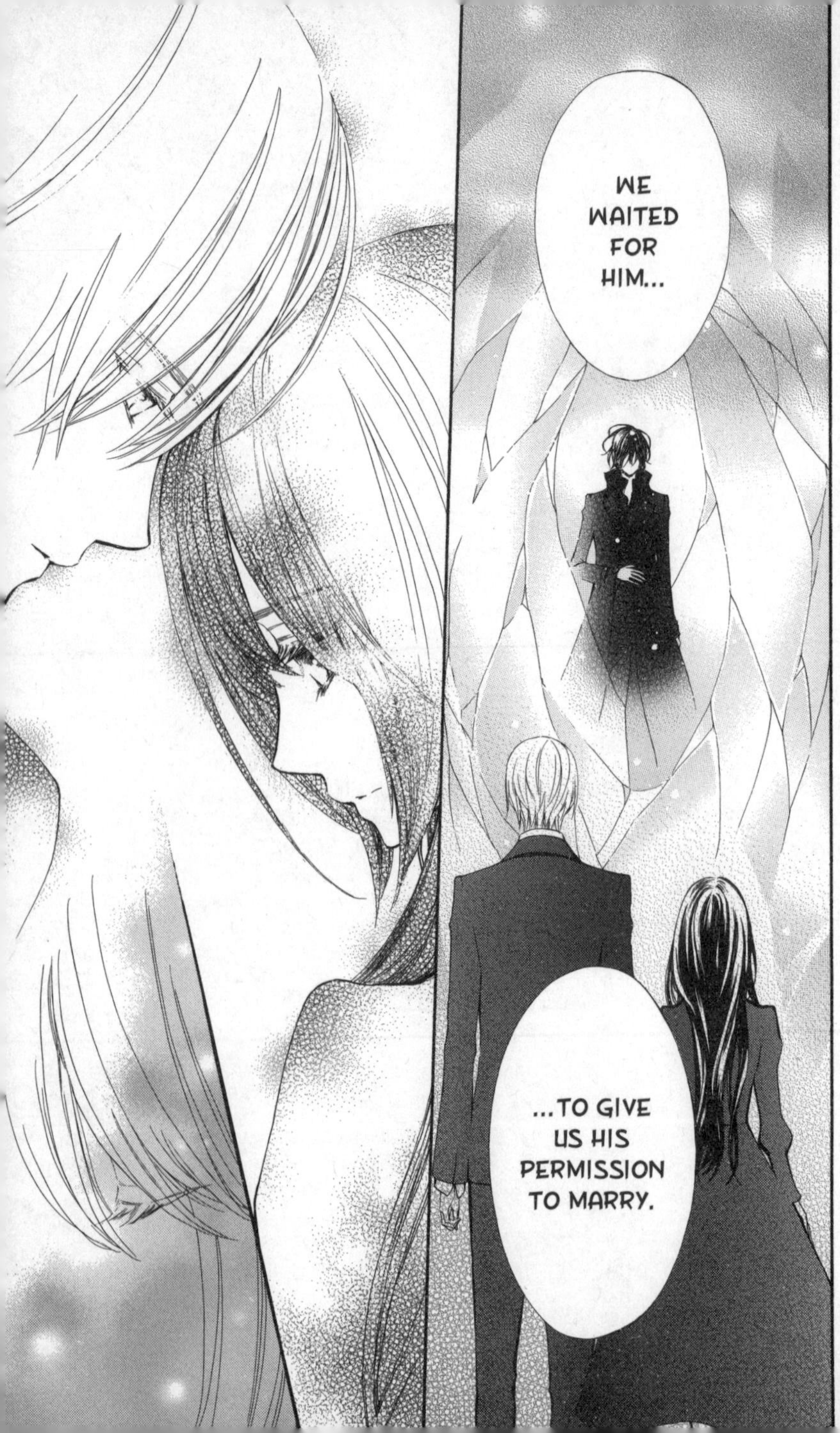
WE WAITED FOR HIM...
...TO GIVE US HIS PERMISSION TO MARRY.

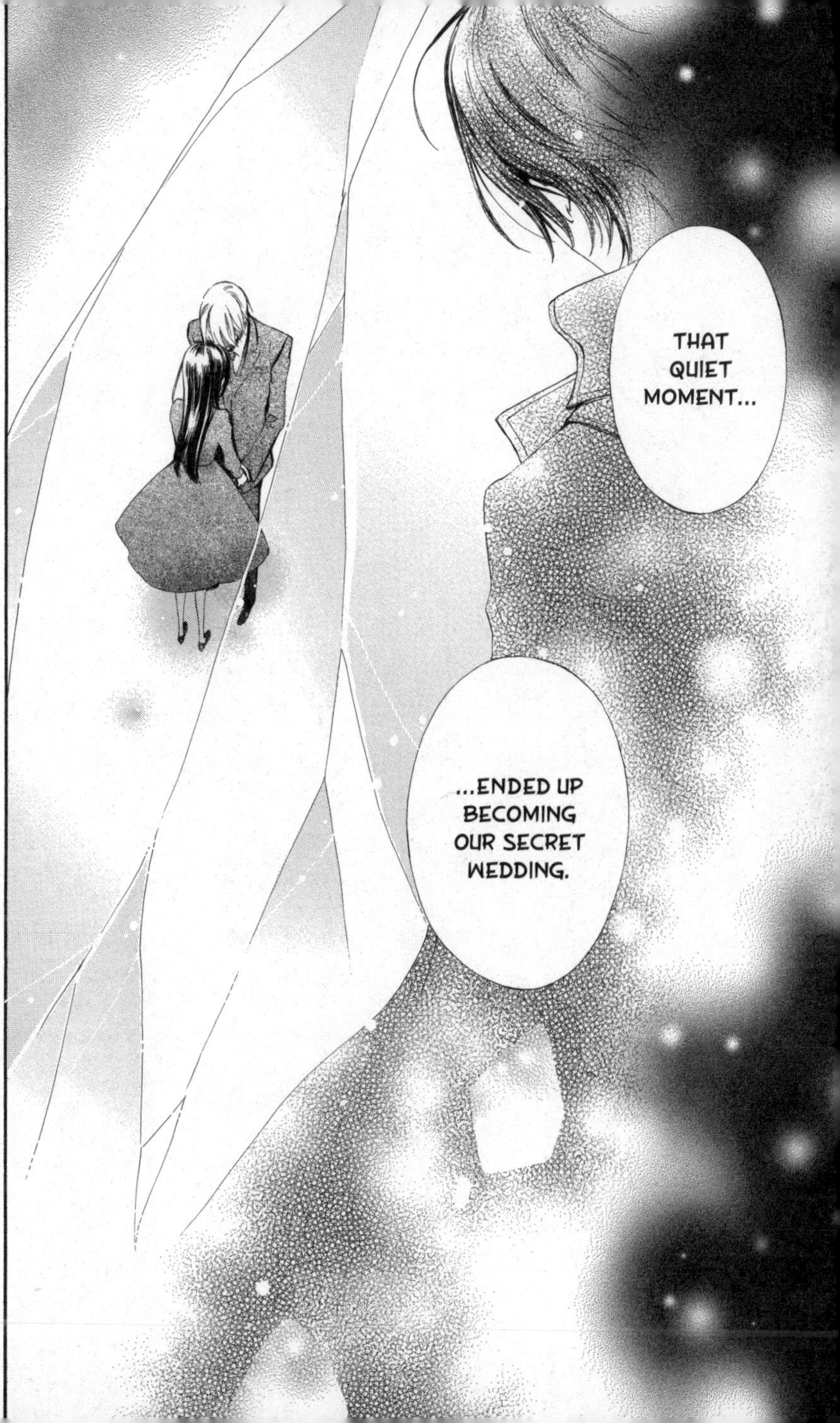
THAT QUIET MOMENT...
...ENDED UP BECOMING OUR SECRET WEDDING.

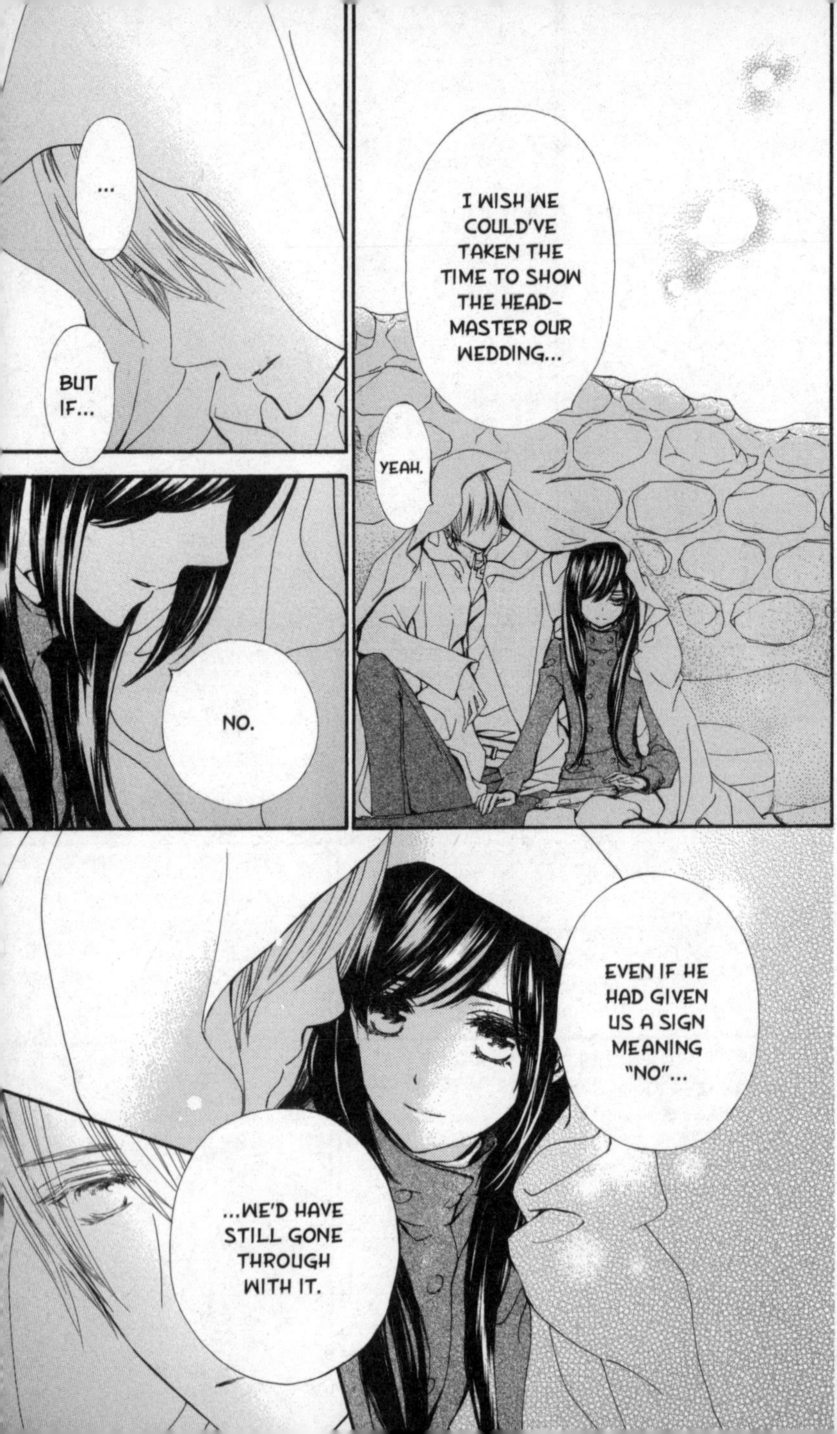
I WISH WE COULD'VE TAKEN THE TIME TO SHOW THE HEAD-MASTER OUR WEDDING...
YEAH.
...
BUT IF...
NO.
EVEN IF HE HAD GIVEN US A SIGN MEANING "NO"...
...WE'D HAVE STILL GONE THROUGH WITH IT.

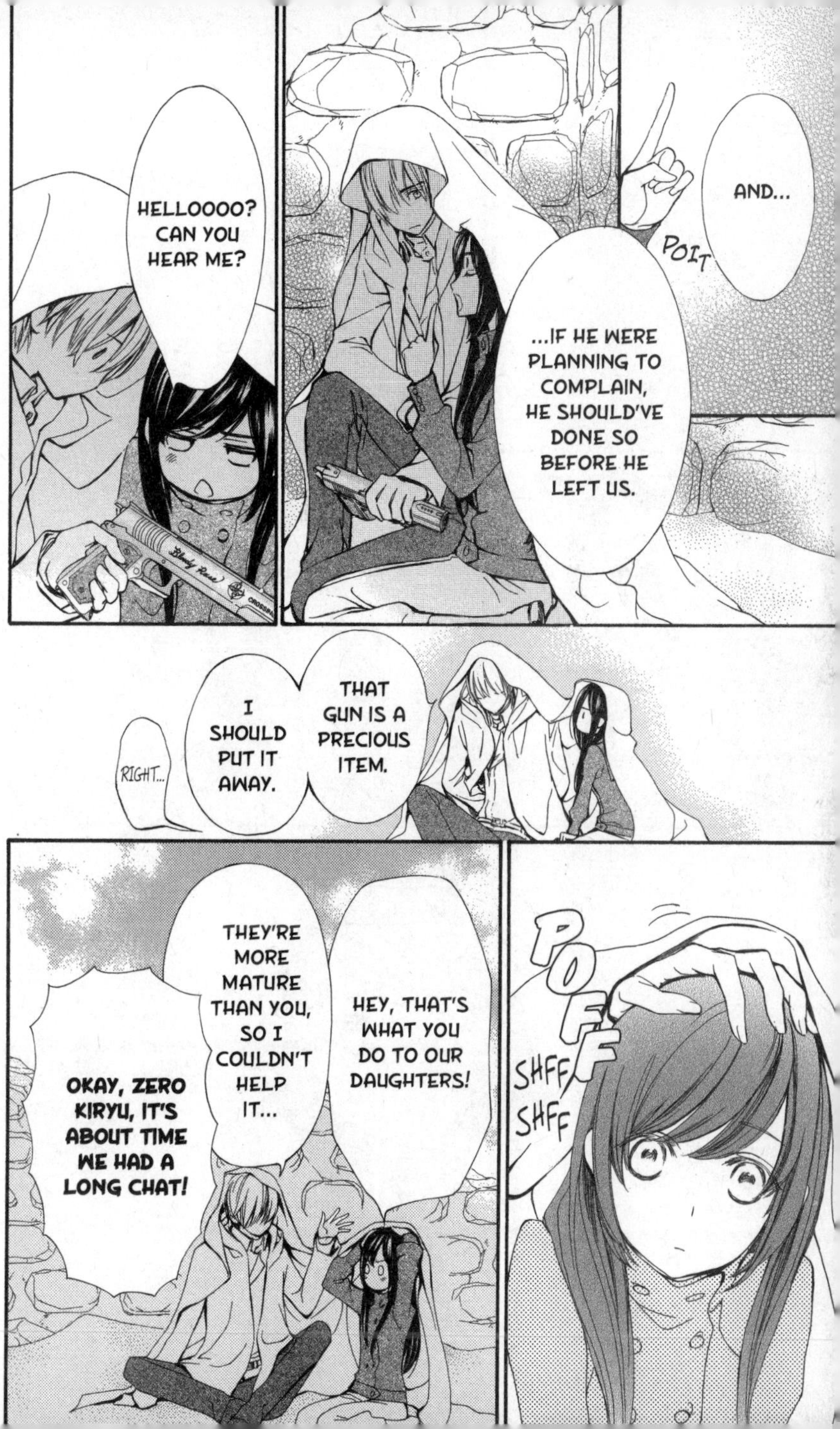
AND...
POIT
...IF HE WERE PLANNING TO COMPLAIN, HE SHOULD'VE DONE SO BEFORE HE LEFT US.
HELLOOOO? CAN YOU HEAR ME?
THAT GUN IS A PRECIOUS ITEM.
I SHOULD PUT IT AWAY.
RIGHT...
POFF
SHFF SHFF
HEY, THAT'S WHAT YOU DO TO OUR DAUGHTERS!
THEY'RE MORE MATURE THAN YOU, SO I COULDN'T HELP IT...
OKAY, ZERO KIRYU, IT'S ABOUT TIME WE HAD A LONG CHAT!

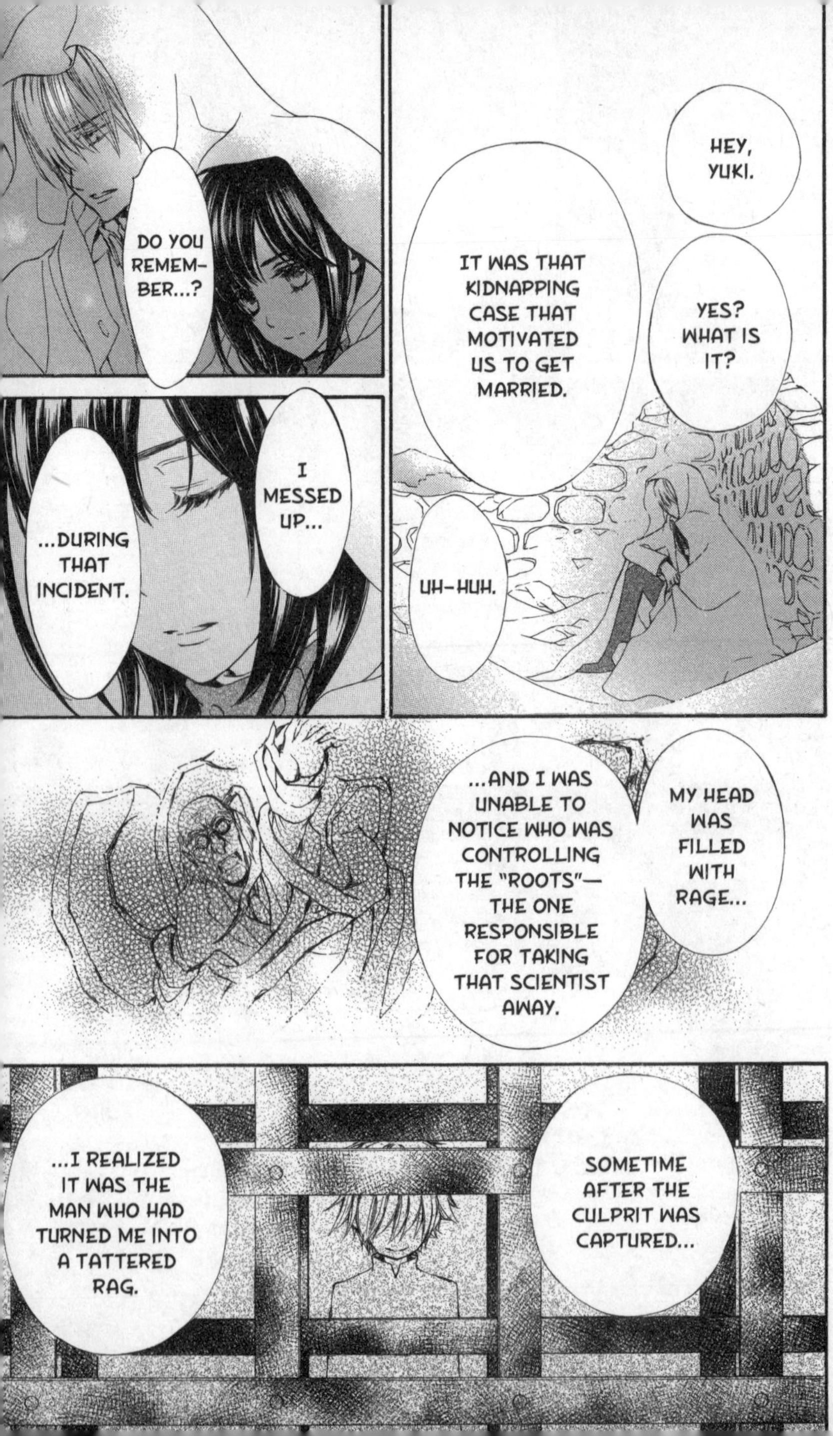
HEY, YUKI.
YES? WHAT IS IT?
IT WAS THAT KIDNAPPING CASE THAT MOTIVATED US TO GET MARRIED.
UH-HUH.
DO YOU REMEM-BER...?
I MESSED UP...
...DURING THAT INCIDENT.
MY HEAD WAS FILLED WITH RAGE...
...AND I WAS UNABLE TO NOTICE WHO WAS CONTROLLING THE "ROOTS"—THE ONE RESPONSIBLE FOR TAKING THAT SCIENTIST AWAY.
SOMETIME AFTER THE CULPRIT WAS CAPTURED...
...I REALIZED IT WAS THE MAN WHO HAD TURNED ME INTO A TATTERED RAG.

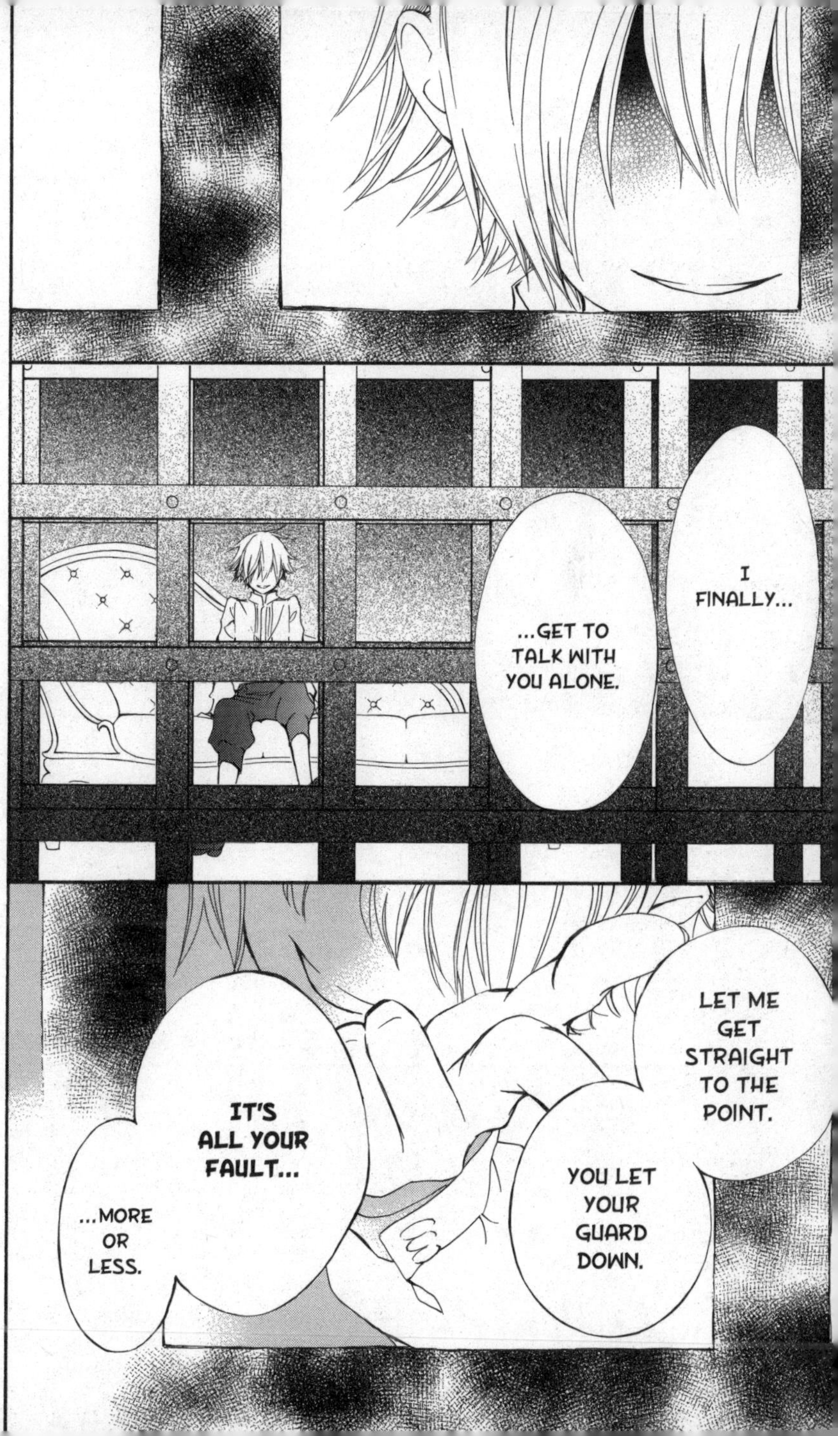
I FINALLY...
...GET TO TALK WITH YOU ALONE.
LET ME GET STRAIGHT TO THE POINT.
YOU LET YOUR GUARD DOWN.
IT'S ALL YOUR FAULT...
...MORE OR LESS.

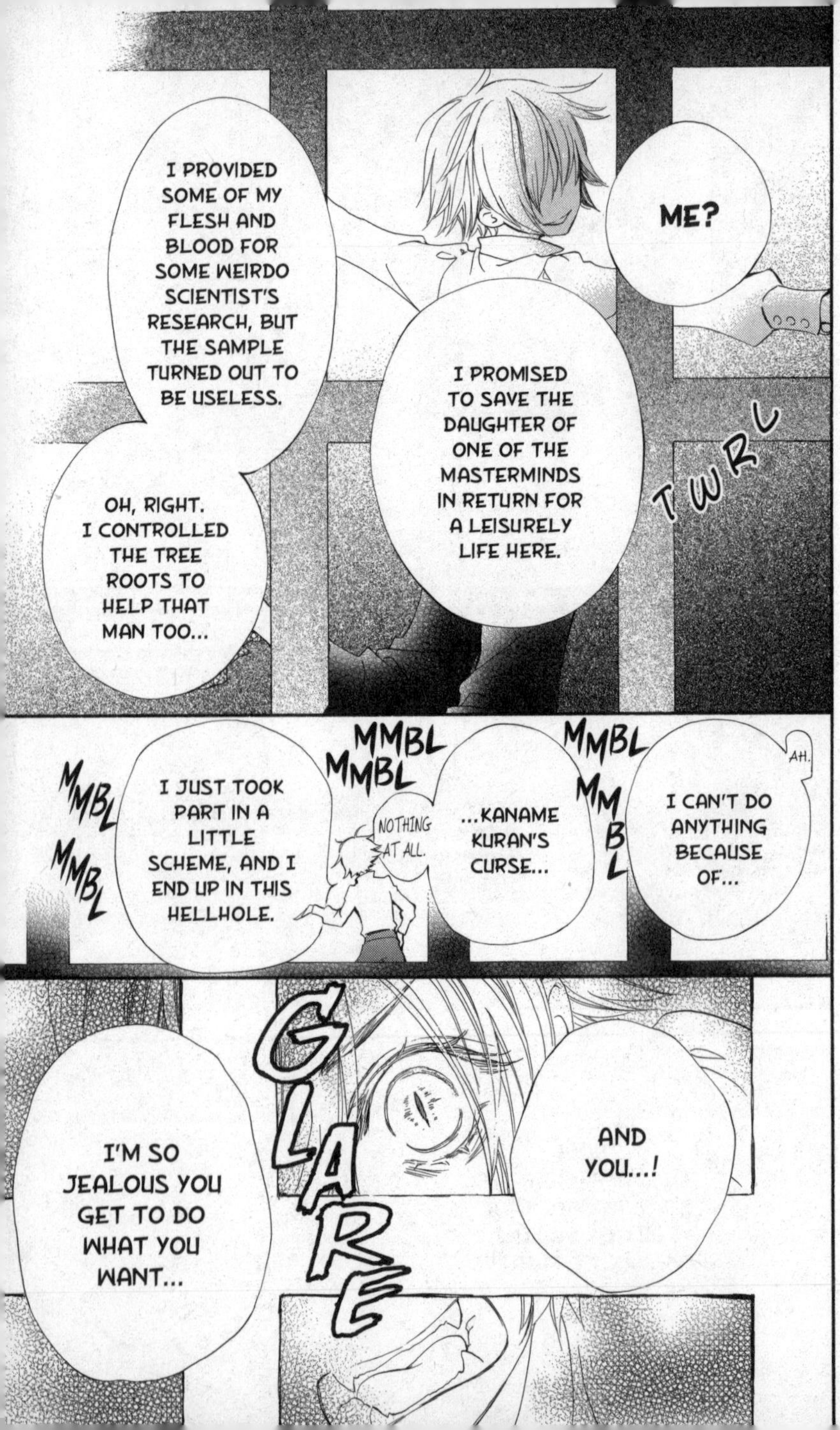
ME?
I PROMISED TO SAVE THE DAUGHTER OF ONE OF THE MASTERMINDS IN RETURN FOR A LEISURELY LIFE HERE.
TWRL
I PROVIDED SOME OF MY FLESH AND BLOOD FOR SOME WEIRDO SCIENTIST'S RESEARCH, BUT THE SAMPLE TURNED OUT TO BE USELESS.
OH, RIGHT. I CONTROLLED THE TREE ROOTS TO HELP THAT MAN TOO...
AH.
I CAN'T DO ANYTHING BECAUSE OF...
MMBL
MMBL
...KANAME KURAN'S CURSE...
MMBL
MMBL
NOTHING AT ALL.
I JUST TOOK PART IN A LITTLE SCHEME, AND I END UP IN THIS HELLHOLE.
MMBL
MMBL
AND YOU...!
GLARE
I'M SO JEALOUS YOU GET TO DO WHAT YOU WANT...

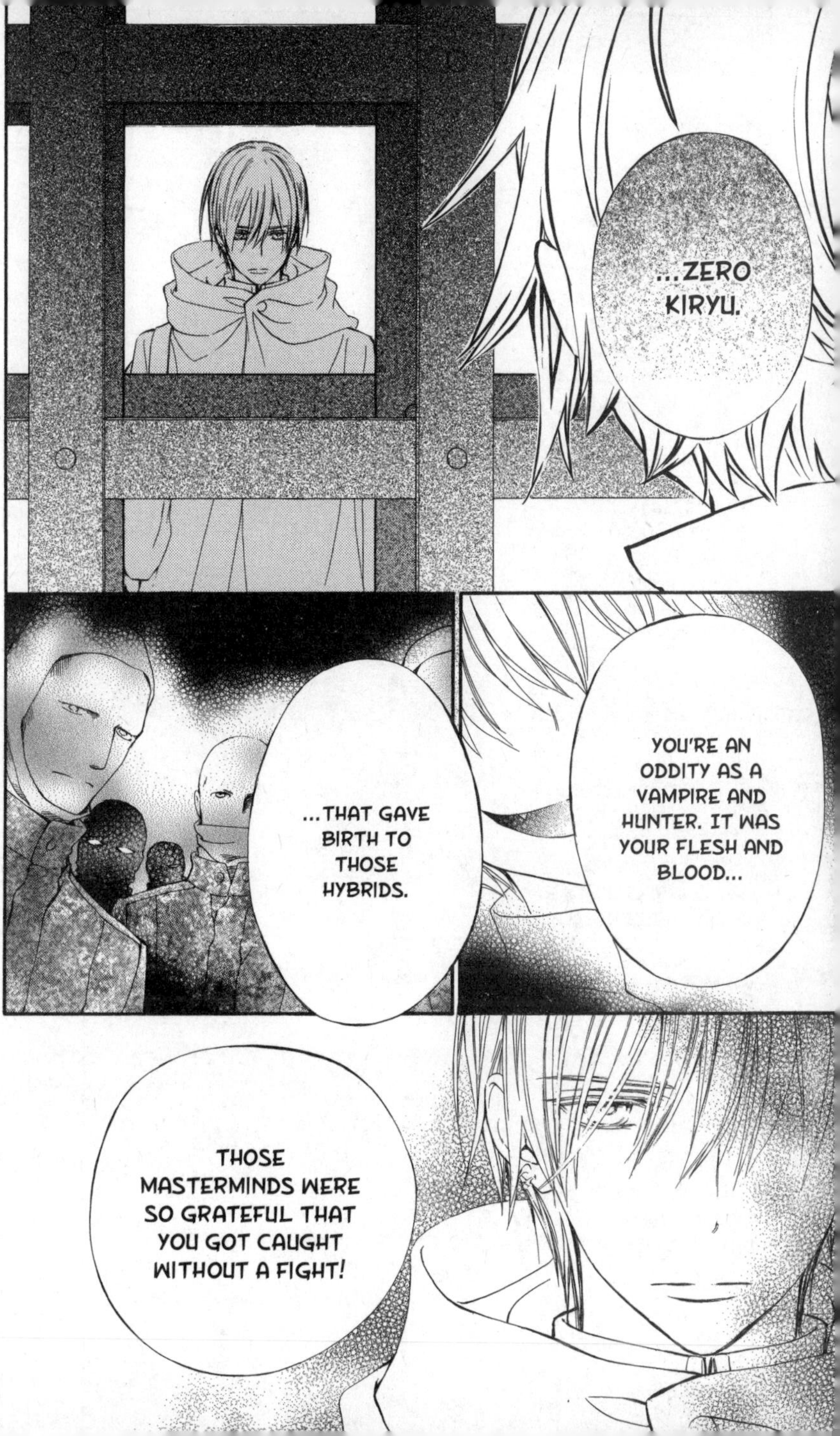
...ZERO KIRYU.
YOU'RE AN ODDITY AS A VAMPIRE AND HUNTER. IT WAS YOUR FLESH AND BLOOD...
...THAT GAVE BIRTH TO THOSE HYBRIDS.
THOSE MASTERMINDS WERE SO GRATEFUL THAT YOU GOT CAUGHT WITHOUT A FIGHT!

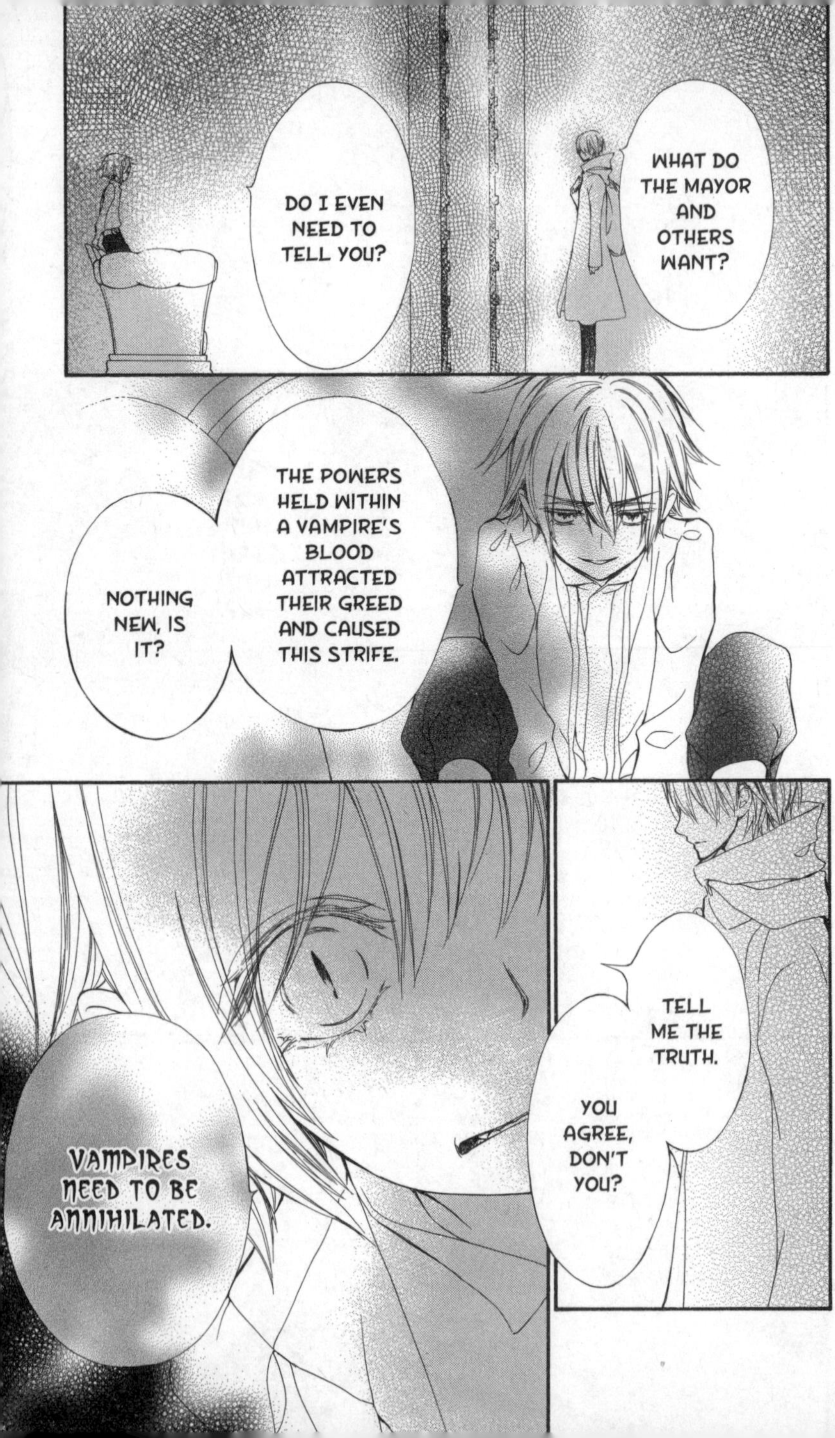
WHAT DO THE MAYOR AND OTHERS WANT?
DO I EVEN NEED TO TELL YOU?
THE POWERS HELD WITHIN A VAMPIRE'S BLOOD ATTRACTED THEIR GREED AND CAUSED THIS STRIFE.
NOTHING NEW, IS IT?
TELL ME THE TRUTH.
YOU AGREE, DON'T YOU?
VAMPIRES NEED TO BE ANNIHILATED.

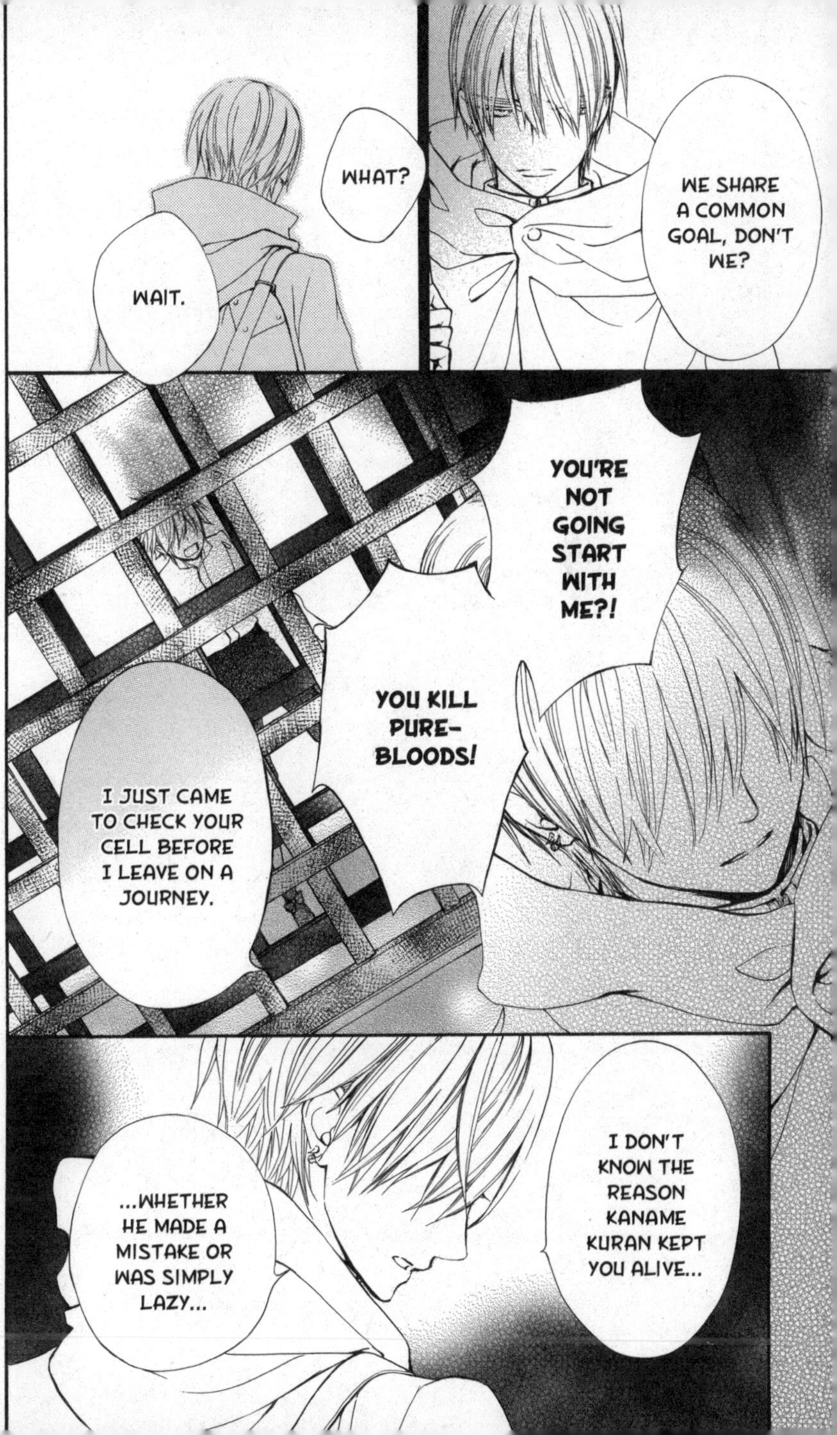
WE SHARE A COMMON GOAL, DON'T WE?
WHAT?
WAIT.
YOU'RE NOT GOING START WITH ME?!
YOU KILL PURE-BLOODS!
I JUST CAME TO CHECK YOUR CELL BEFORE I LEAVE ON A JOURNEY.
I DON'T KNOW THE REASON KANAME KURAN KEPT YOU ALIVE...
...WHETHER HE MADE A MISTAKE OR WAS SIMPLY LAZY...

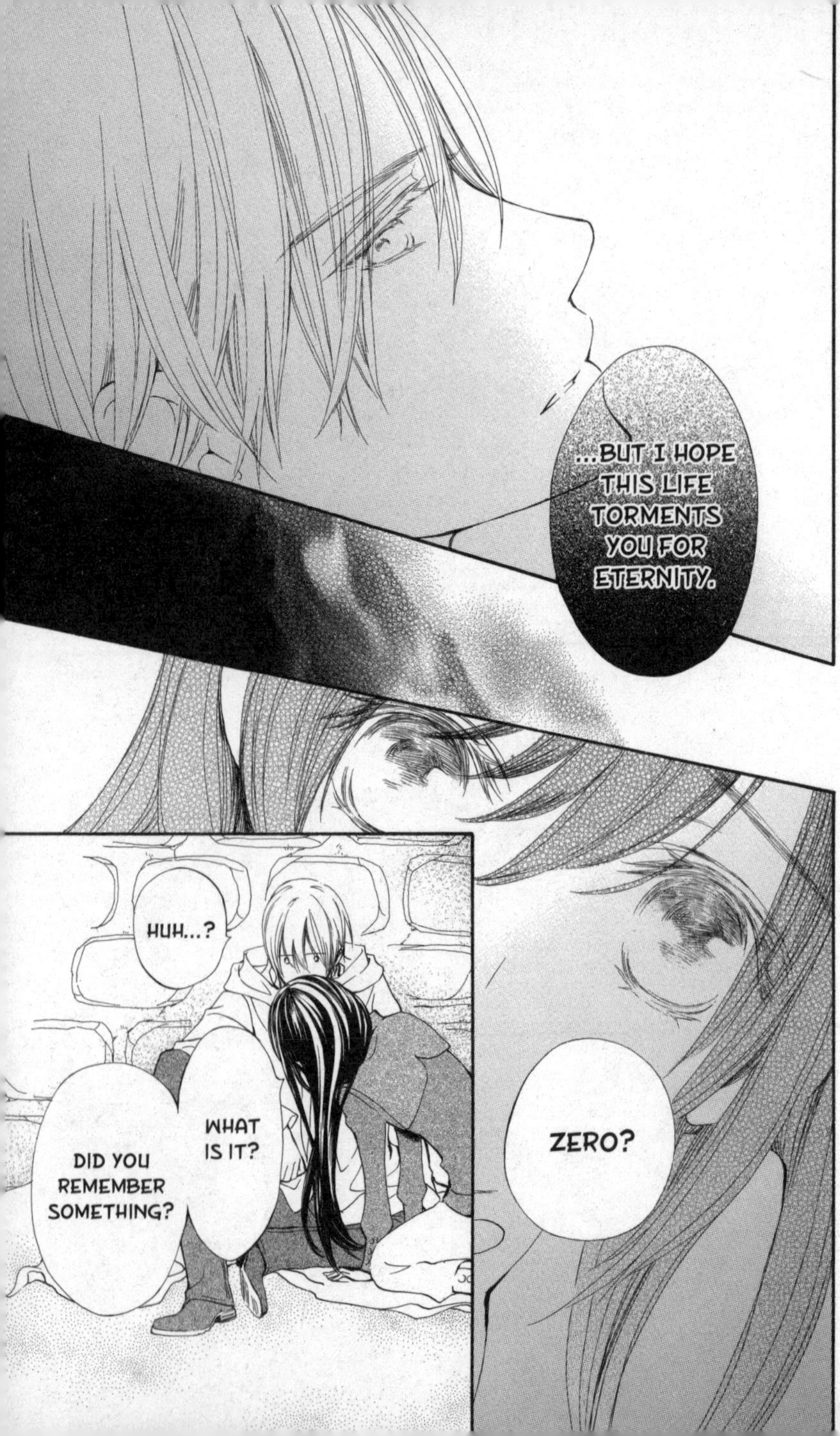
...BUT I HOPE THIS LIFE TORMENTS YOU FOR ETERNITY.
ZERO?
HUH...?
WHAT IS IT?
DID YOU REMEMBER SOMETHING?

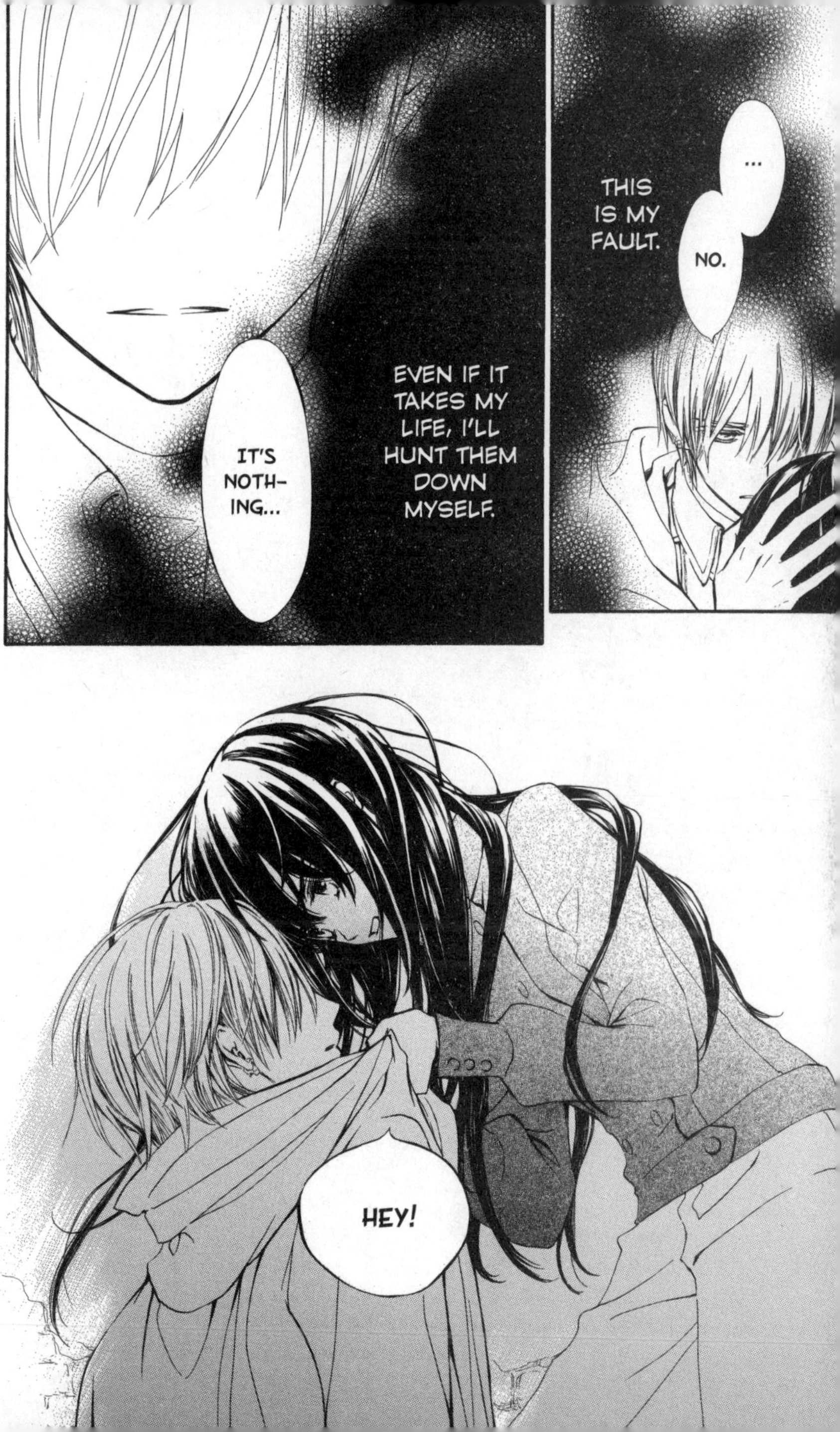
...
THIS IS MY FAULT.
NO.
EVEN IF IT TAKES MY LIFE, I'LL HUNT THEM DOWN MYSELF.
IT'S NOTHING...
HEY!

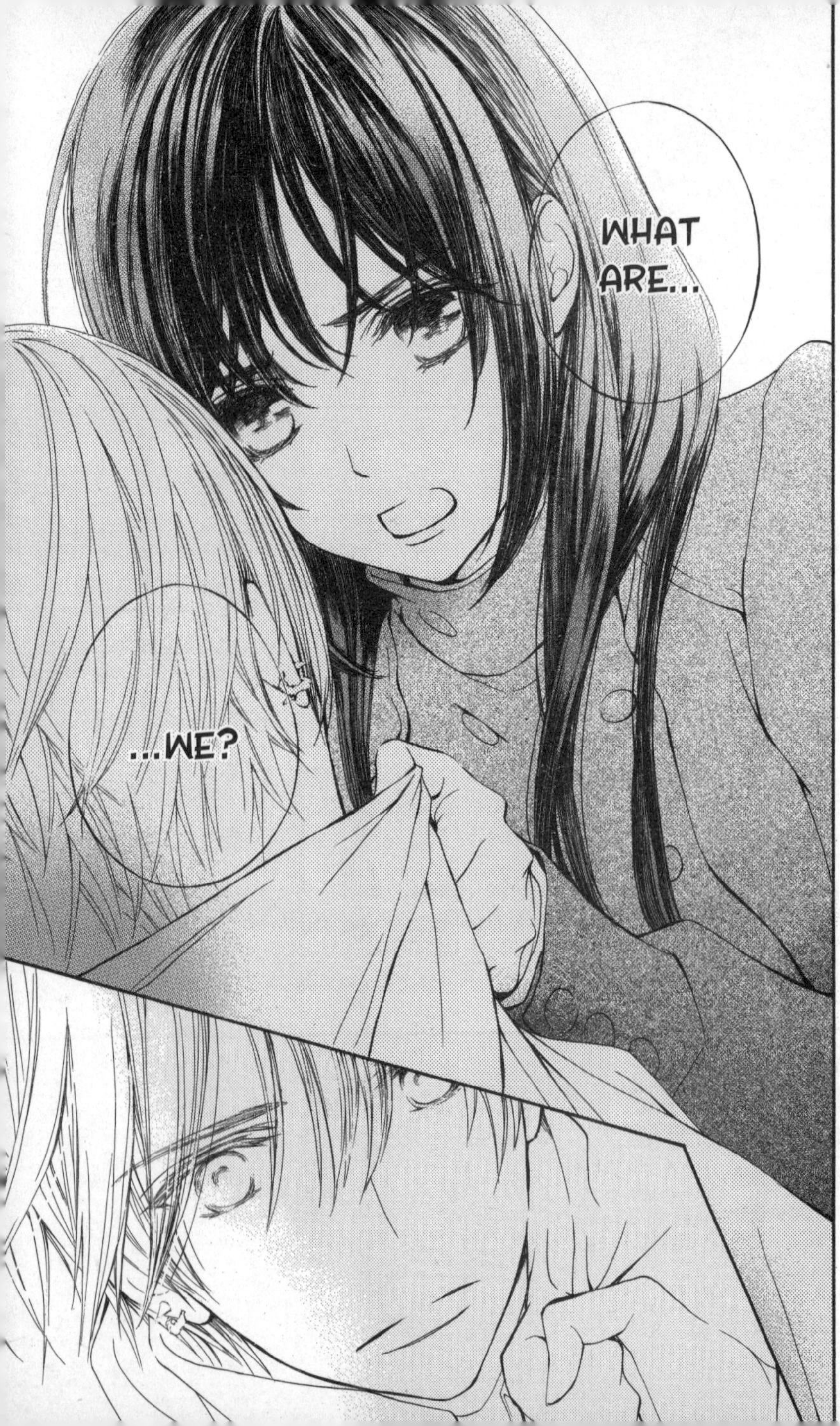
WHAT ARE...
...WE?

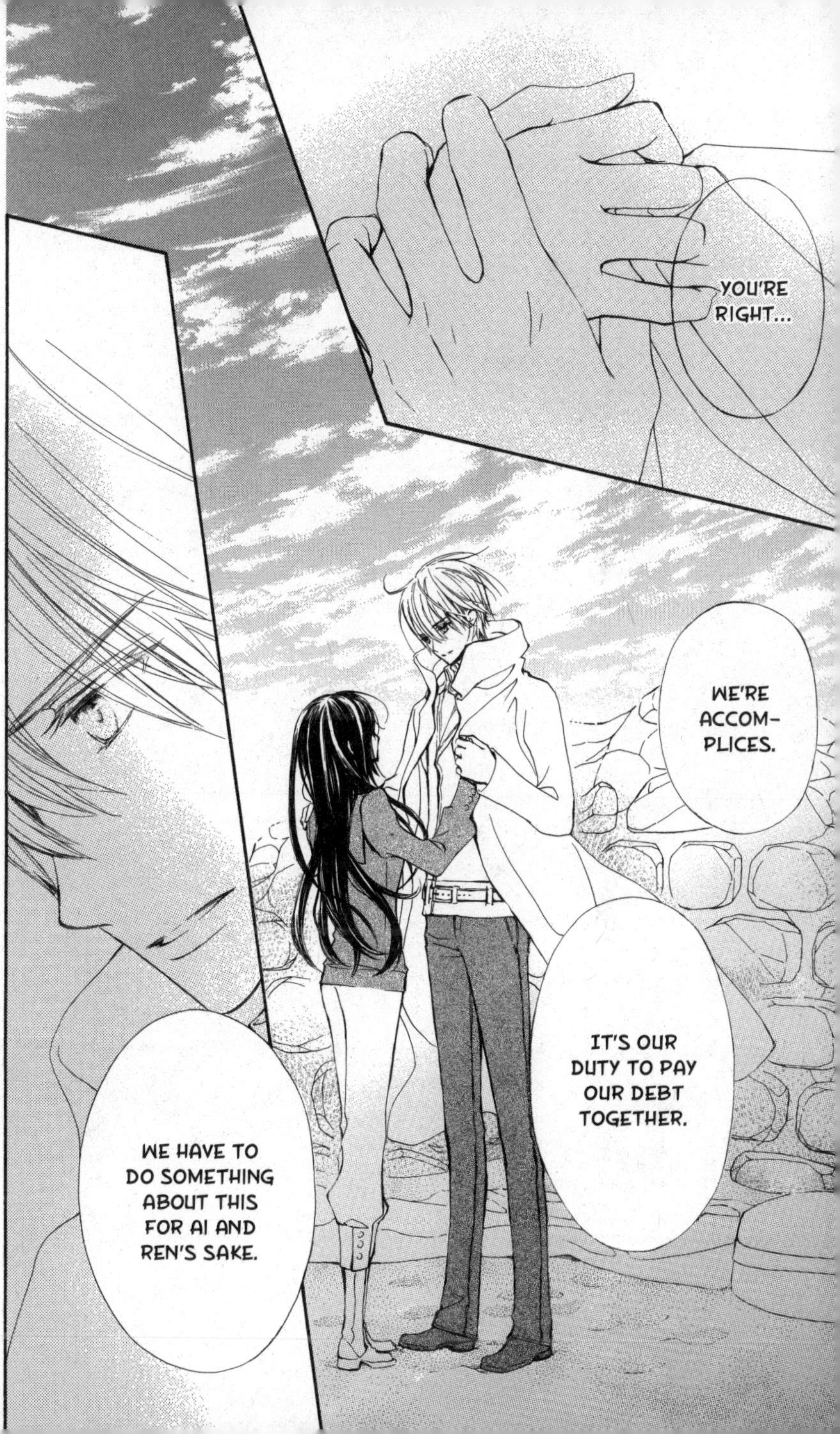
YOU'RE RIGHT...
WE'RE ACCOMPLICES.
IT'S OUR DUTY TO PAY OUR DEBT TOGETHER.
WE HAVE TO DO SOMETHING ABOUT THIS FOR AI AND REN'S SAKE.

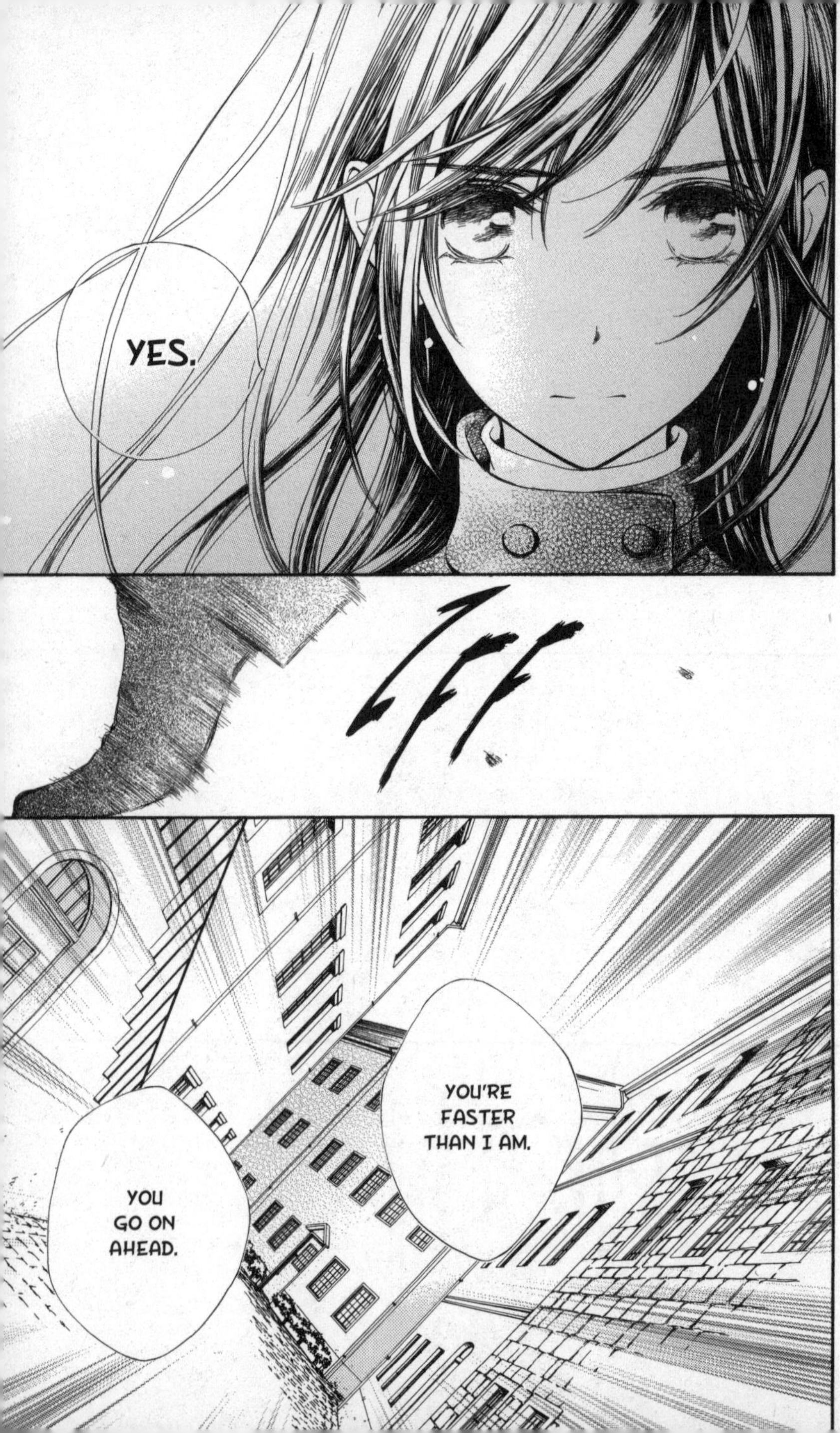
YES.
YOU'RE FASTER THAN I AM.
YOU GO ON AHEAD.

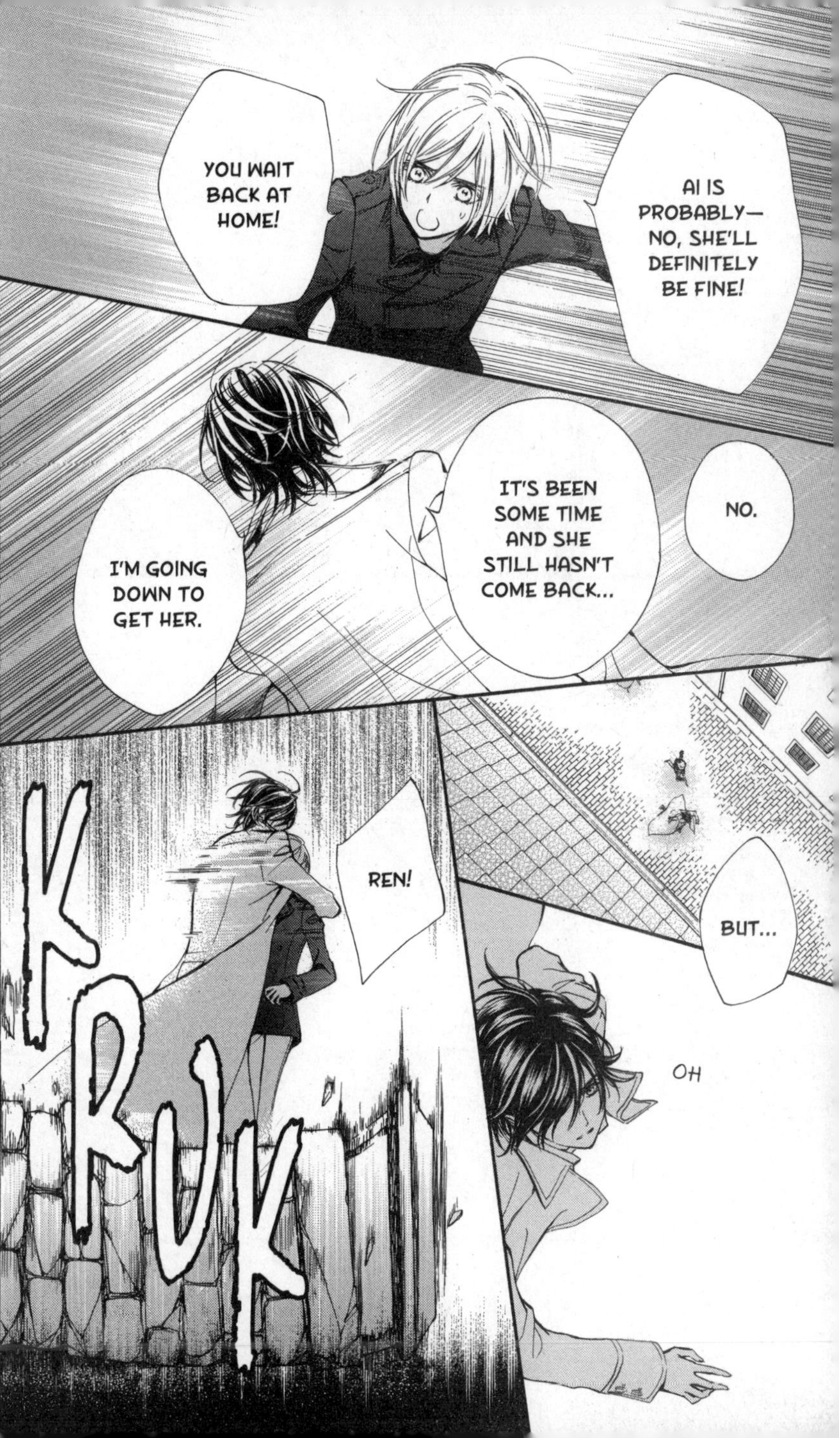
AI IS PROBABLY— NO, SHE'LL DEFINITELY BE FINE!
YOU WAIT BACK AT HOME!
NO.
IT'S BEEN SOME TIME AND SHE STILL HASN'T COME BACK...
I'M GOING DOWN TO GET HER.
BUT...
OH
REN!
KRUK

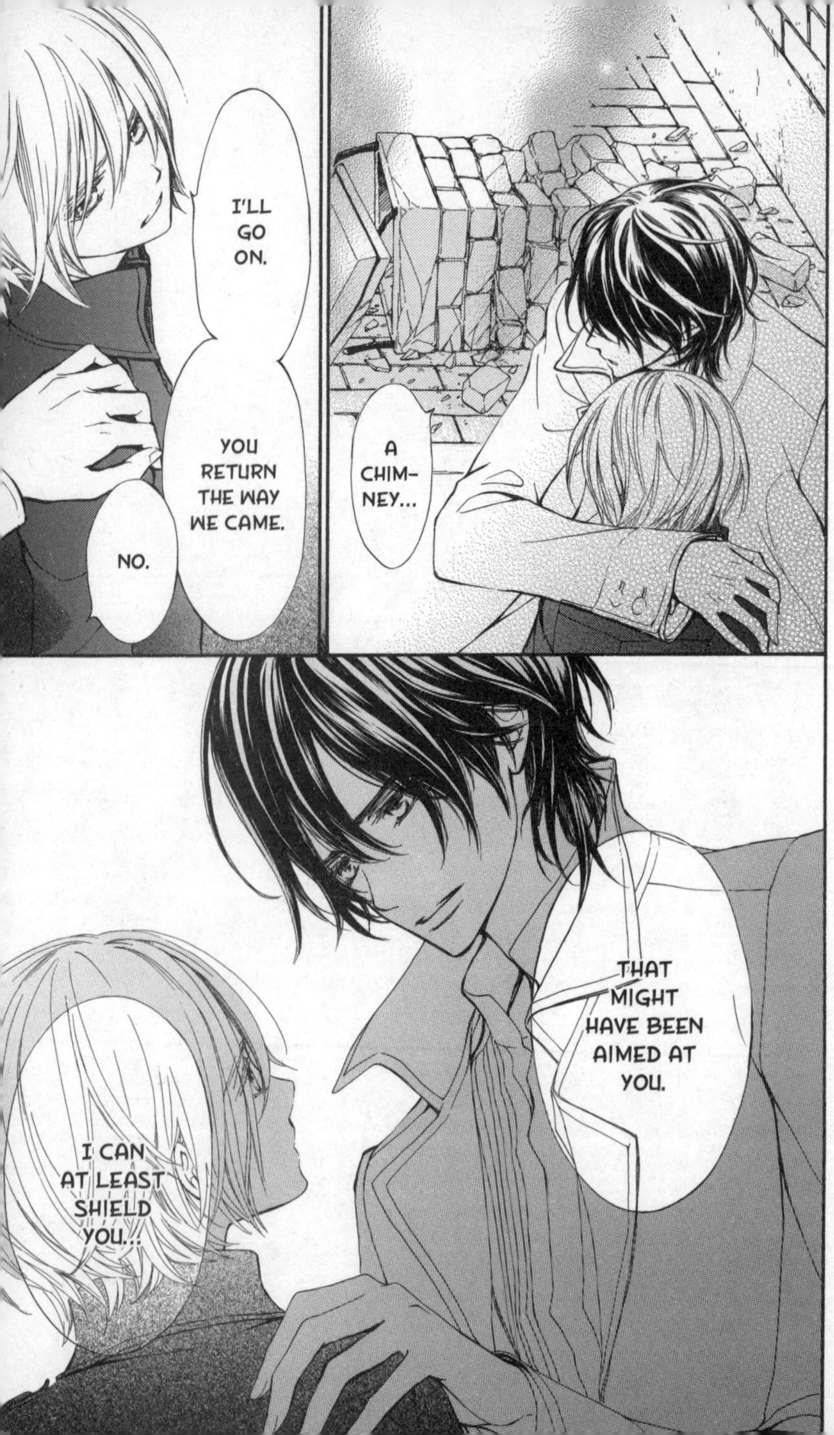
A CHIMNEY...
I'LL GO ON.
YOU RETURN THE WAY WE CAME.
NO.
THAT MIGHT HAVE BEEN AIMED AT YOU.
I CAN AT LEAST SHIELD YOU...

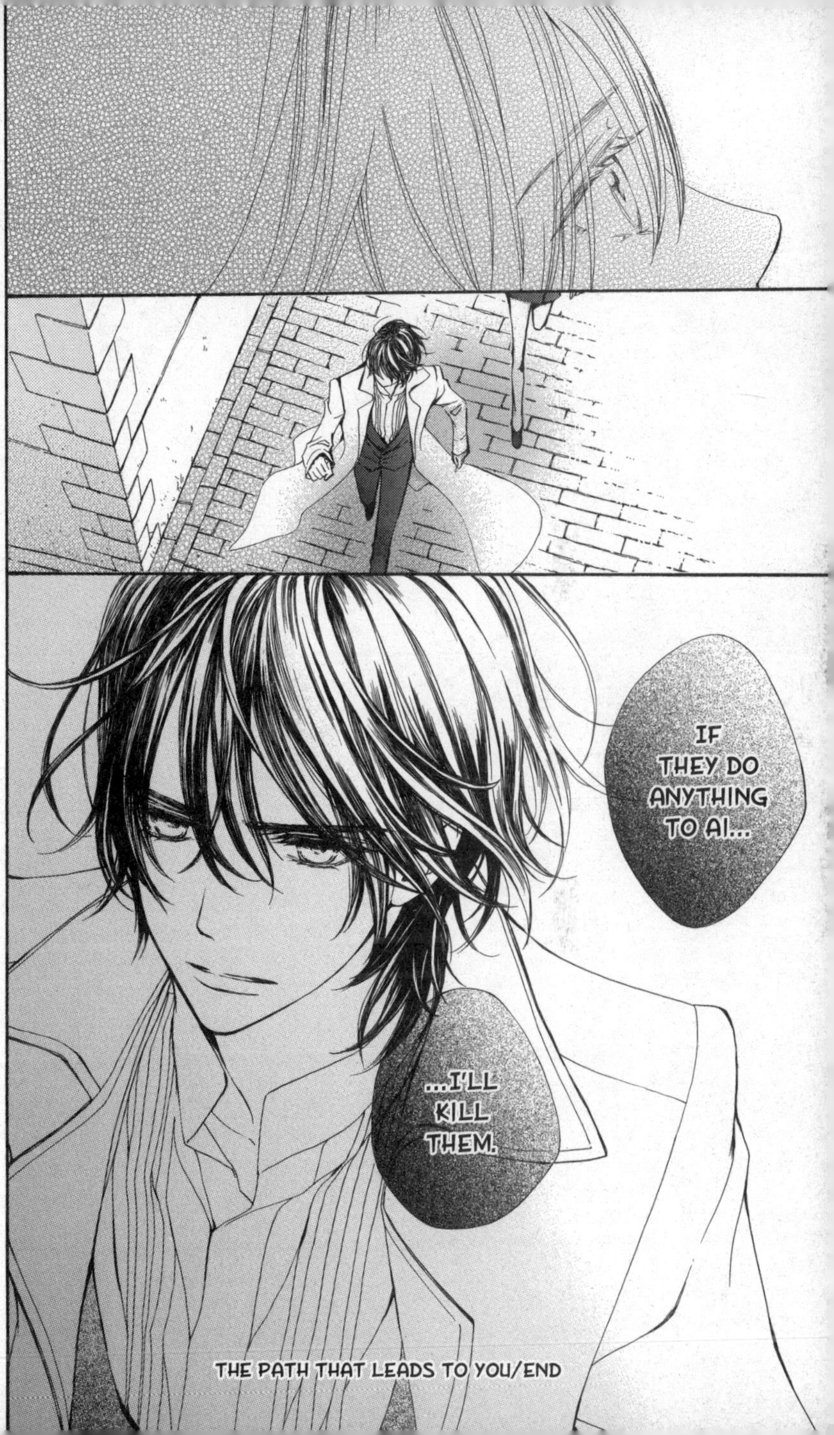
IF THEY DO ANYTHING TO AI...
...I'LL KILL THEM.
THE PATH THAT LEADS TO YOU/END

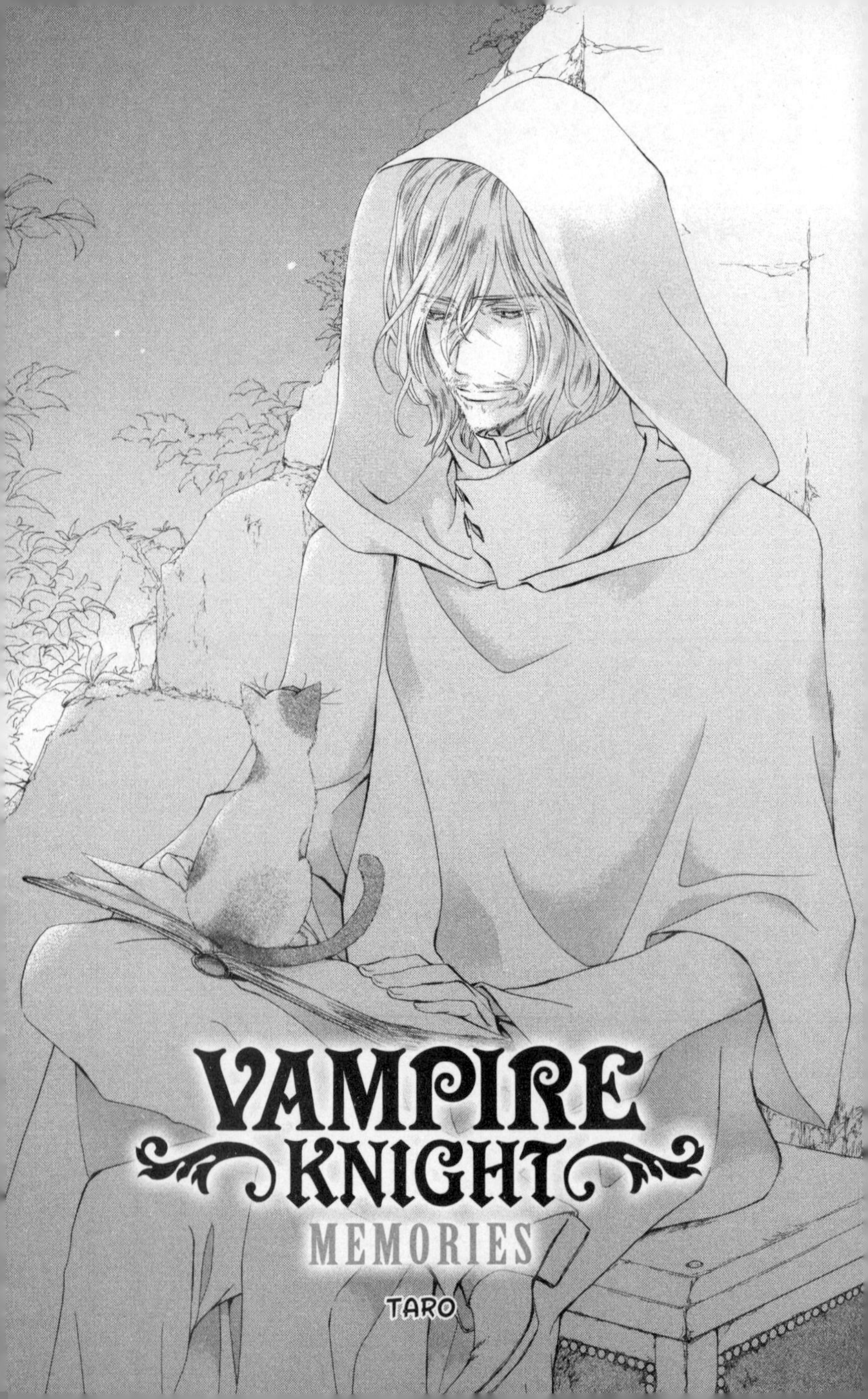
VAMPIRE KNIGHT
MEMORIES
TARO

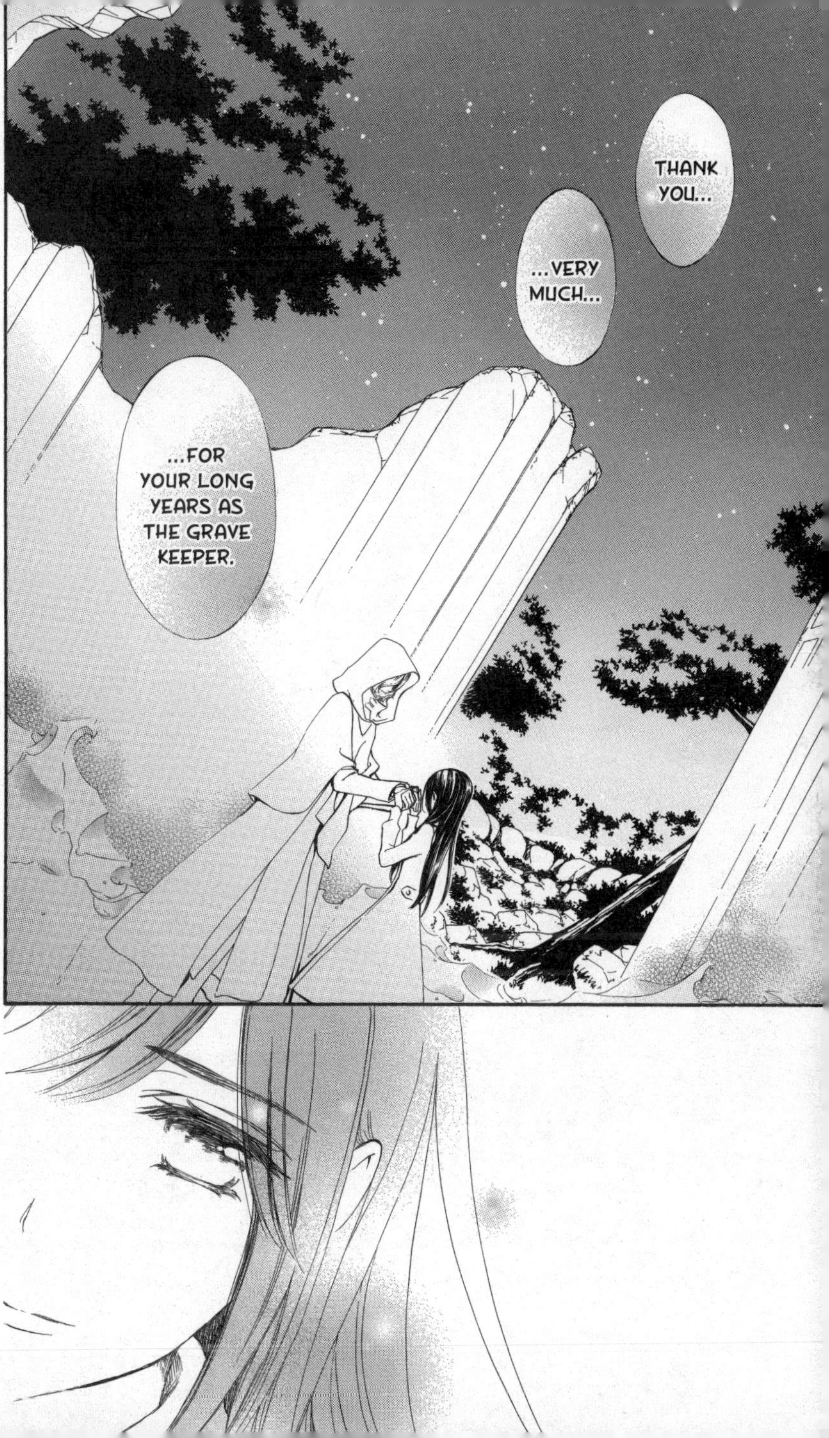
THANK YOU...
...VERY MUCH...
...FOR YOUR LONG YEARS AS THE GRAVE KEEPER.

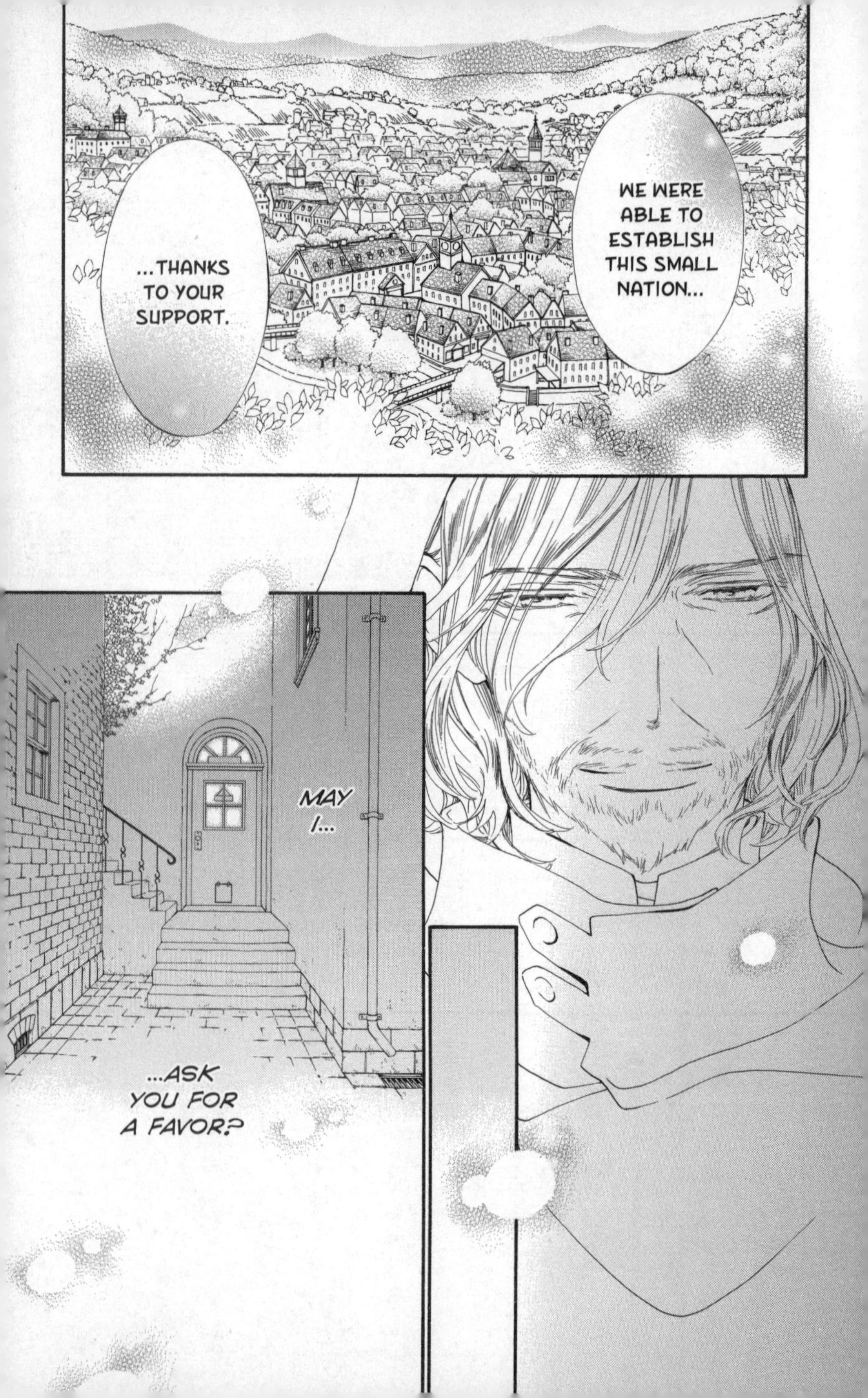
WE WERE ABLE TO ESTABLISH THIS SMALL NATION...
...THANKS TO YOUR SUPPORT.
MAY I...
...ASK YOU FOR A FAVOR?

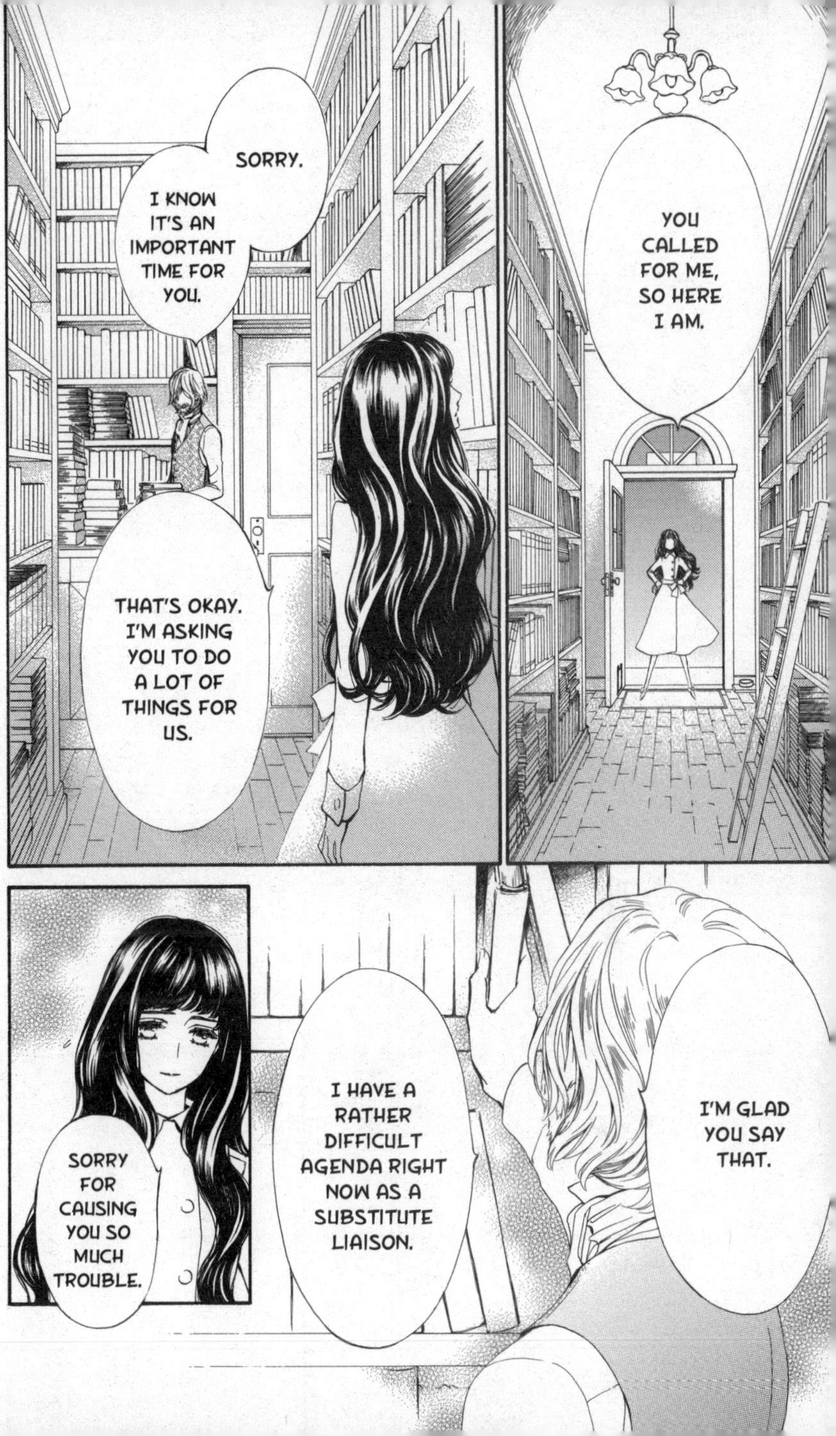
YOU CALLED FOR ME, SO HERE I AM.
SORRY.
I KNOW IT'S AN IMPORTANT TIME FOR YOU.
THAT'S OKAY. I'M ASKING YOU TO DO A LOT OF THINGS FOR US.
I'M GLAD YOU SAY THAT.
I HAVE A RATHER DIFFICULT AGENDA RIGHT NOW AS A SUBSTITUTE LIAISON.
SORRY FOR CAUSING YOU SO MUCH TROUBLE.

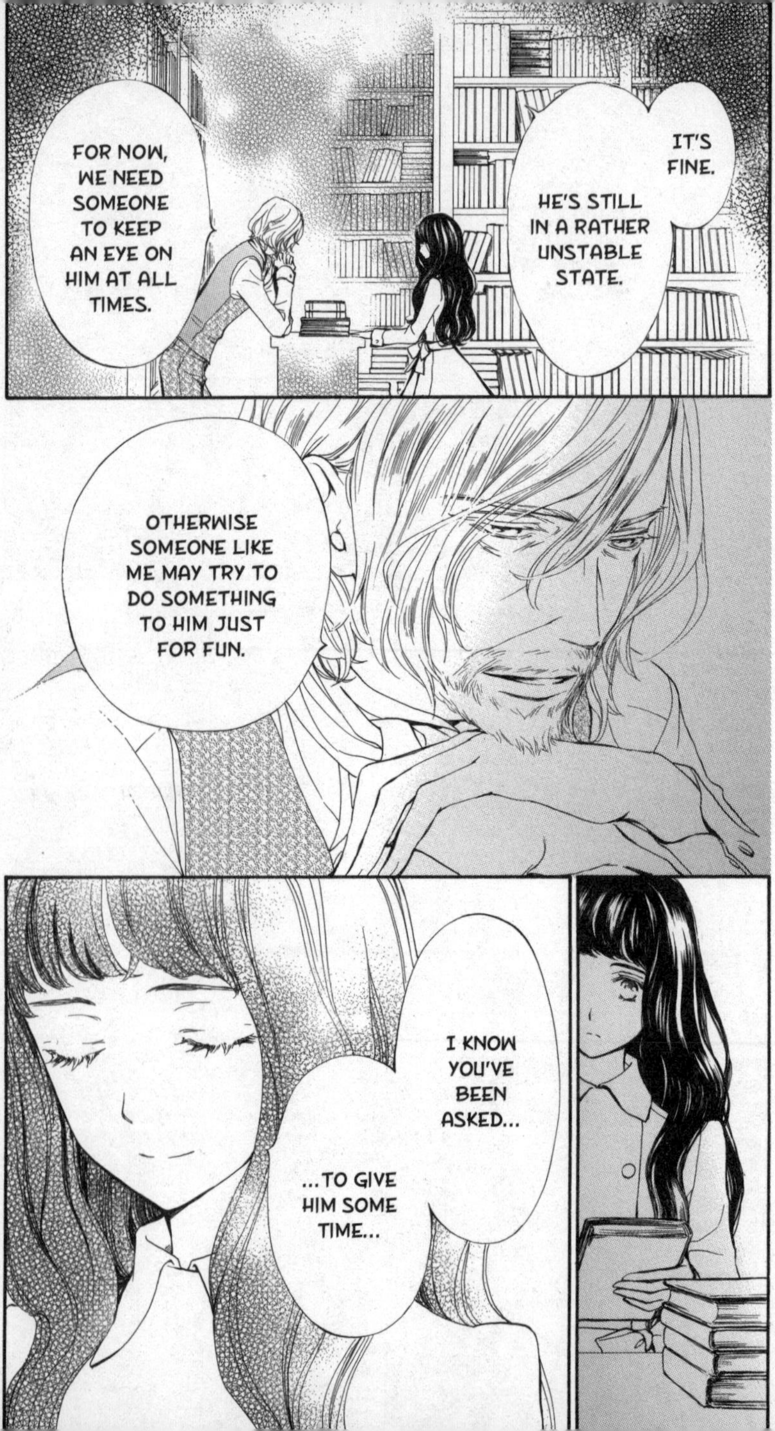
IT'S FINE.
HE'S STILL IN A RATHER UNSTABLE STATE.
FOR NOW, WE NEED SOMEONE TO KEEP AN EYE ON HIM AT ALL TIMES.
OTHERWISE SOMEONE LIKE ME MAY TRY TO DO SOMETHING TO HIM JUST FOR FUN.
I KNOW YOU'VE BEEN ASKED...
...TO GIVE HIM SOME TIME...

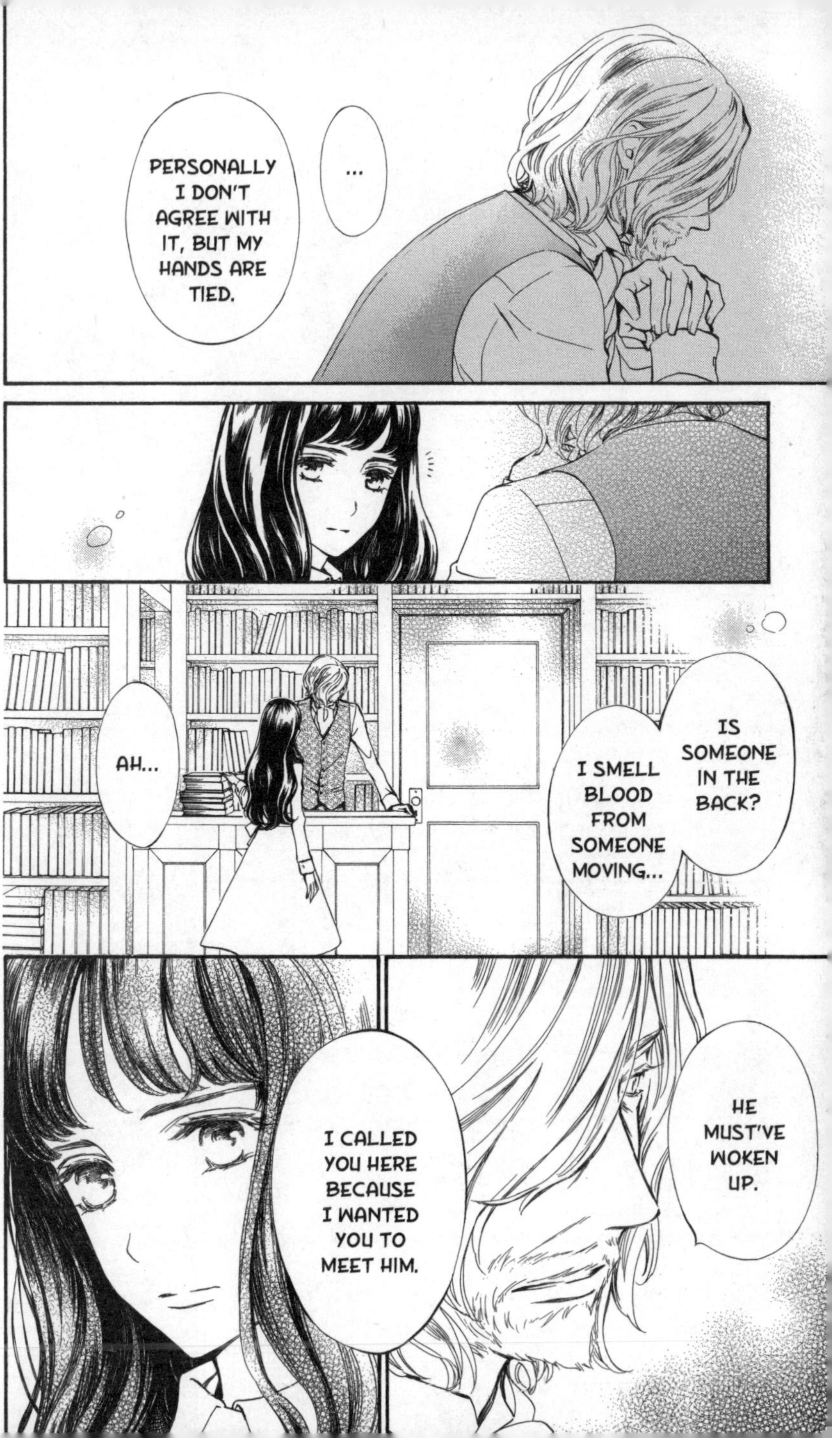
...
PERSONALLY I DON'T AGREE WITH IT, BUT MY HANDS ARE TIED.
IS SOMEONE IN THE BACK?
I SMELL BLOOD FROM SOMEONE MOVING...
AH...
HE MUST'VE WOKEN UP.
I CALLED YOU HERE BECAUSE I WANTED YOU TO MEET HIM.

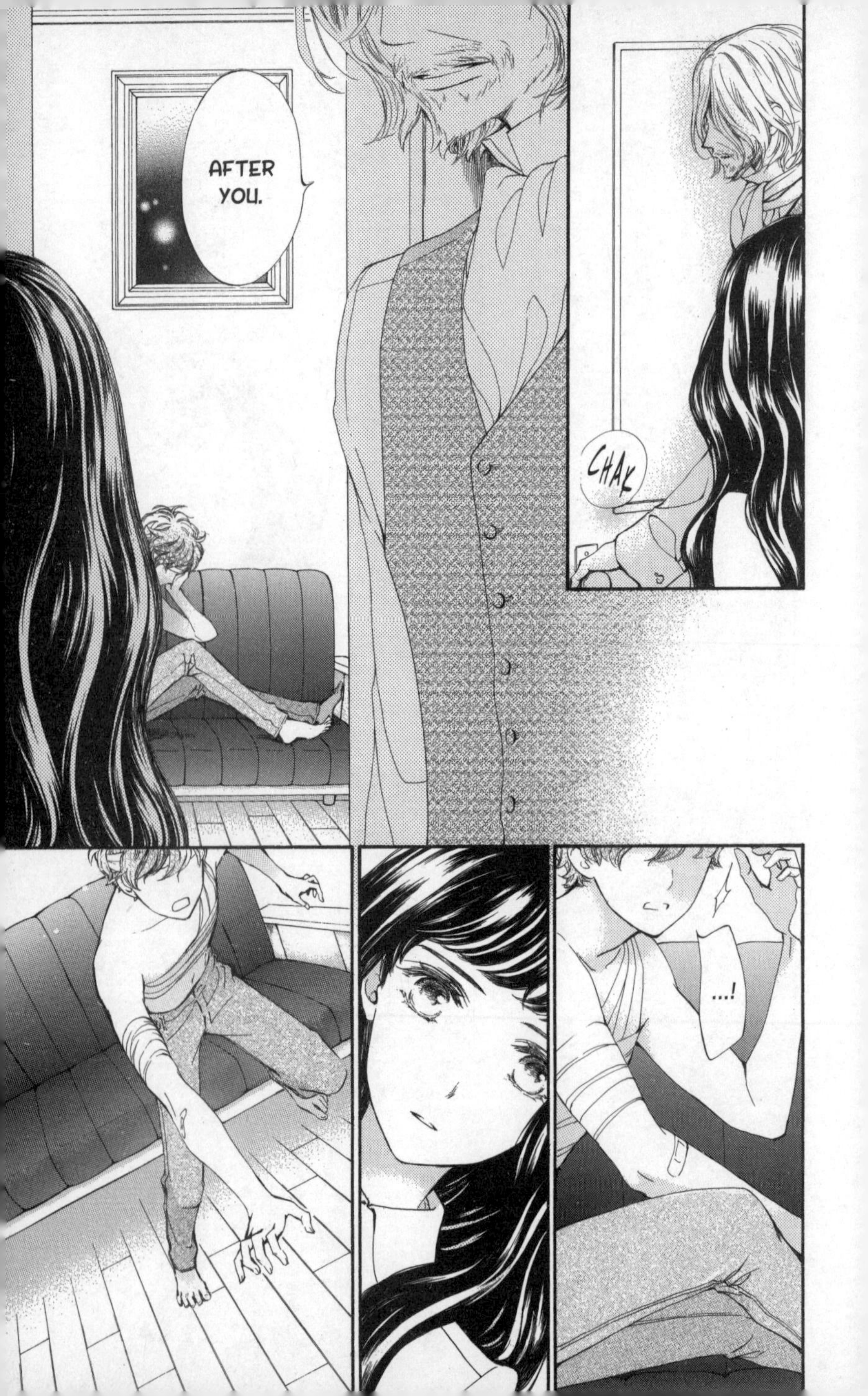
CHAK
AFTER YOU.
...!

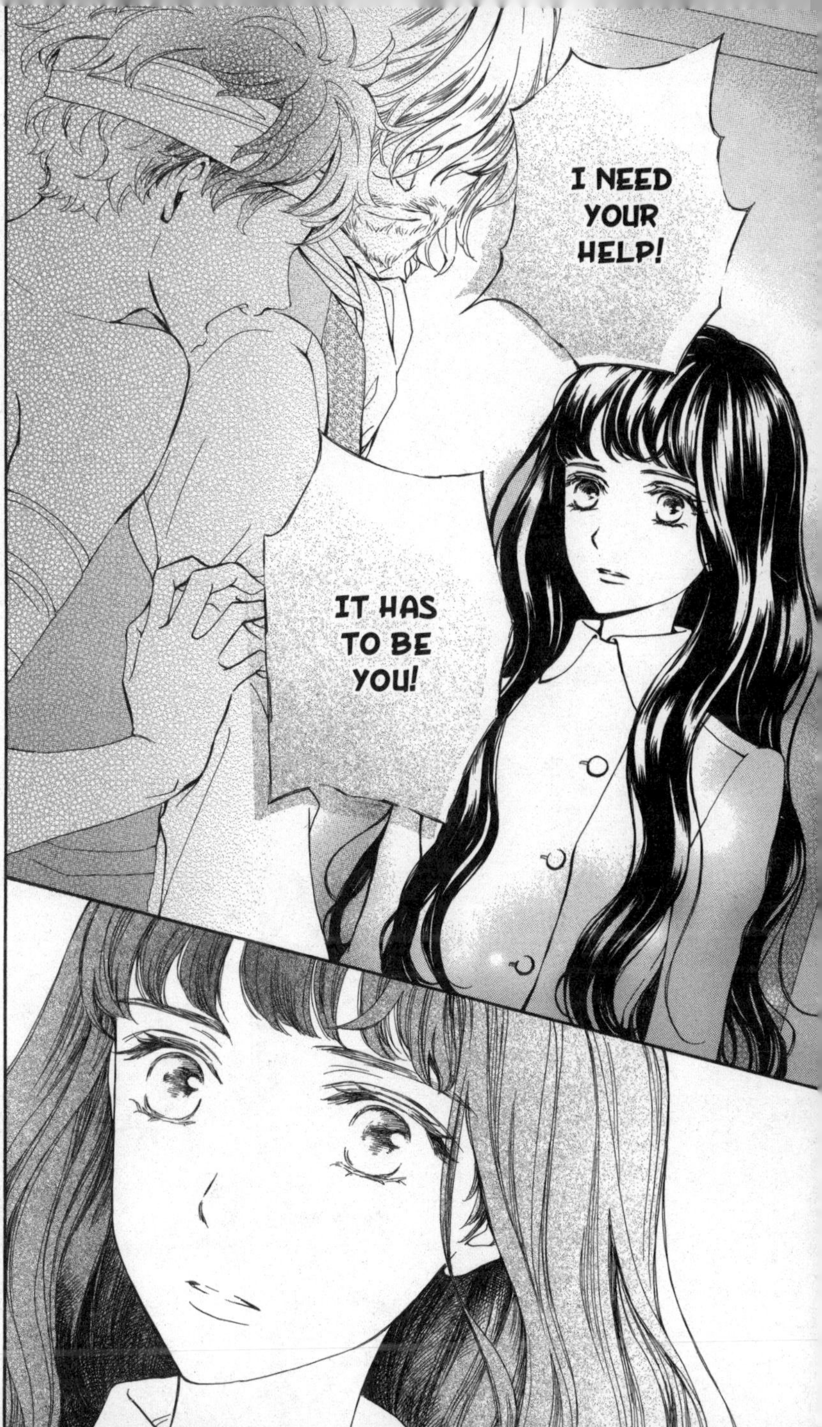
I NEED YOUR HELP!
IT HAS TO BE YOU!

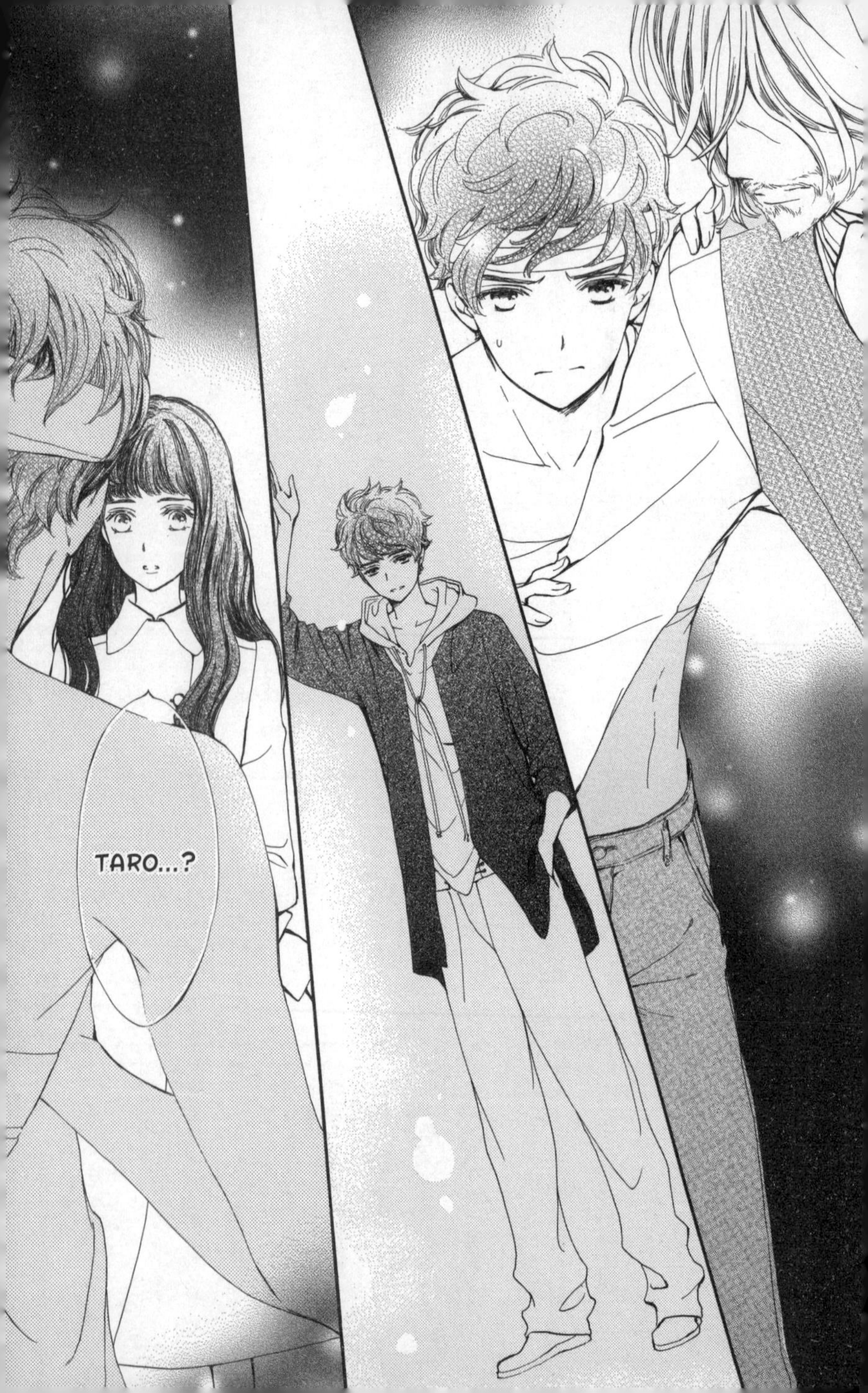
TARO...?

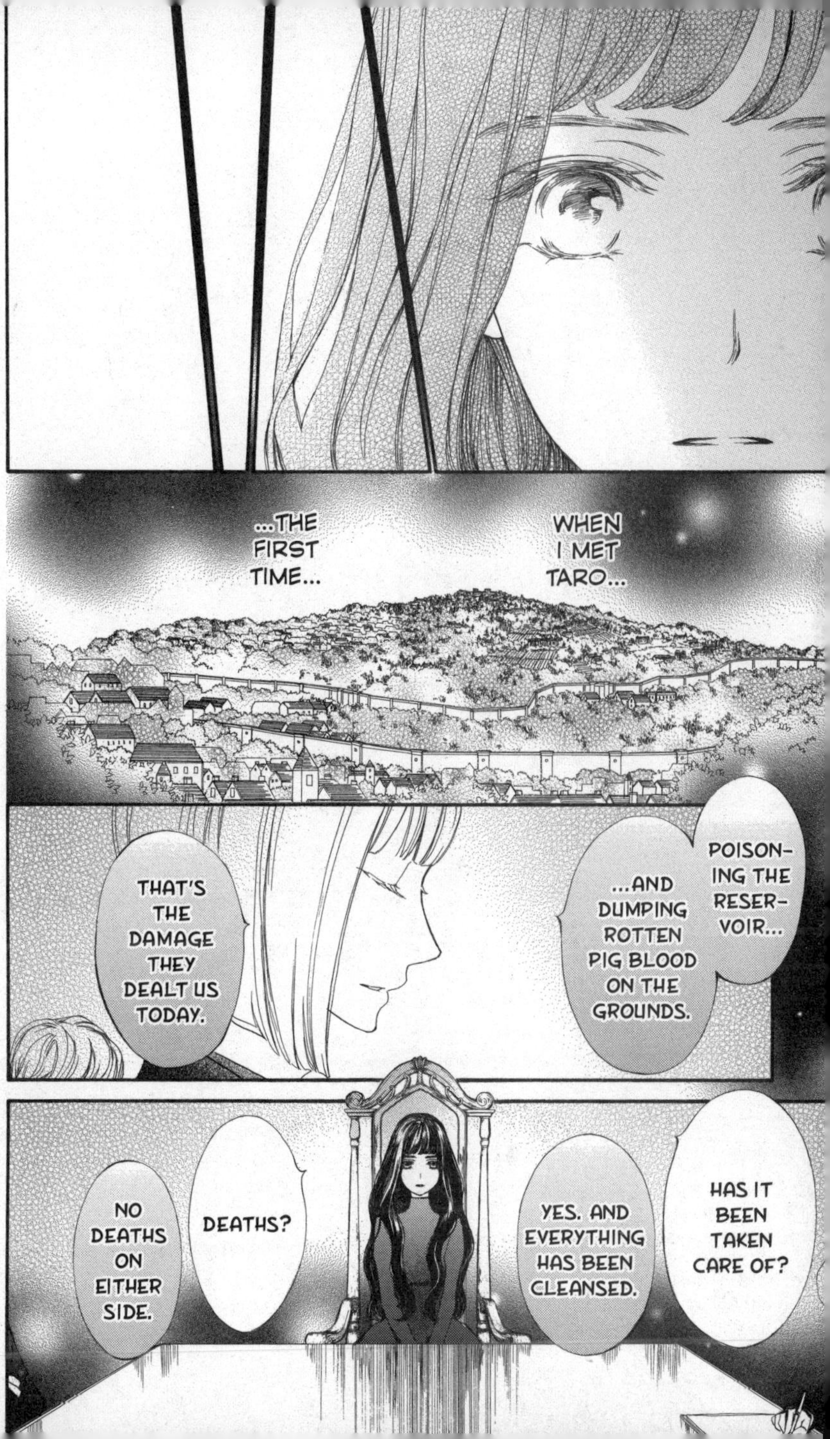
WHEN I MET TARO...
...THE FIRST TIME...
POISON-ING THE RESER-VOIR...
...AND DUMPING ROTTEN PIG BLOOD ON THE GROUNDS.
THAT'S THE DAMAGE THEY DEALT US TODAY.
HAS IT BEEN TAKEN CARE OF?
YES. AND EVERYTHING HAS BEEN CLEANSED.
DEATHS?
NO DEATHS ON EITHER SIDE.

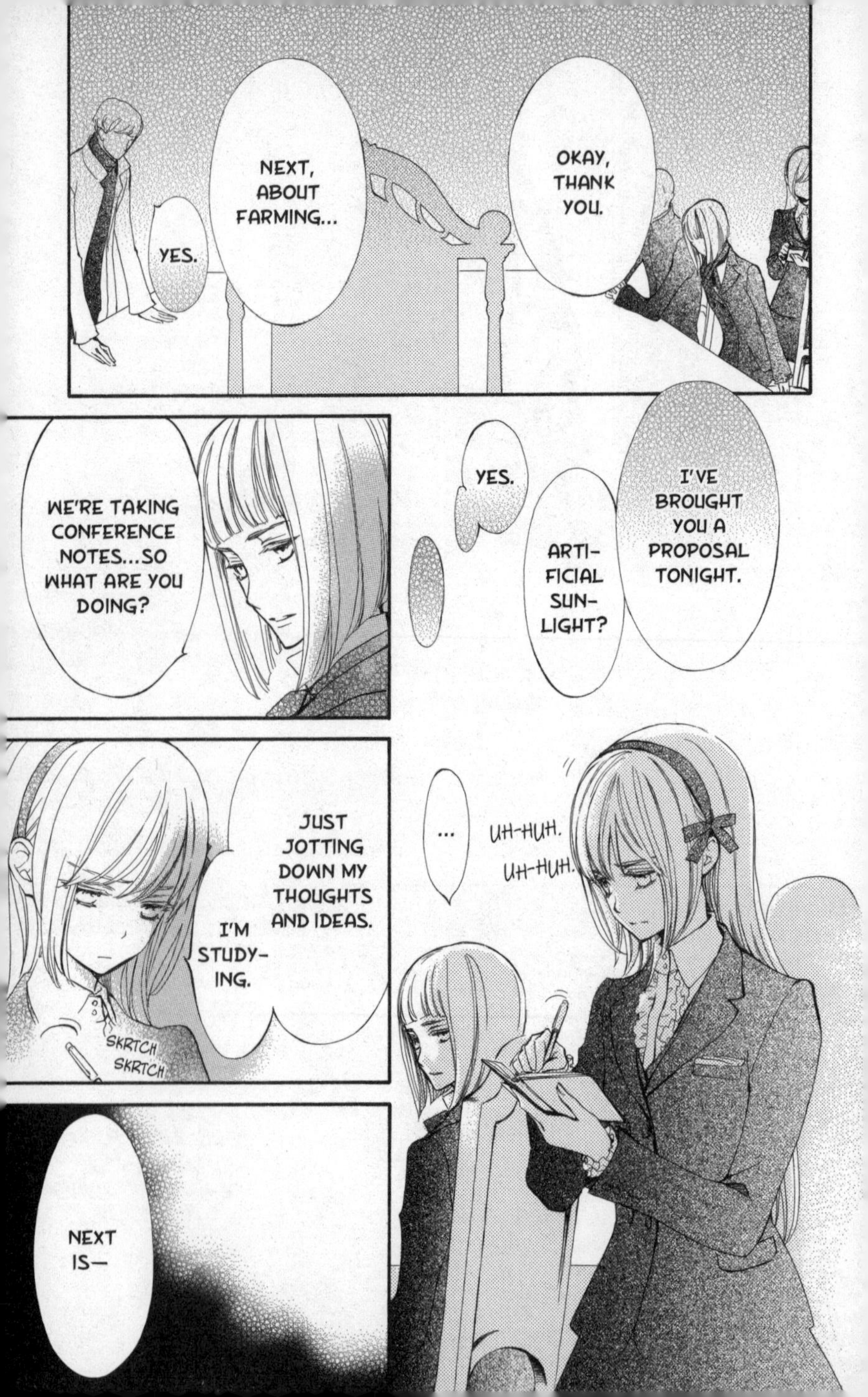
OKAY, THANK YOU.
NEXT, ABOUT FARMING...
YES.
I'VE BROUGHT YOU A PROPOSAL TONIGHT.
ARTI-FICIAL SUN-LIGHT?
YES.
WE'RE TAKING CONFERENCE NOTES...SO WHAT ARE YOU DOING?
UH-HUH. UH-HUH.
...
JUST JOTTING DOWN MY THOUGHTS AND IDEAS.
I'M STUDY-ING.
SKRTCH SKRTCH
NEXT IS—

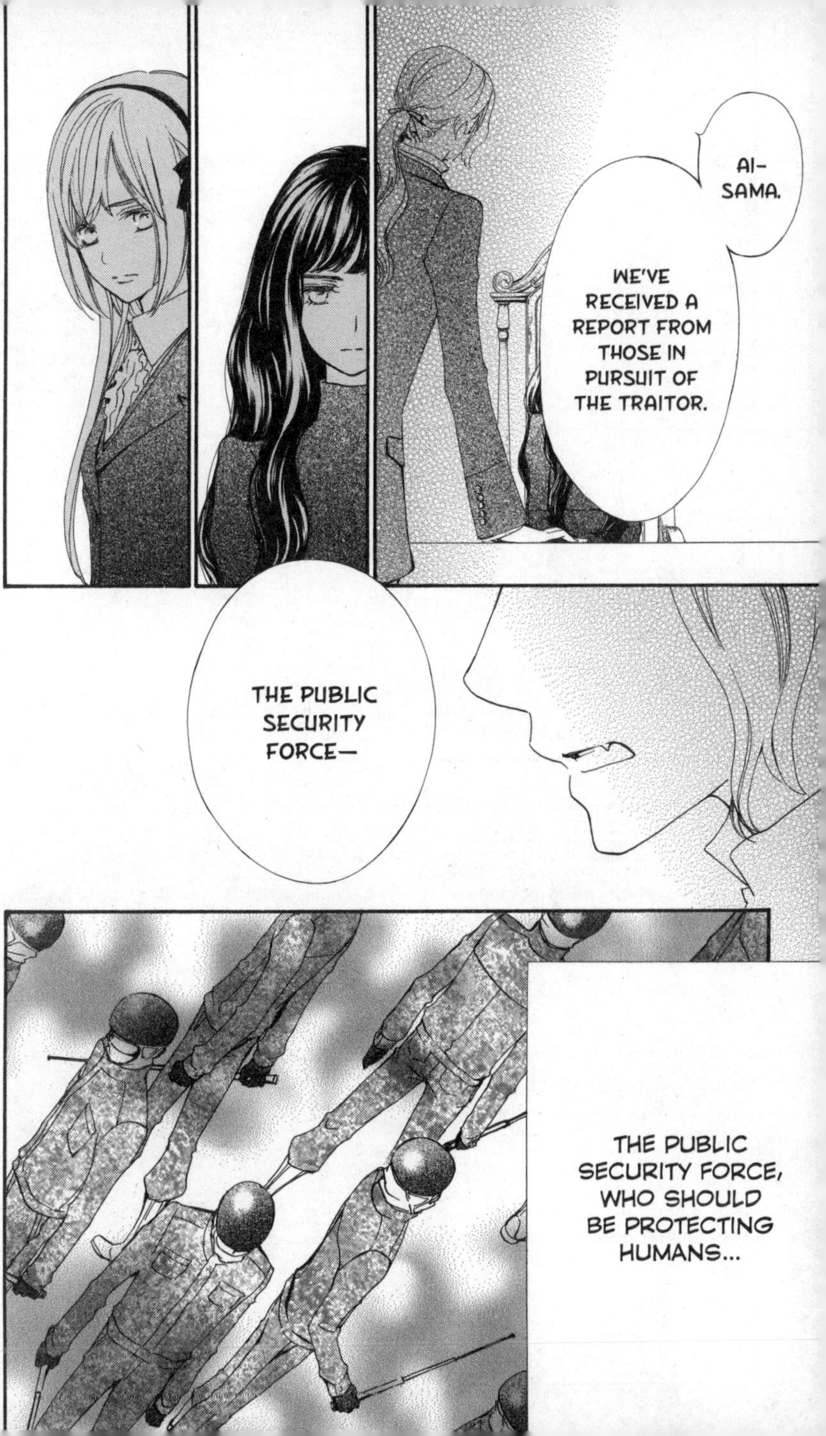
AI-SAMA.
WE'VE RECEIVED A REPORT FROM THOSE IN PURSUIT OF THE TRAITOR.
THE PUBLIC SECURITY FORCE—
THE PUBLIC SECURITY FORCE, WHO SHOULD BE PROTECTING HUMANS...

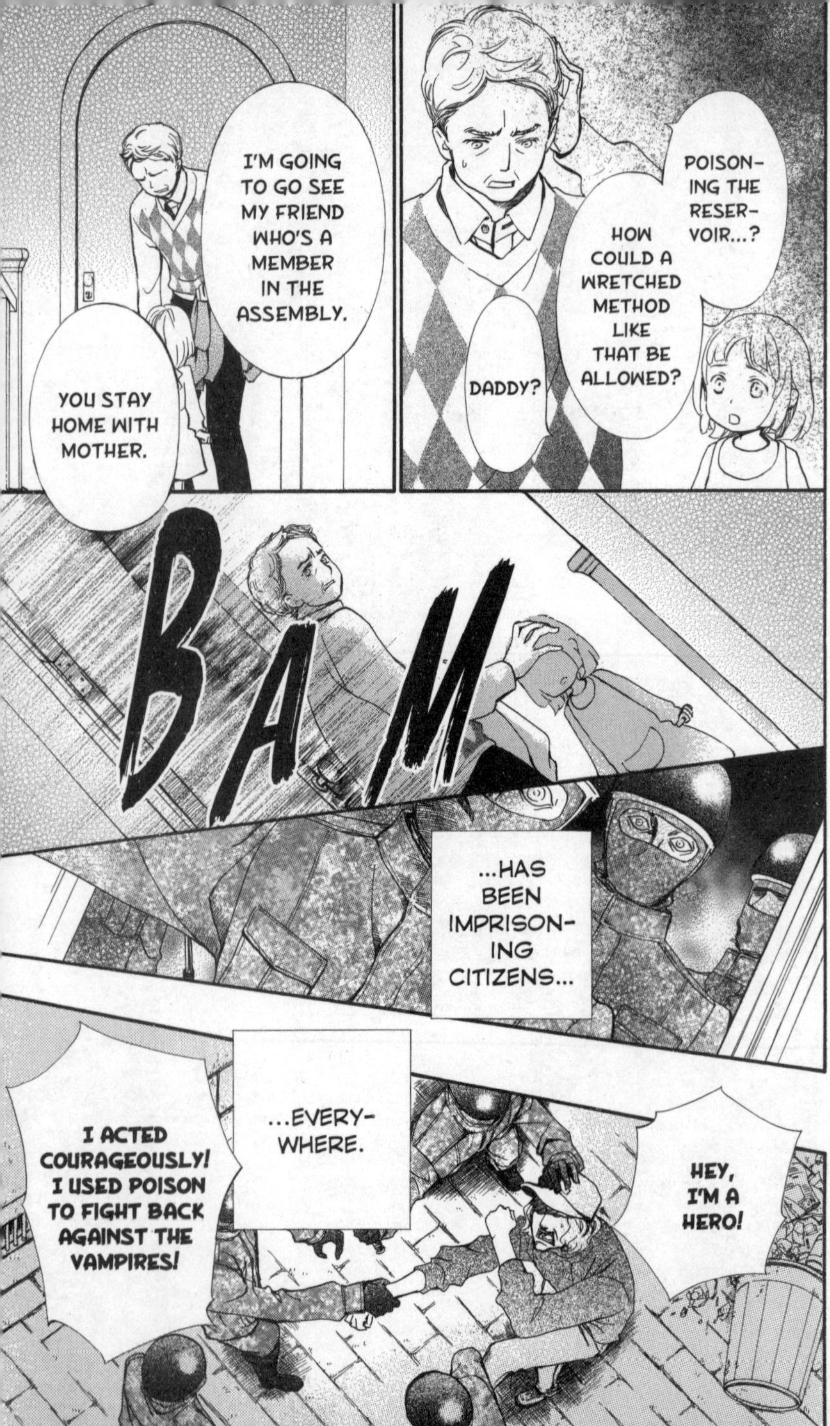
POISONING THE RESERVOIR...?
HOW COULD A WRETCHED METHOD LIKE THAT BE ALLOWED?
DADDY?
I'M GOING TO GO SEE MY FRIEND WHO'S A MEMBER IN THE ASSEMBLY.
YOU STAY HOME WITH MOTHER.
BAM
...HAS BEEN IMPRISONING CITIZENS...
HEY, I'M A HERO!
...EVERYWHERE.
I ACTED COURAGEOUSLY! I USED POISON TO FIGHT BACK AGAINST THE VAMPIRES!

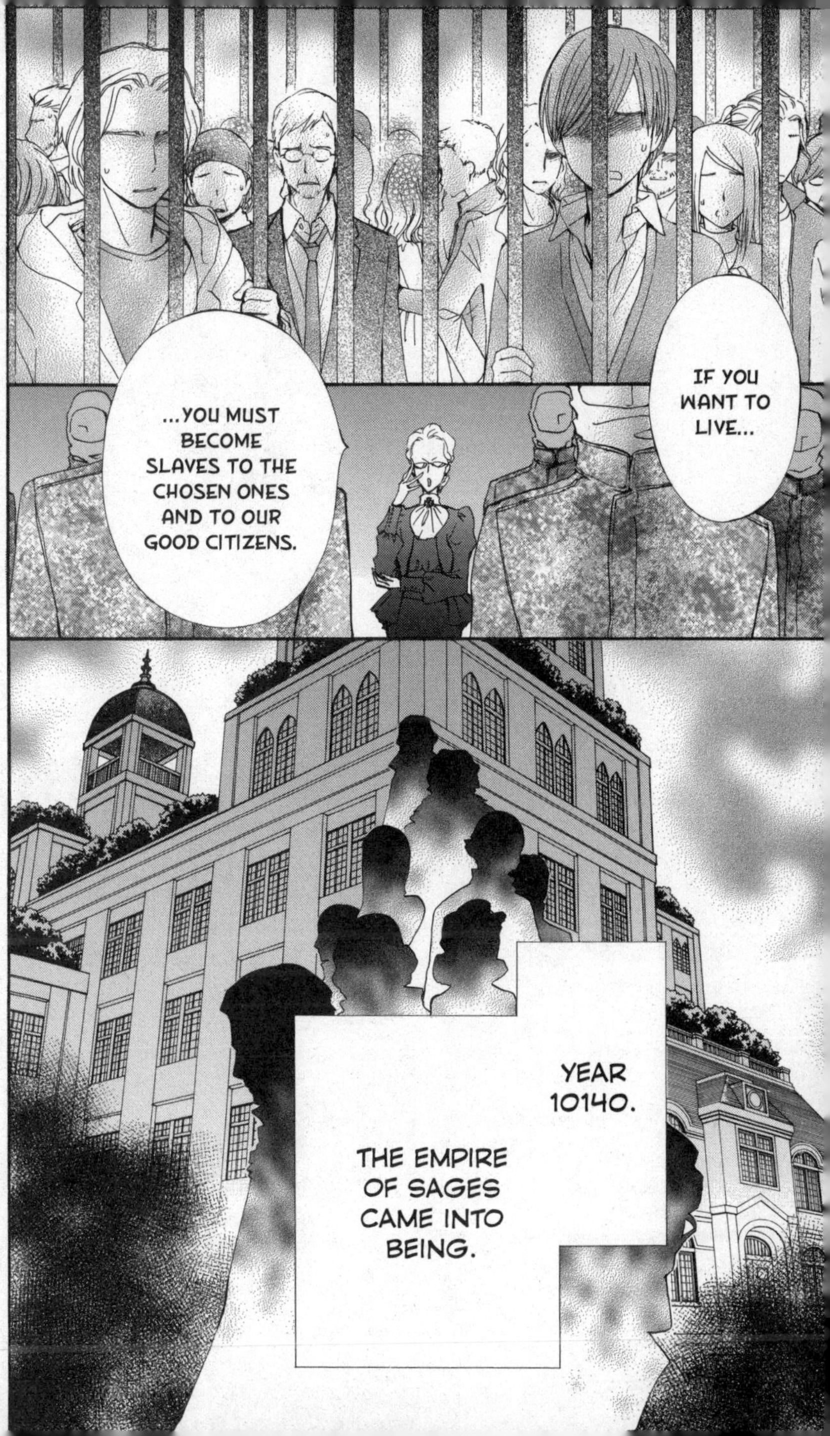
IF YOU WANT TO LIVE...
...YOU MUST BECOME SLAVES TO THE CHOSEN ONES AND TO OUR GOOD CITIZENS.
YEAR 10140.
THE EMPIRE OF SAGES CAME INTO BEING.

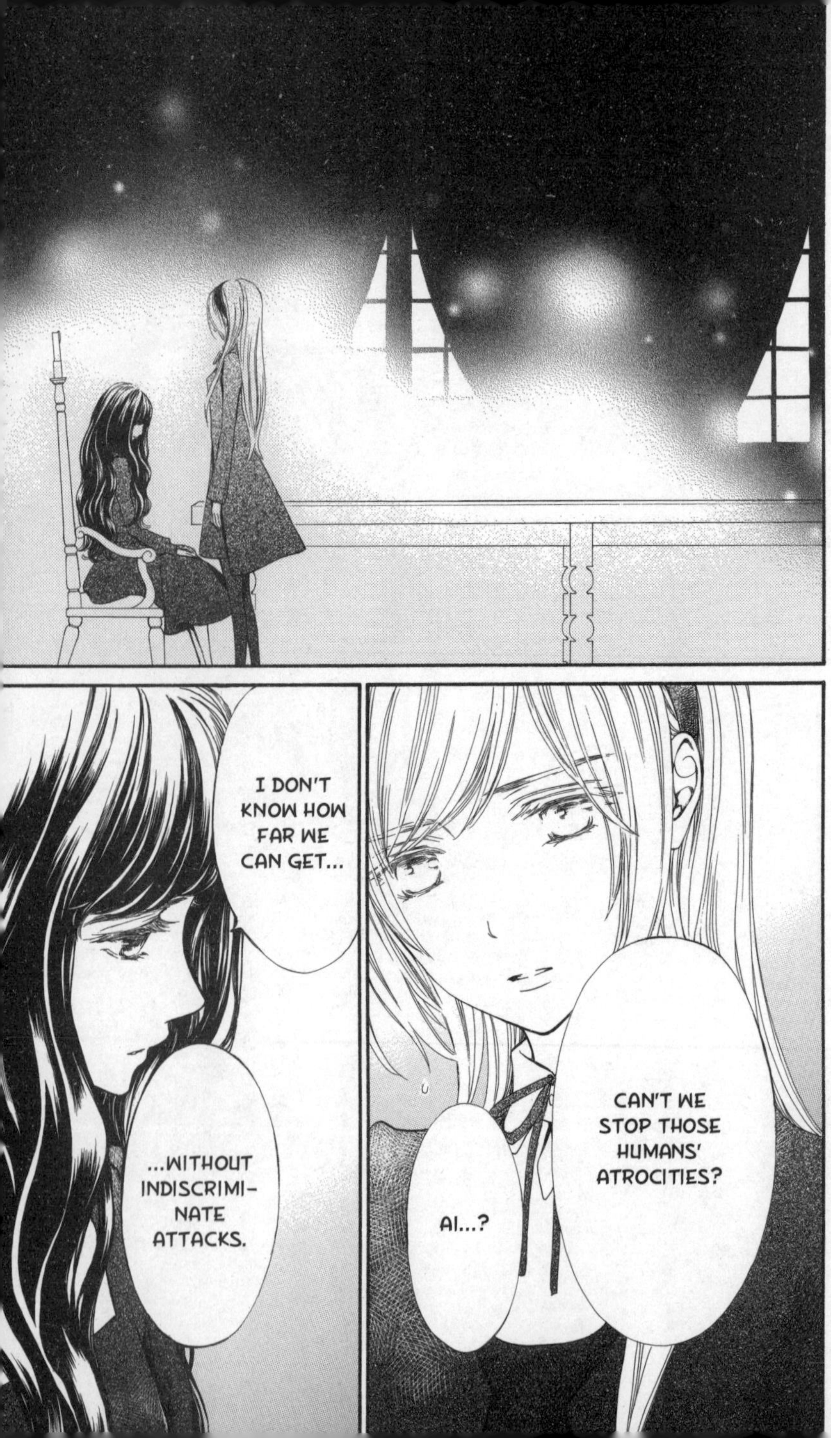
CAN'T WE STOP THOSE HUMANS' ATROCITIES?
AI...?
I DON'T KNOW HOW FAR WE CAN GET...
...WITHOUT INDISCRIMI-NATE ATTACKS.

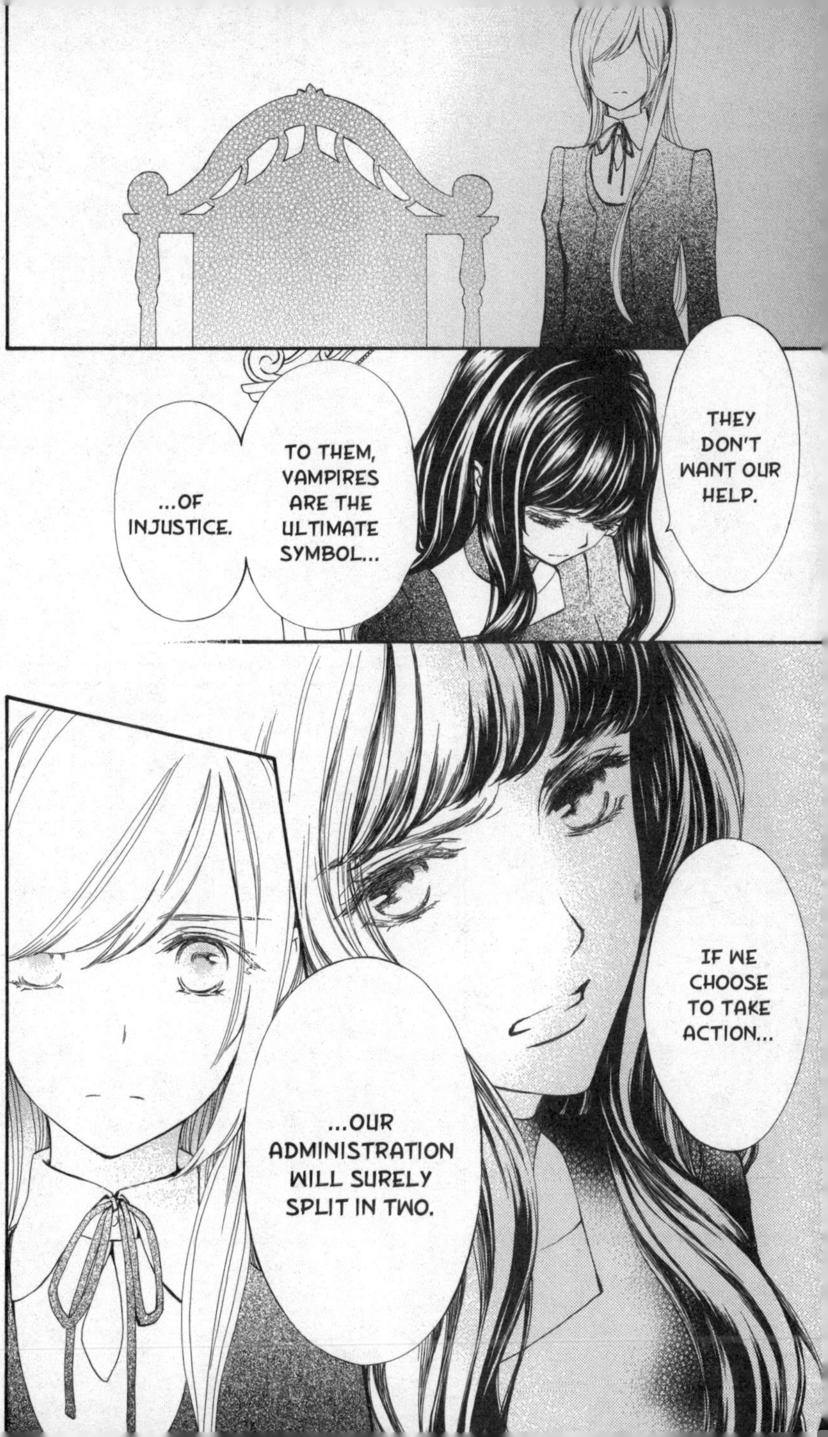
THEY DON'T WANT OUR HELP.
TO THEM, VAMPIRES ARE THE ULTIMATE SYMBOL...
...OF INJUSTICE.
IF WE CHOOSE TO TAKE ACTION...
...OUR ADMINISTRATION WILL SURELY SPLIT IN TWO.

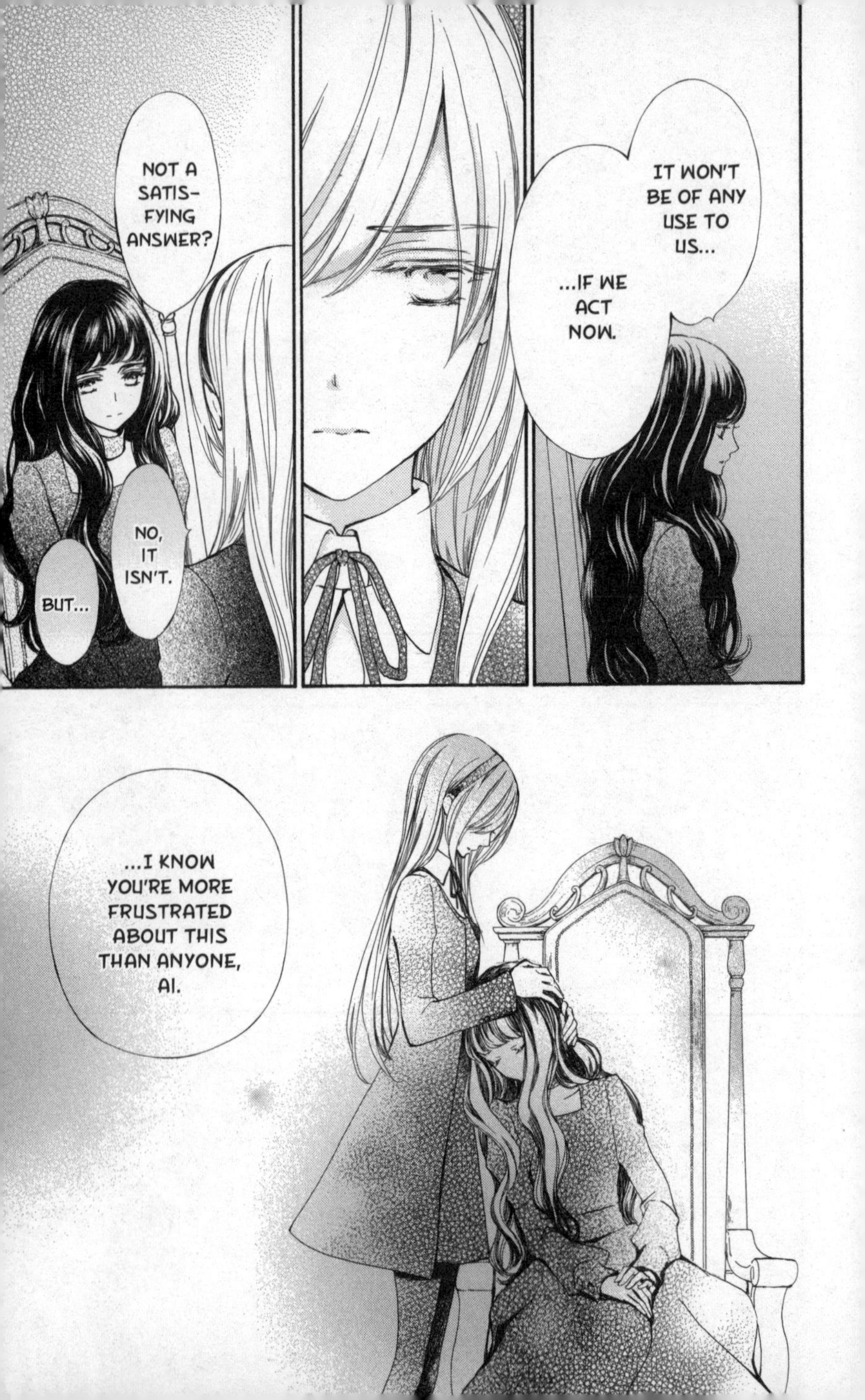
IT WON'T BE OF ANY USE TO US...
...IF WE ACT NOW.
NOT A SATIS-FYING ANSWER?
NO, IT ISN'T.
BUT...
...I KNOW YOU'RE MORE FRUSTRATED ABOUT THIS THAN ANYONE, AI.

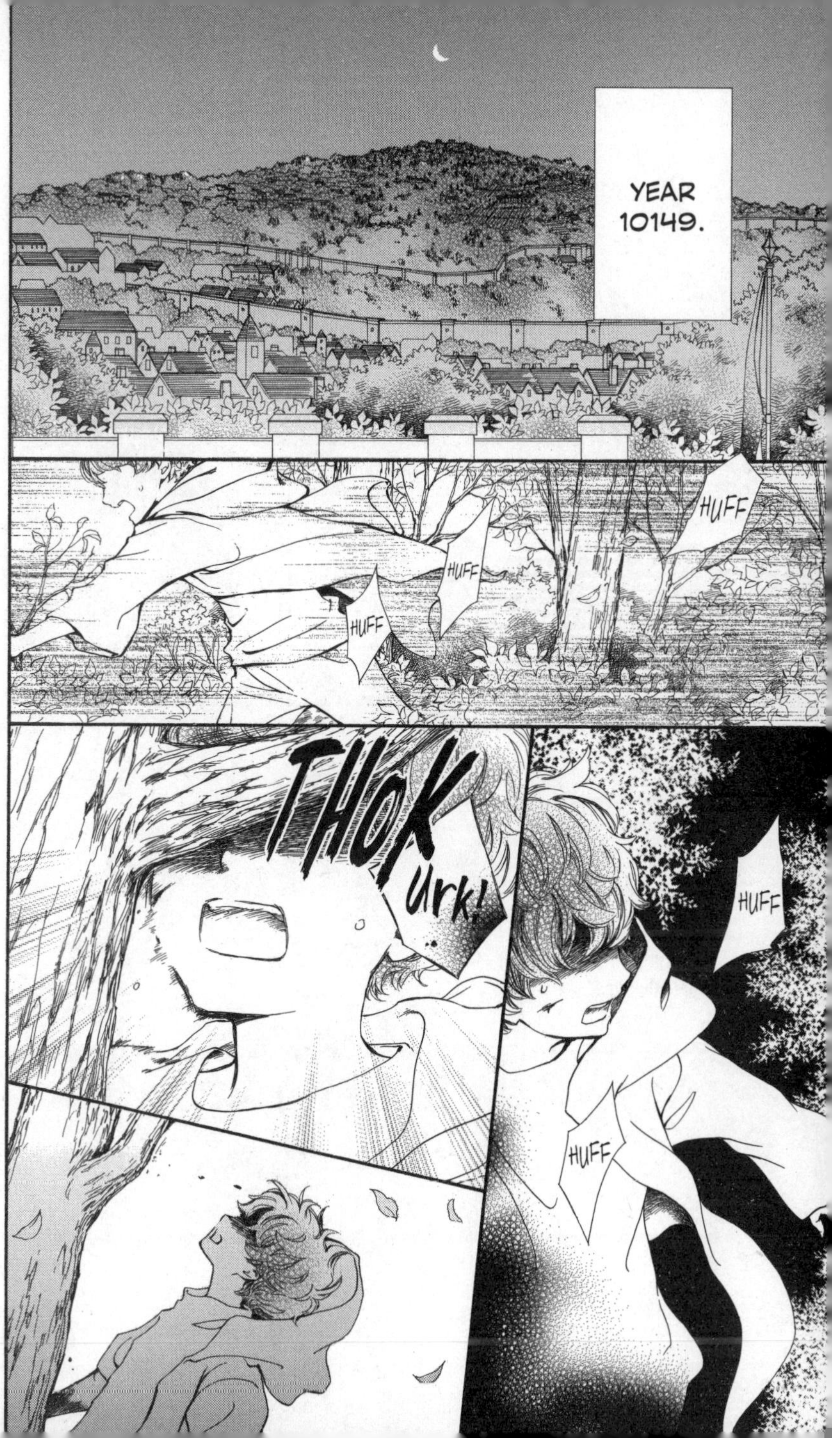
YEAR 10149.
HUFF
HUFF
HUFF
HUFF
HUFF
THOK
urk!

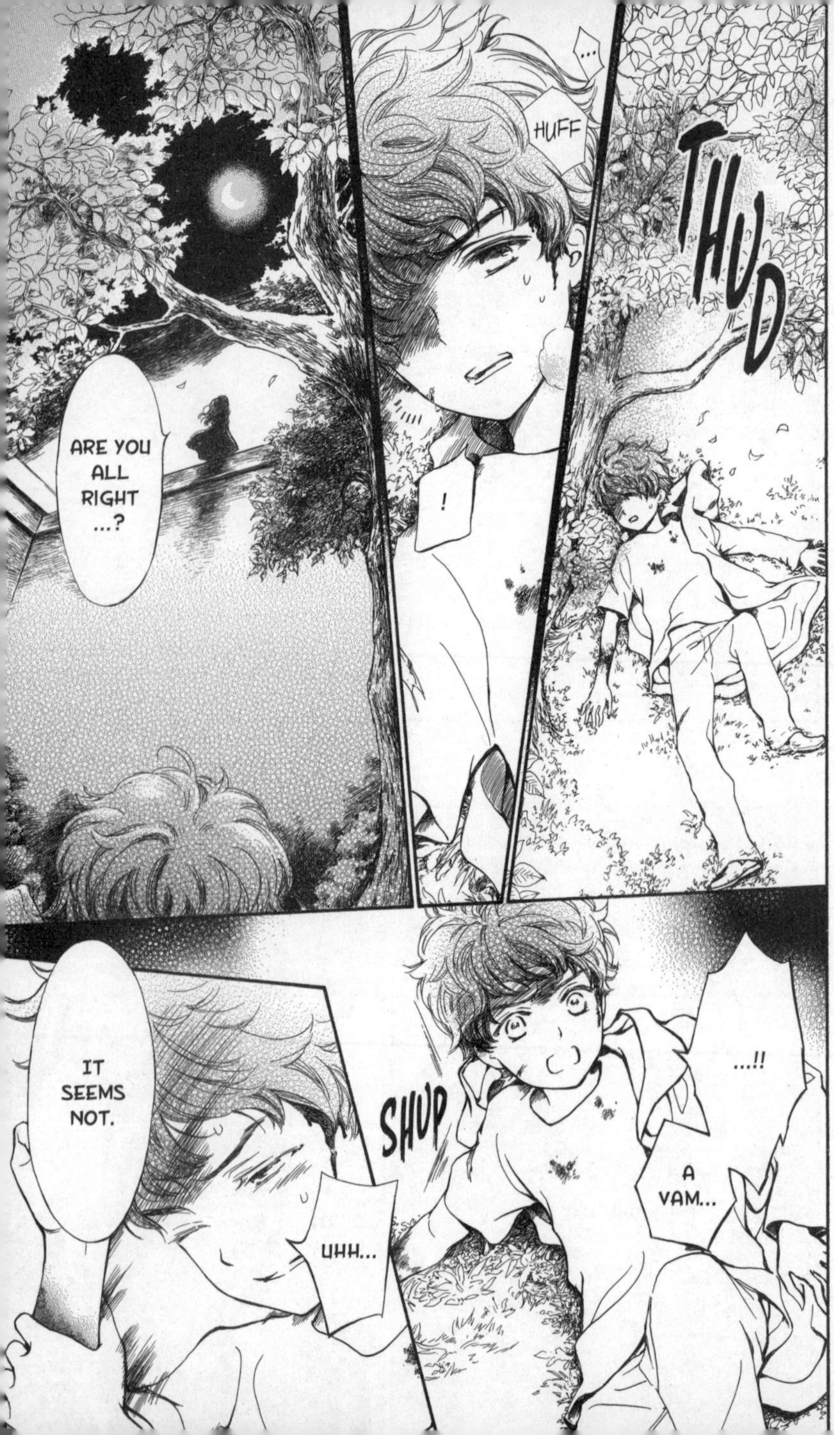
THUD
...
HUFF
!
ARE YOU ALL RIGHT ...?
...!!
A VAM...
SHUP
IT SEEMS NOT.
UHH...

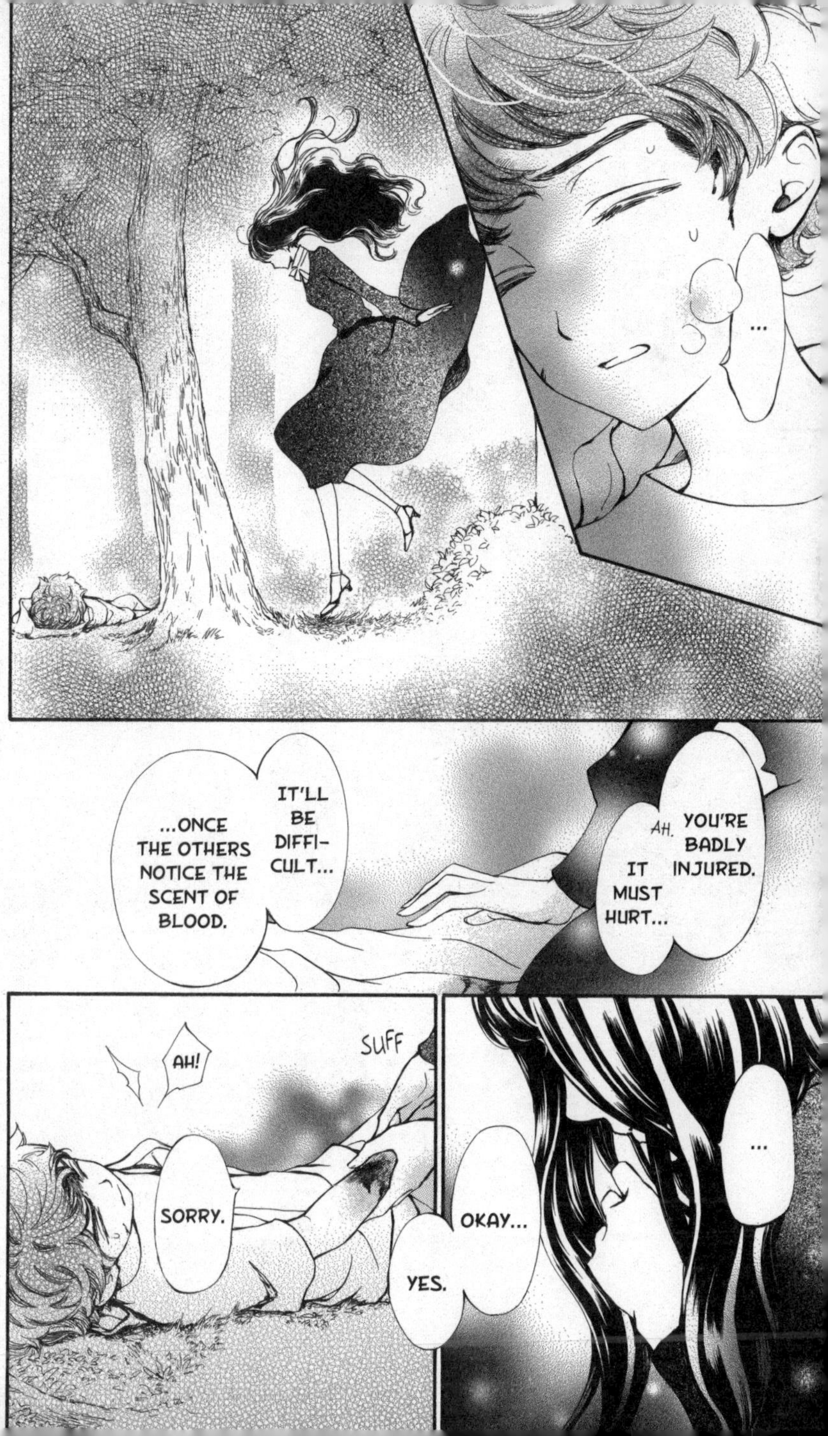
...
AH.
YOU'RE BADLY INJURED.
IT MUST HURT...
IT'LL BE DIFFI-CULT...
...ONCE THE OTHERS NOTICE THE SCENT OF BLOOD.
...
OKAY...
YES.
SUFF
AH!
SORRY.

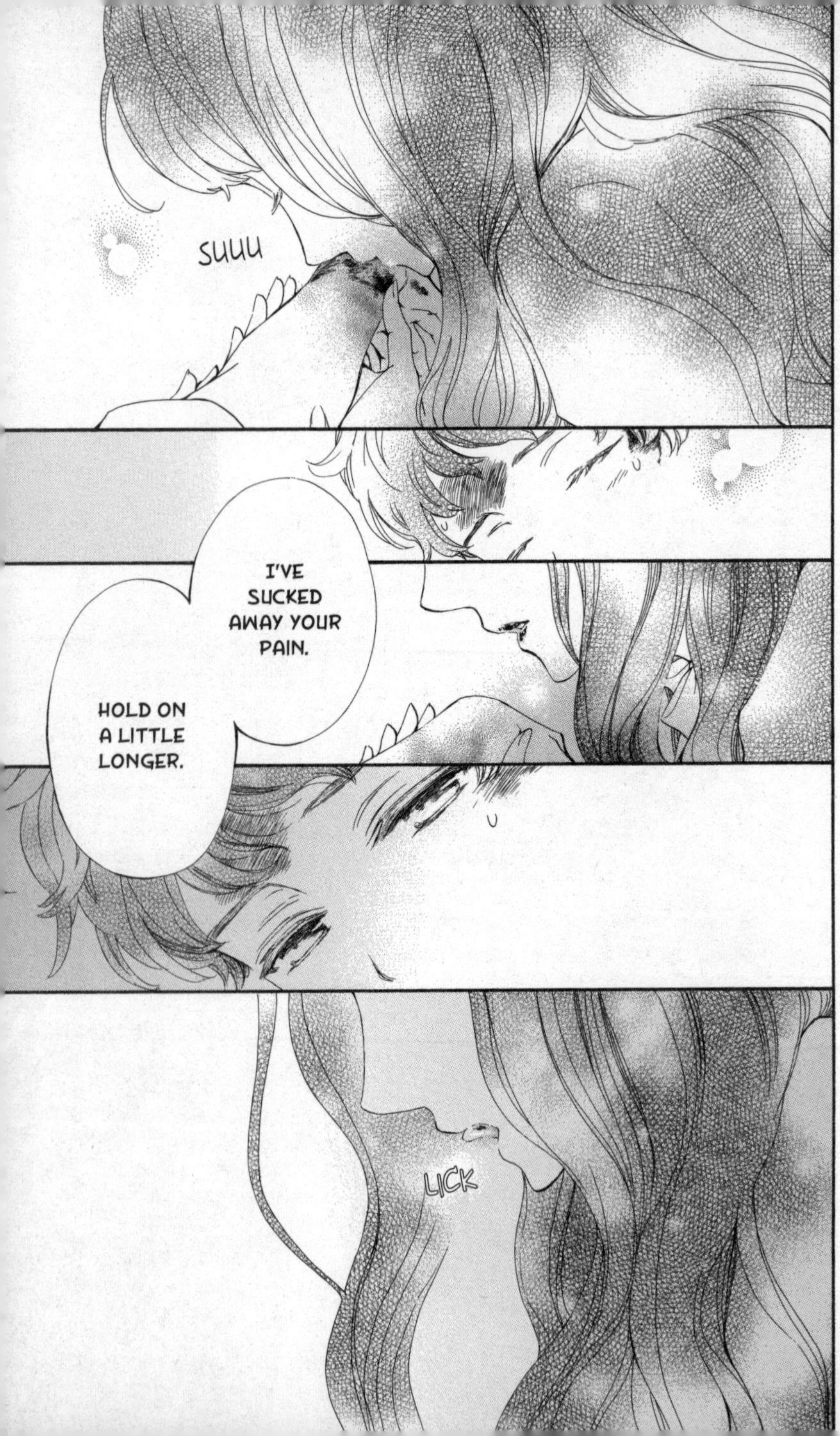
SUUU
I'VE SUCKED AWAY YOUR PAIN.
HOLD ON A LITTLE LONGER.
LICK

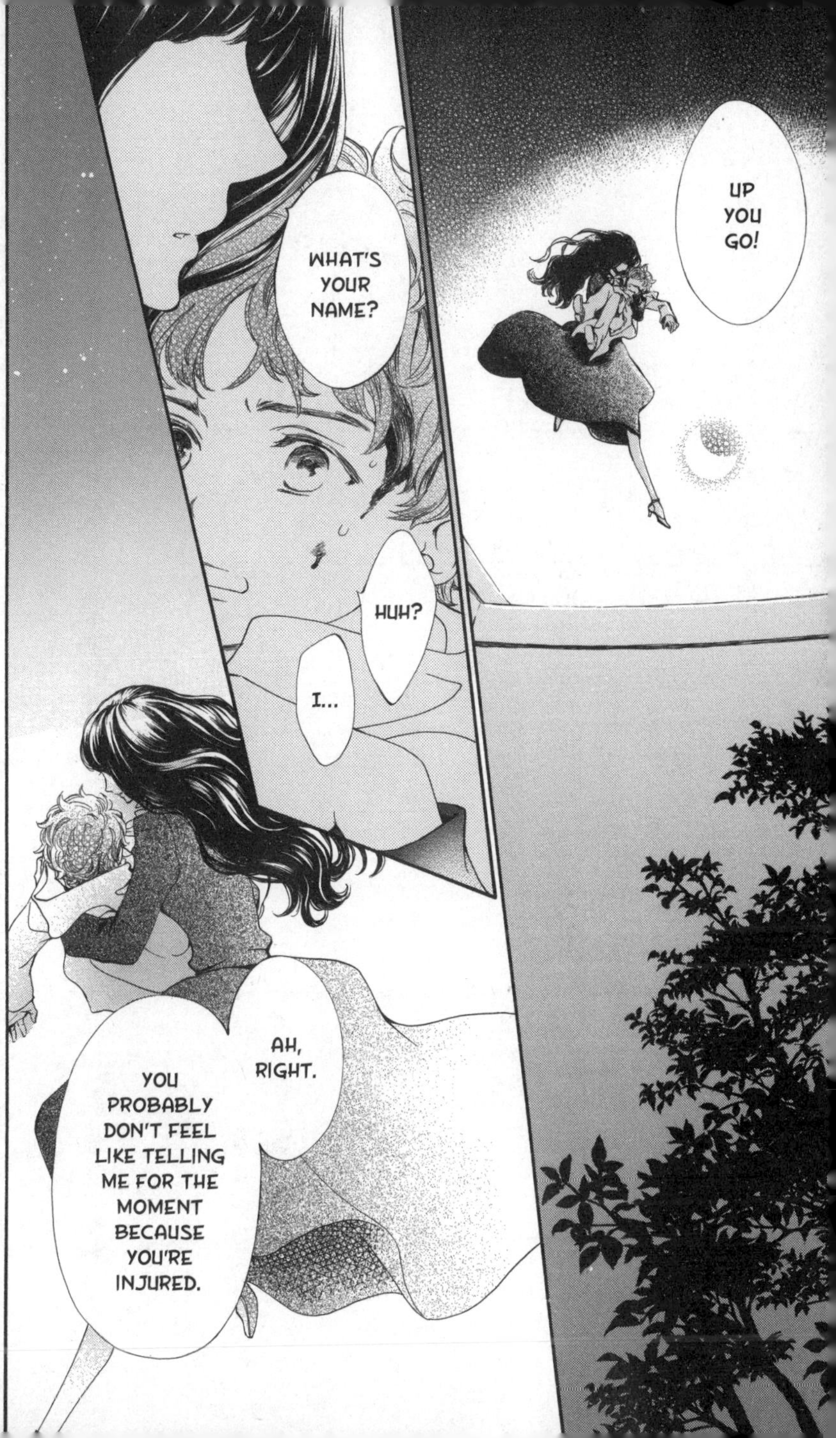
UP YOU GO!
WHAT'S YOUR NAME?
HUH?
I...
AH, RIGHT.
YOU PROBABLY DON'T FEEL LIKE TELLING ME FOR THE MOMENT BECAUSE YOU'RE INJURED.

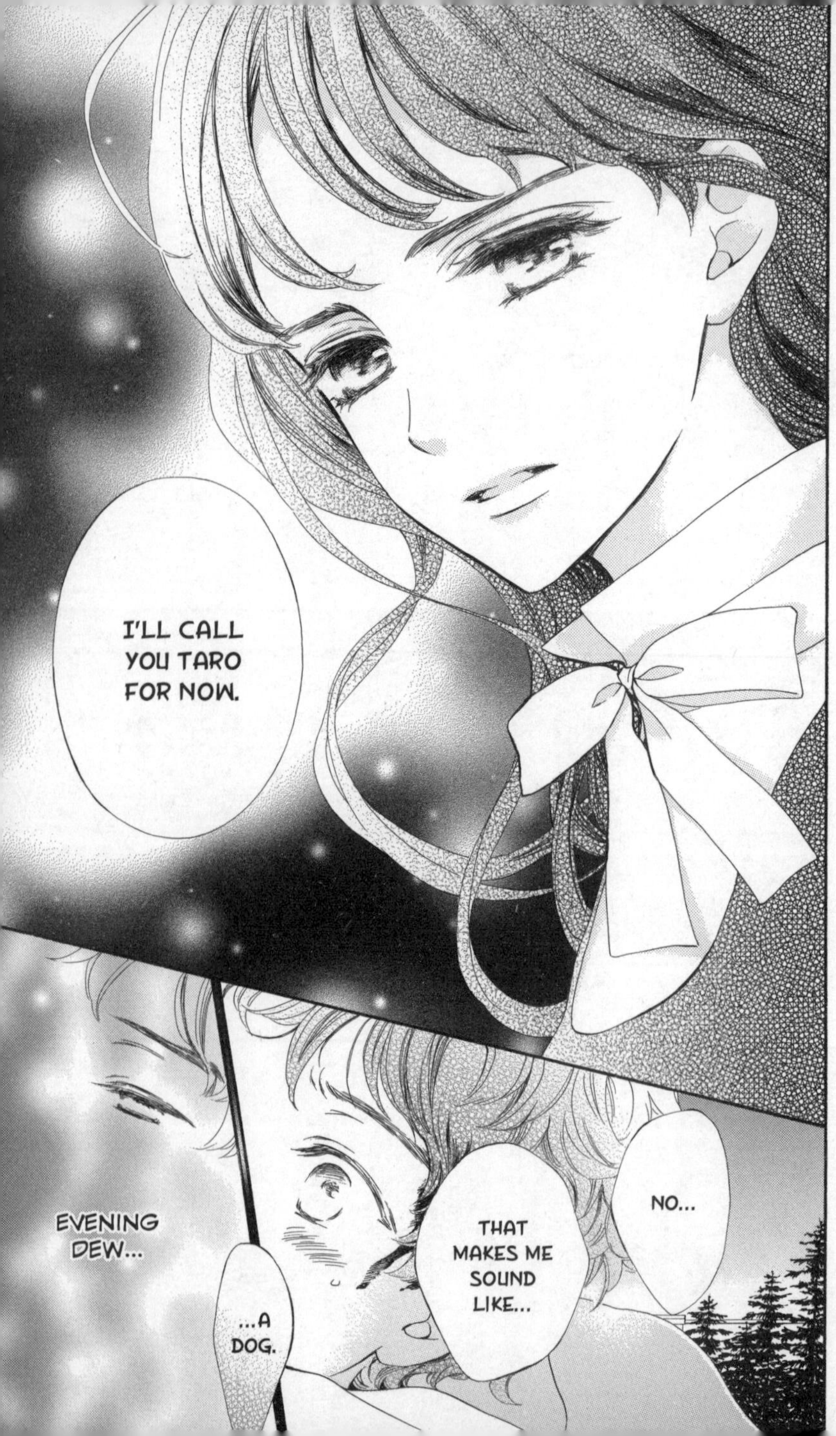
I'LL CALL YOU TARO FOR NOW.
NO...
THAT MAKES ME SOUND LIKE...
...A DOG.
EVENING DEW...

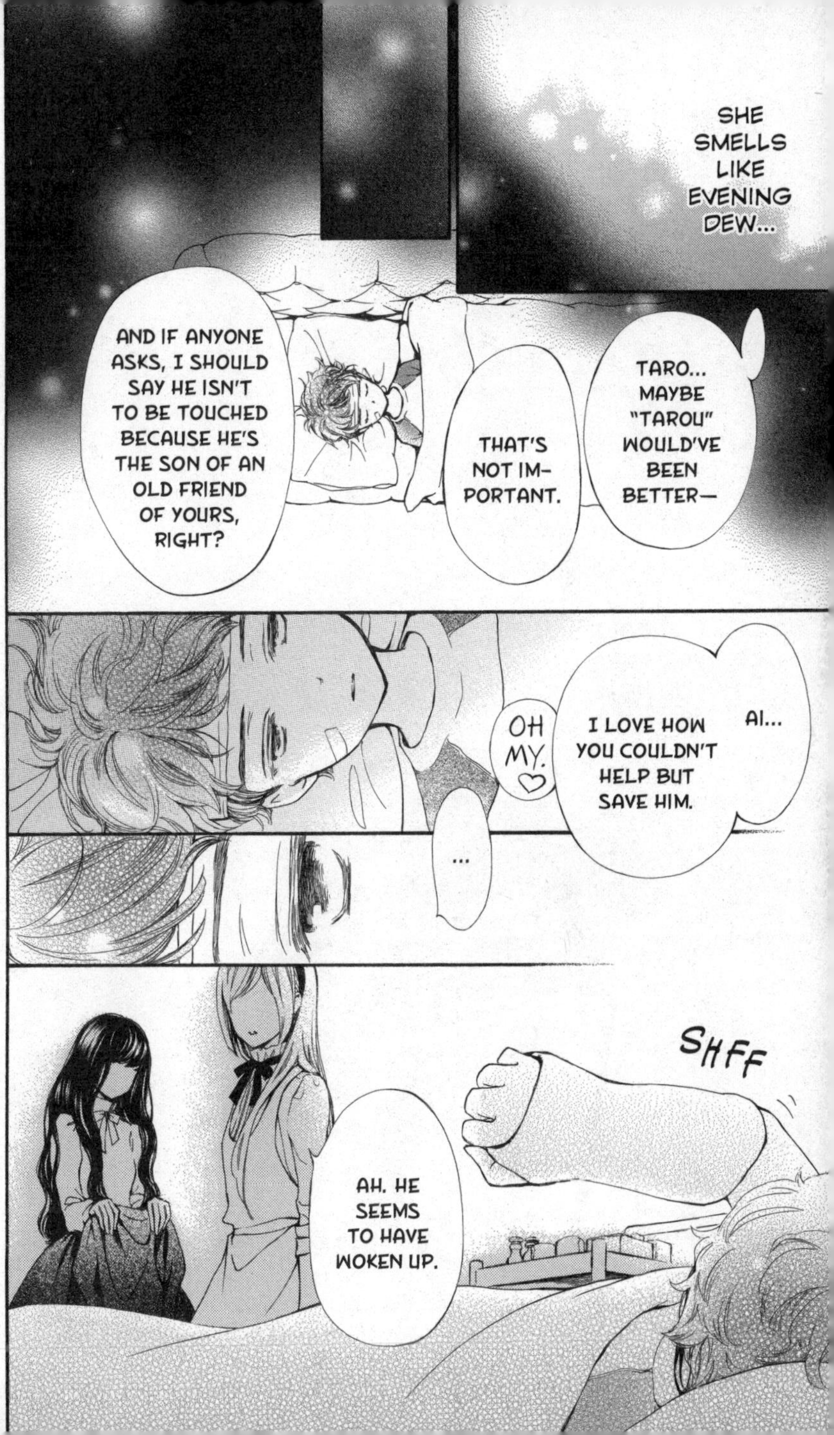
SHE SMELLS LIKE EVENING DEW...
TARO... MAYBE "TAROU" WOULD'VE BEEN BETTER—
THAT'S NOT IM-PORTANT.
AND IF ANYONE ASKS, I SHOULD SAY HE ISN'T TO BE TOUCHED BECAUSE HE'S THE SON OF AN OLD FRIEND OF YOURS, RIGHT?
AI...
I LOVE HOW YOU COULDN'T HELP BUT SAVE HIM.
OH MY. ♡
...
SHFF
AH. HE SEEMS TO HAVE WOKEN UP.

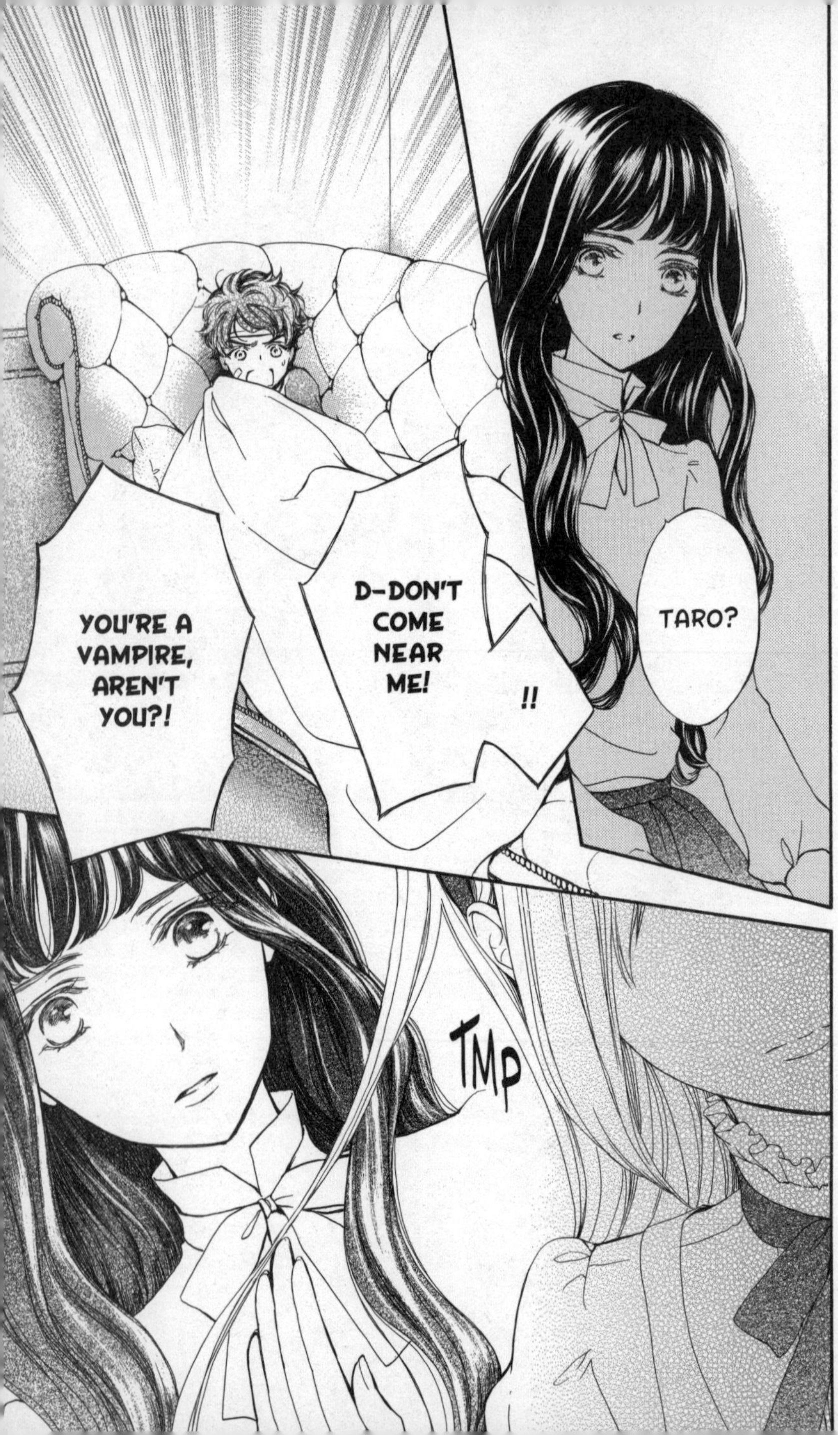
TARO?
!!
D-DON'T COME NEAR ME!
YOU'RE A VAMPIRE, AREN'T YOU?!
TMP

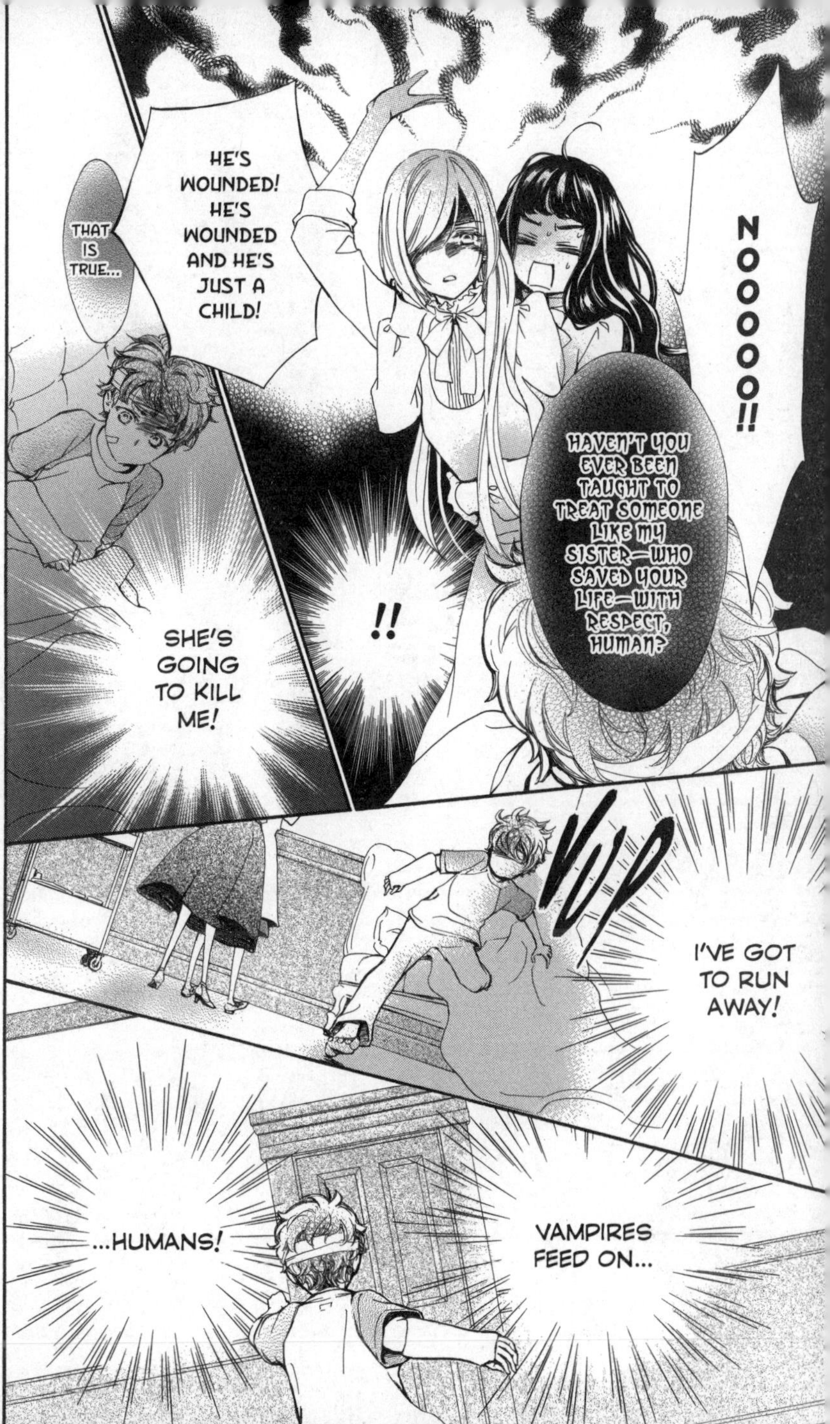
NOOOOO!!
HE'S WOUNDED! HE'S WOUNDED AND HE'S JUST A CHILD!
HAVEN'T YOU EVER BEEN TAUGHT TO TREAT SOMEONE LIKE MY SISTER—WHO SAVED YOUR LIFE—WITH RESPECT, HUMAN?
!!
THAT IS TRUE...
SHE'S GOING TO KILL ME!
VIP
I'VE GOT TO RUN AWAY!
VAMPIRES FEED ON...
...HUMANS!

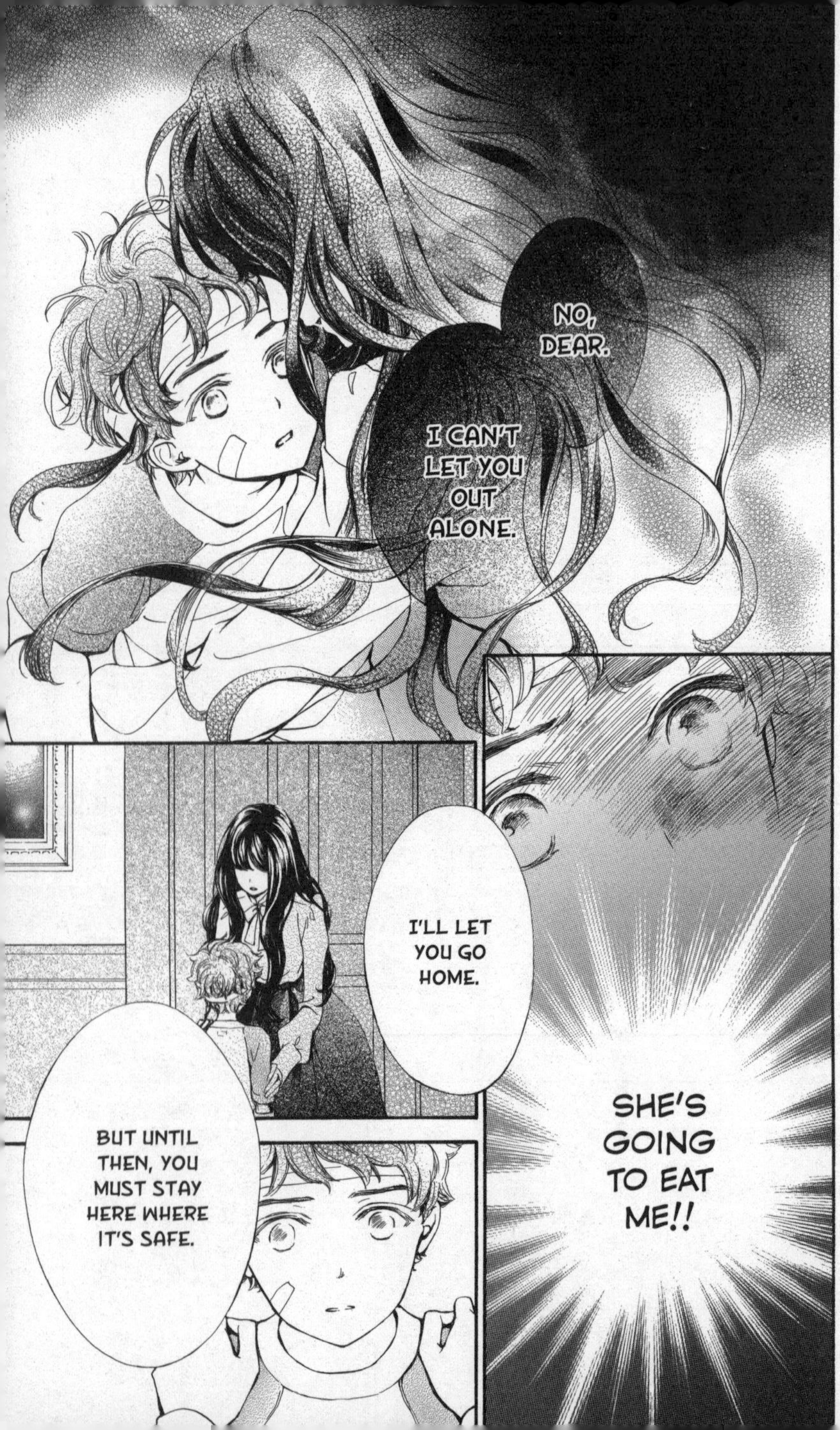
NO, DEAR.
I CAN'T LET YOU OUT ALONE.
SHE'S GOING TO EAT ME!!
I'LL LET YOU GO HOME.
BUT UNTIL THEN, YOU MUST STAY HERE WHERE IT'S SAFE.

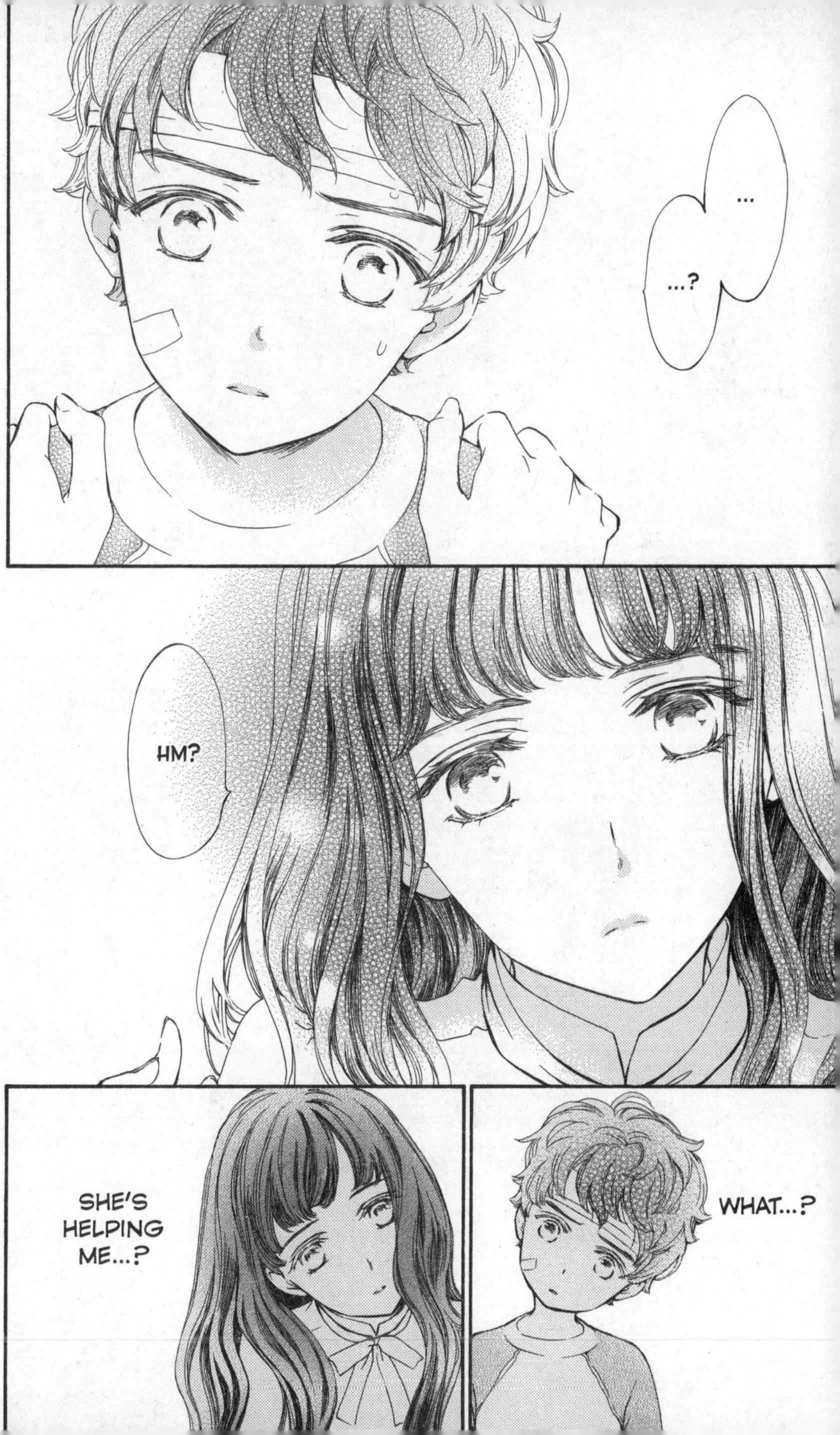
...
...?
HM?
WHAT...?
SHE'S HELPING ME...?

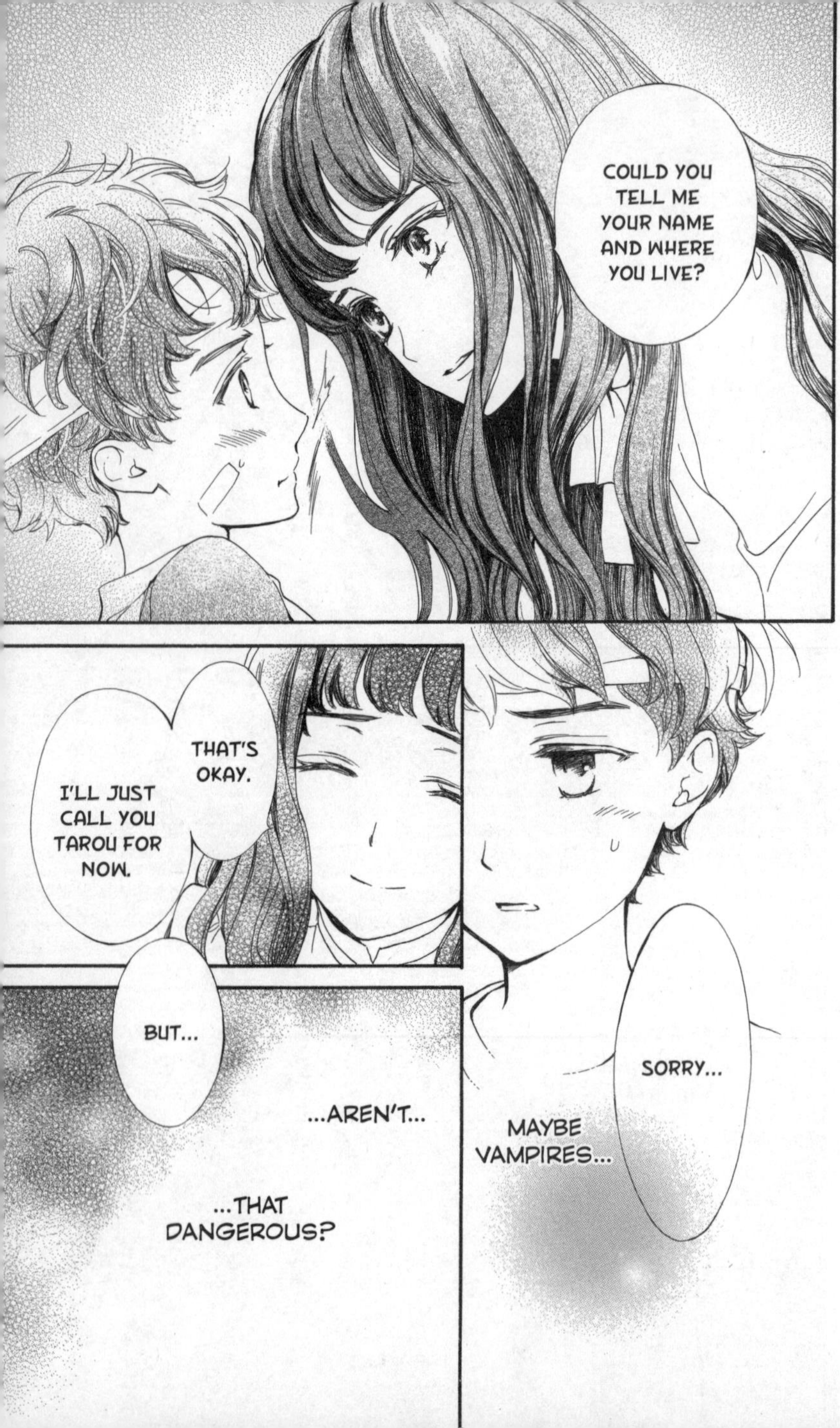
COULD YOU TELL ME YOUR NAME AND WHERE YOU LIVE?
SORRY...
THAT'S OKAY.
I'LL JUST CALL YOU TAROU FOR NOW.
BUT...
MAYBE VAMPIRES...
...AREN'T...
...THAT DANGEROUS?

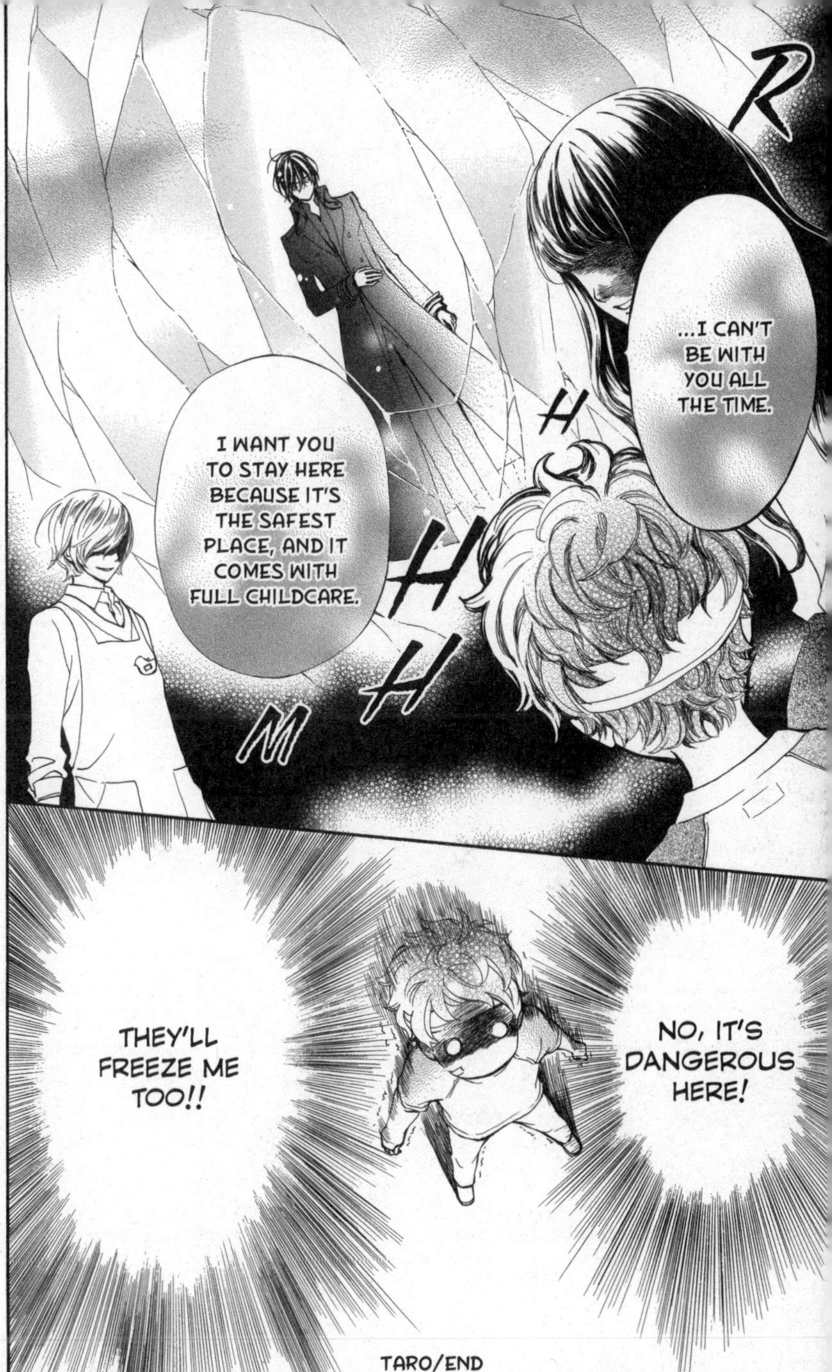
RHHHHM
...I CAN'T BE WITH YOU ALL THE TIME.
I WANT YOU TO STAY HERE BECAUSE IT'S THE SAFEST PLACE, AND IT COMES WITH FULL CHILDCARE.
NO, IT'S DANGEROUS HERE!
THEY'LL FREEZE ME TOO!!
TARO/END

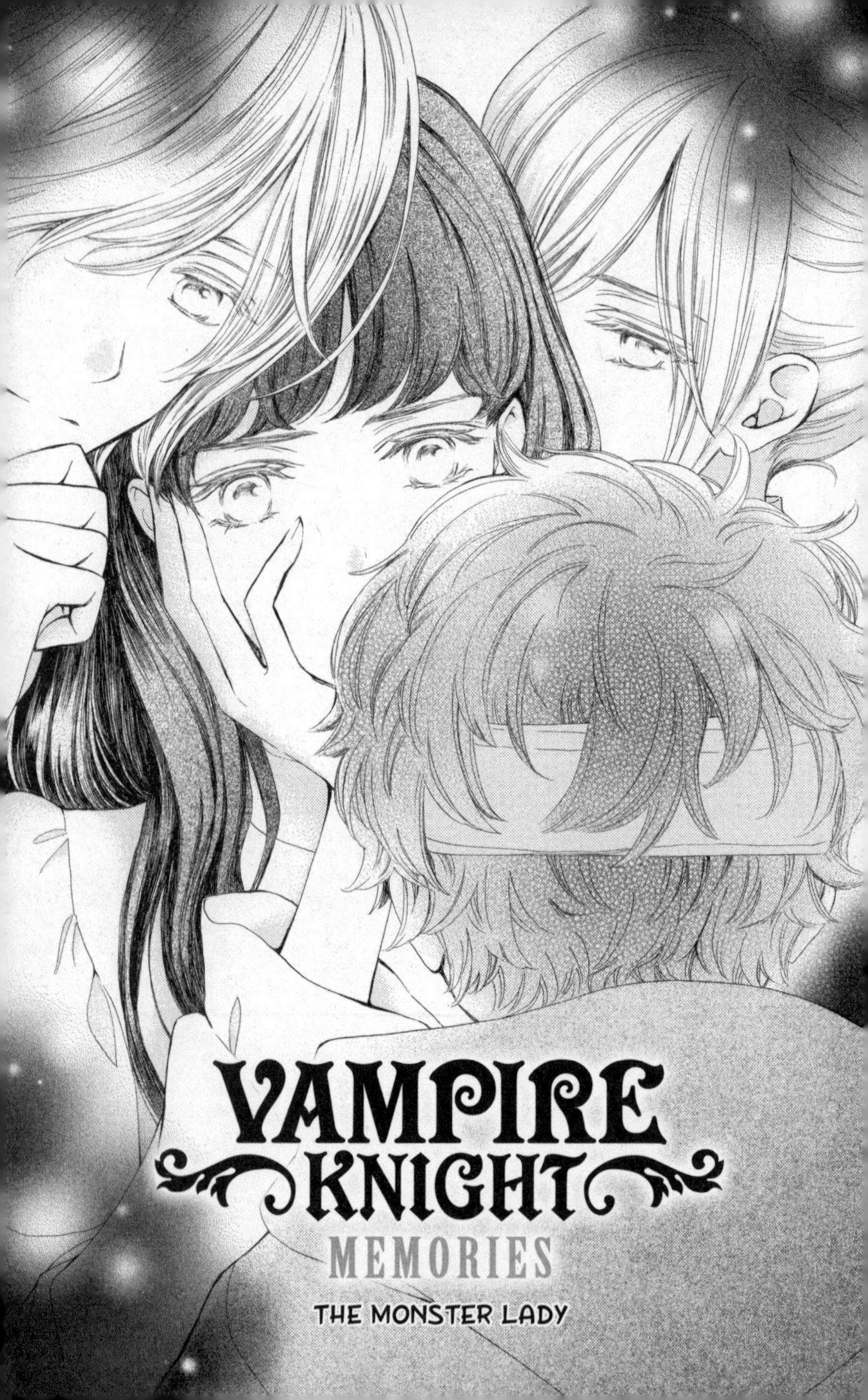
VAMPIRE KNIGHT
MEMORIES
THE MONSTER LADY

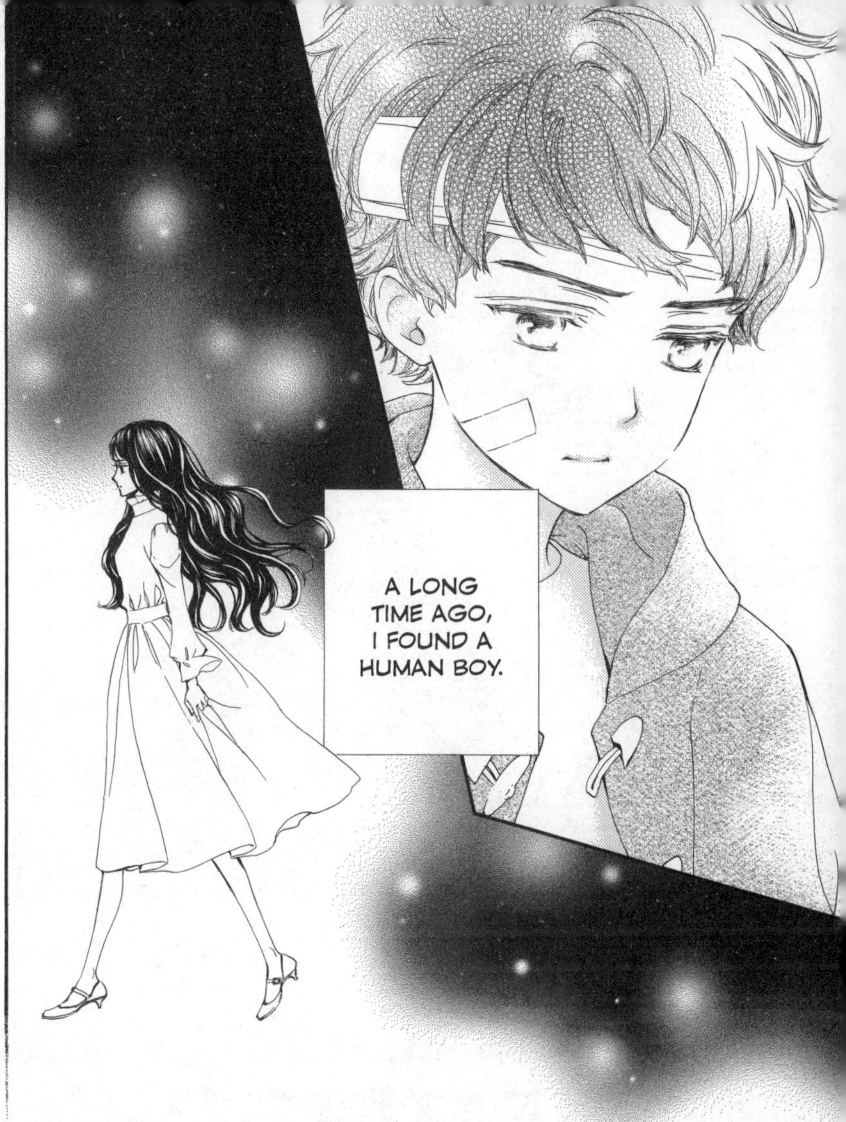
A LONG TIME AGO, I FOUND A HUMAN BOY.

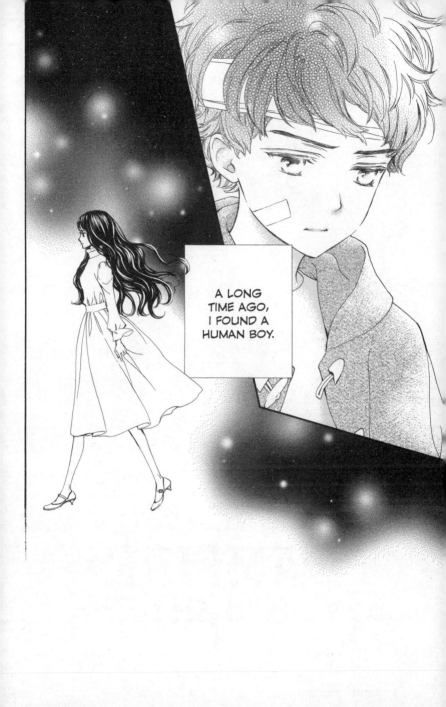

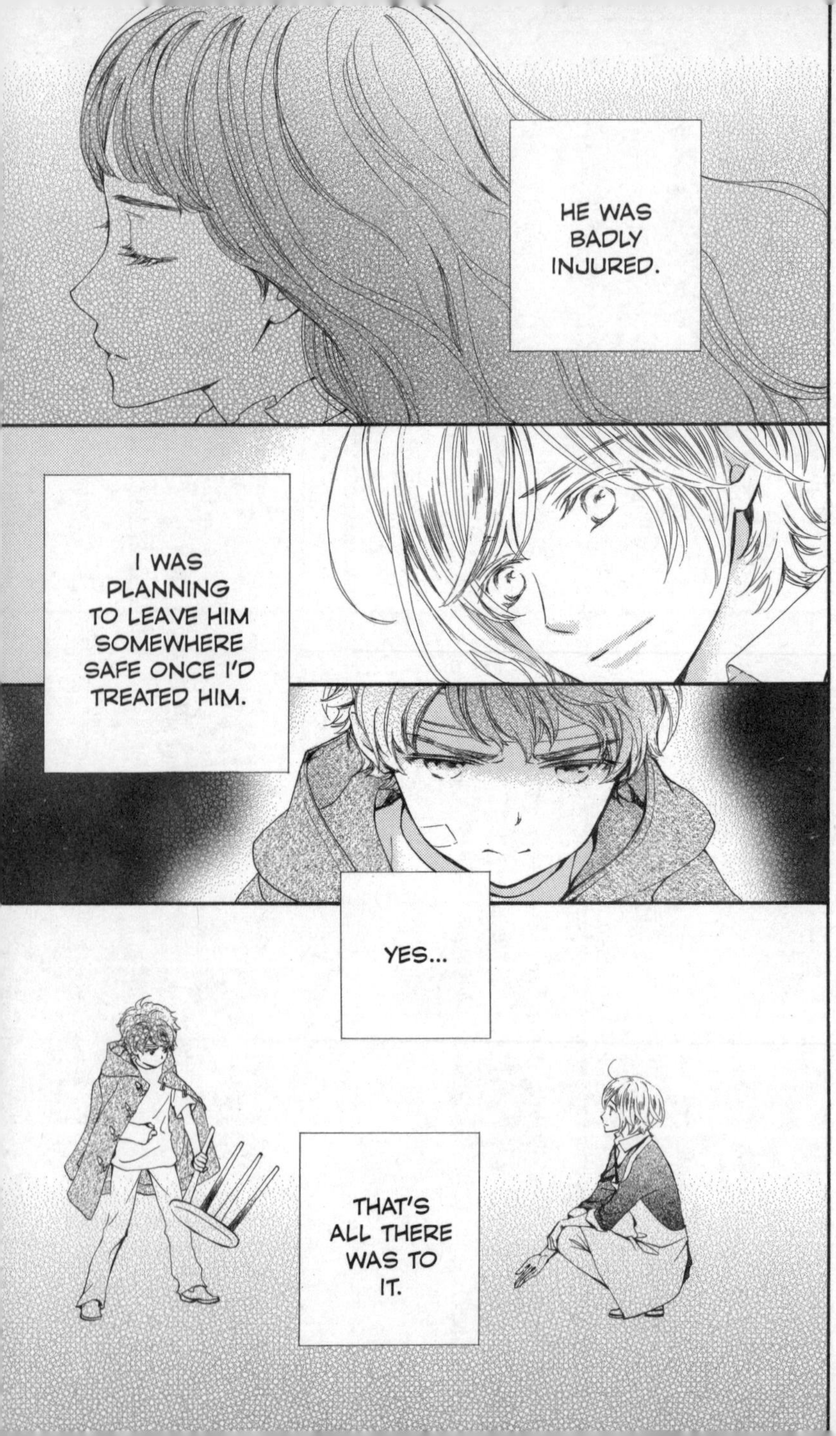
HE WAS BADLY INJURED.
I WAS PLANNING TO LEAVE HIM SOMEWHERE SAFE ONCE I'D TREATED HIM.
YES...
THAT'S ALL THERE WAS TO IT.

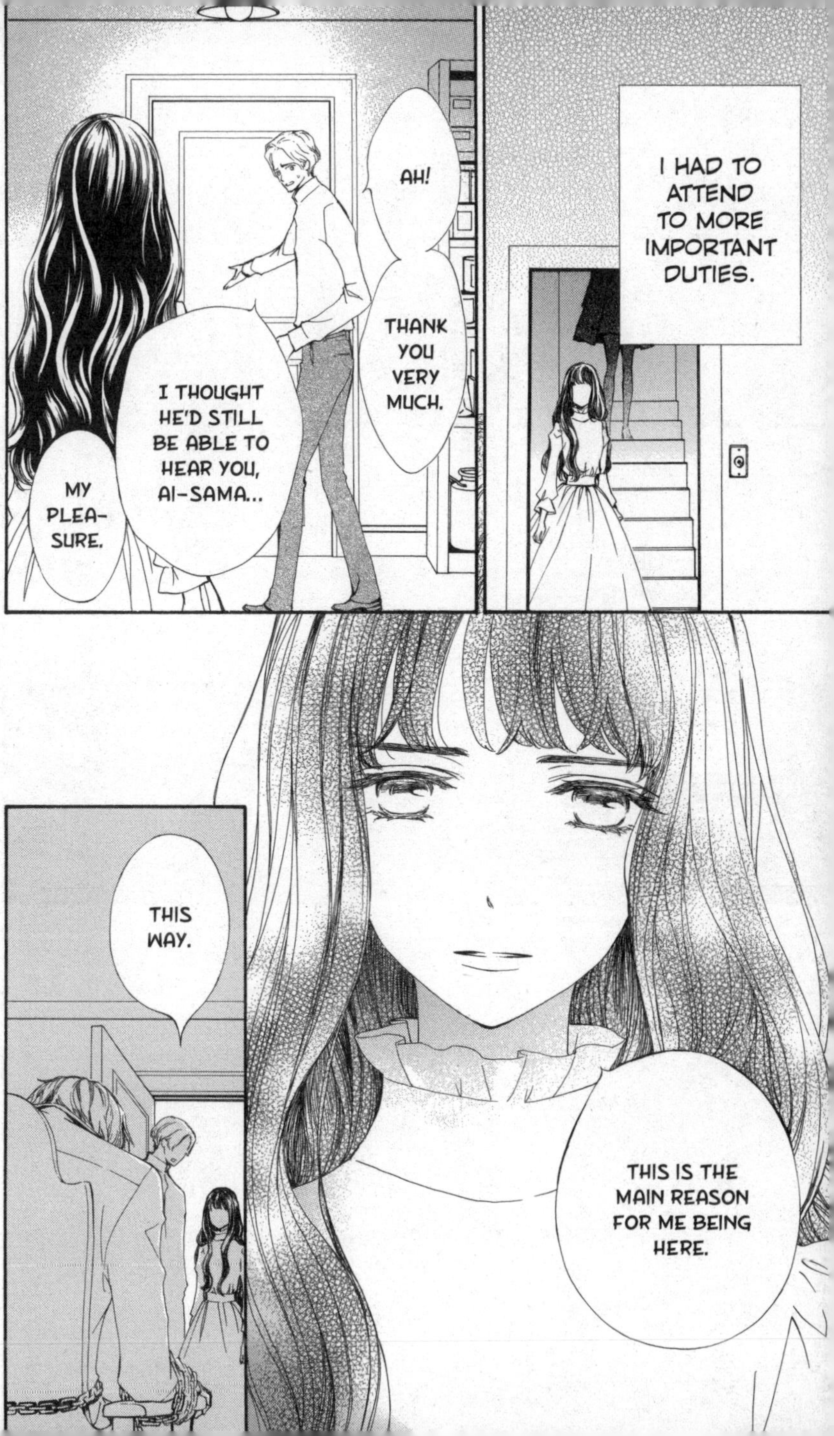
I HAD TO ATTEND TO MORE IMPORTANT DUTIES.
AH!
THANK YOU VERY MUCH.
I THOUGHT HE'D STILL BE ABLE TO HEAR YOU, AI-SAMA...
MY PLEA-SURE.
THIS IS THE MAIN REASON FOR ME BEING HERE.
THIS WAY.

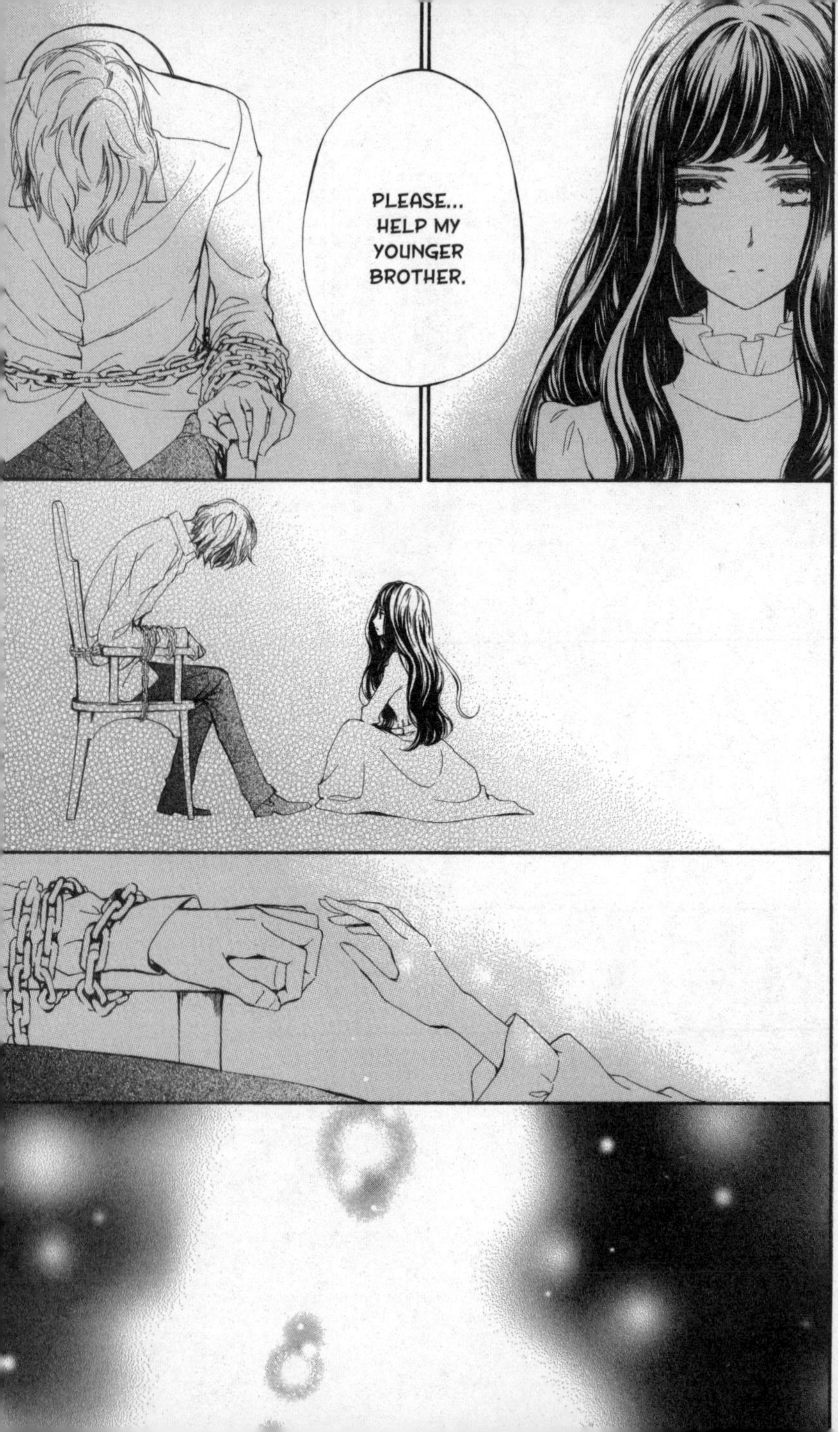
PLEASE... HELP MY YOUNGER BROTHER.

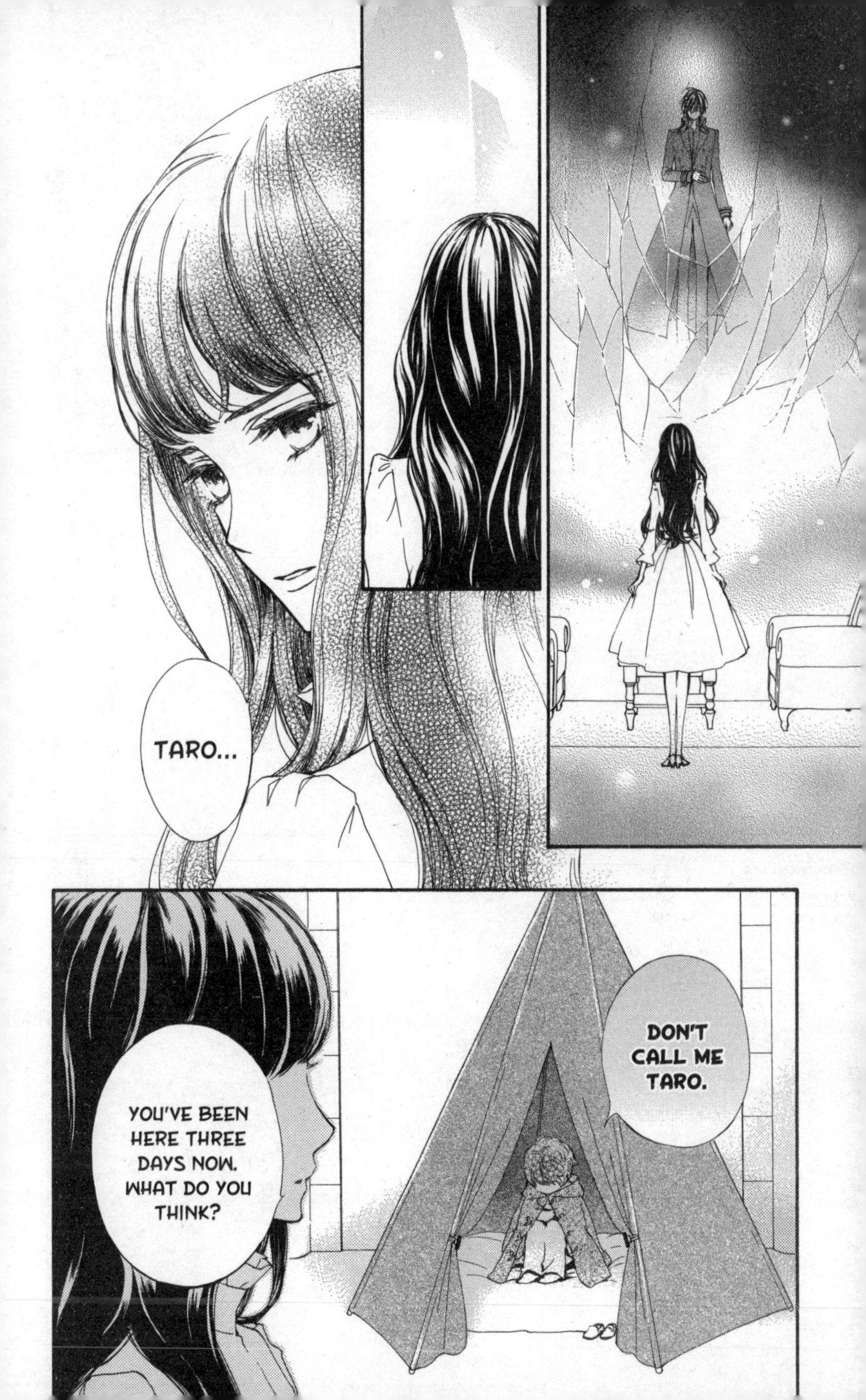
TARO...
DON'T CALL ME TARO.
YOU'VE BEEN HERE THREE DAYS NOW. WHAT DO YOU THINK?

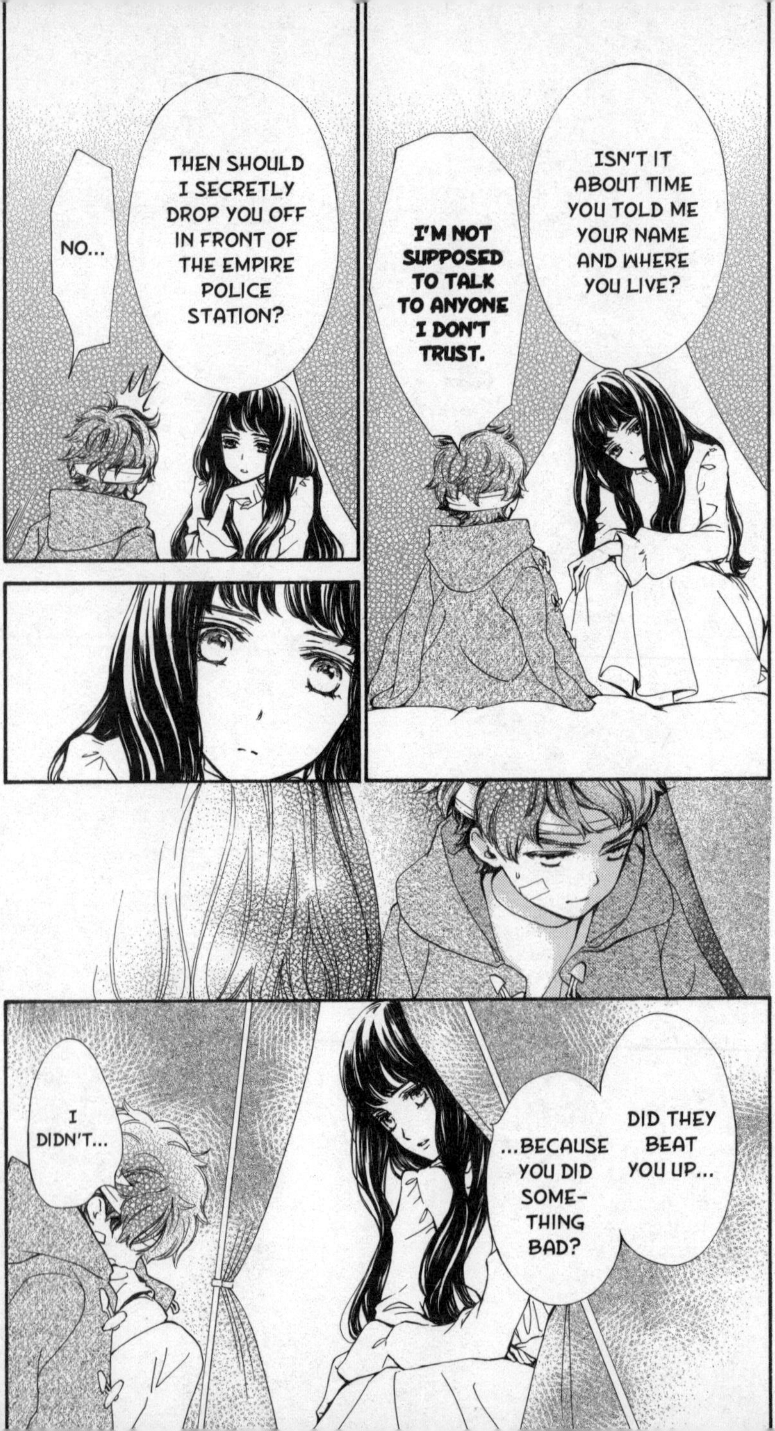
ISN'T IT ABOUT TIME YOU TOLD ME YOUR NAME AND WHERE YOU LIVE?
I'M NOT SUPPOSED TO TALK TO ANYONE I DON'T TRUST.
THEN SHOULD I SECRETLY DROP YOU OFF IN FRONT OF THE EMPIRE POLICE STATION?
NO...
DID THEY BEAT YOU UP...
...BECAUSE YOU DID SOME-THING BAD?
I DIDN'T...

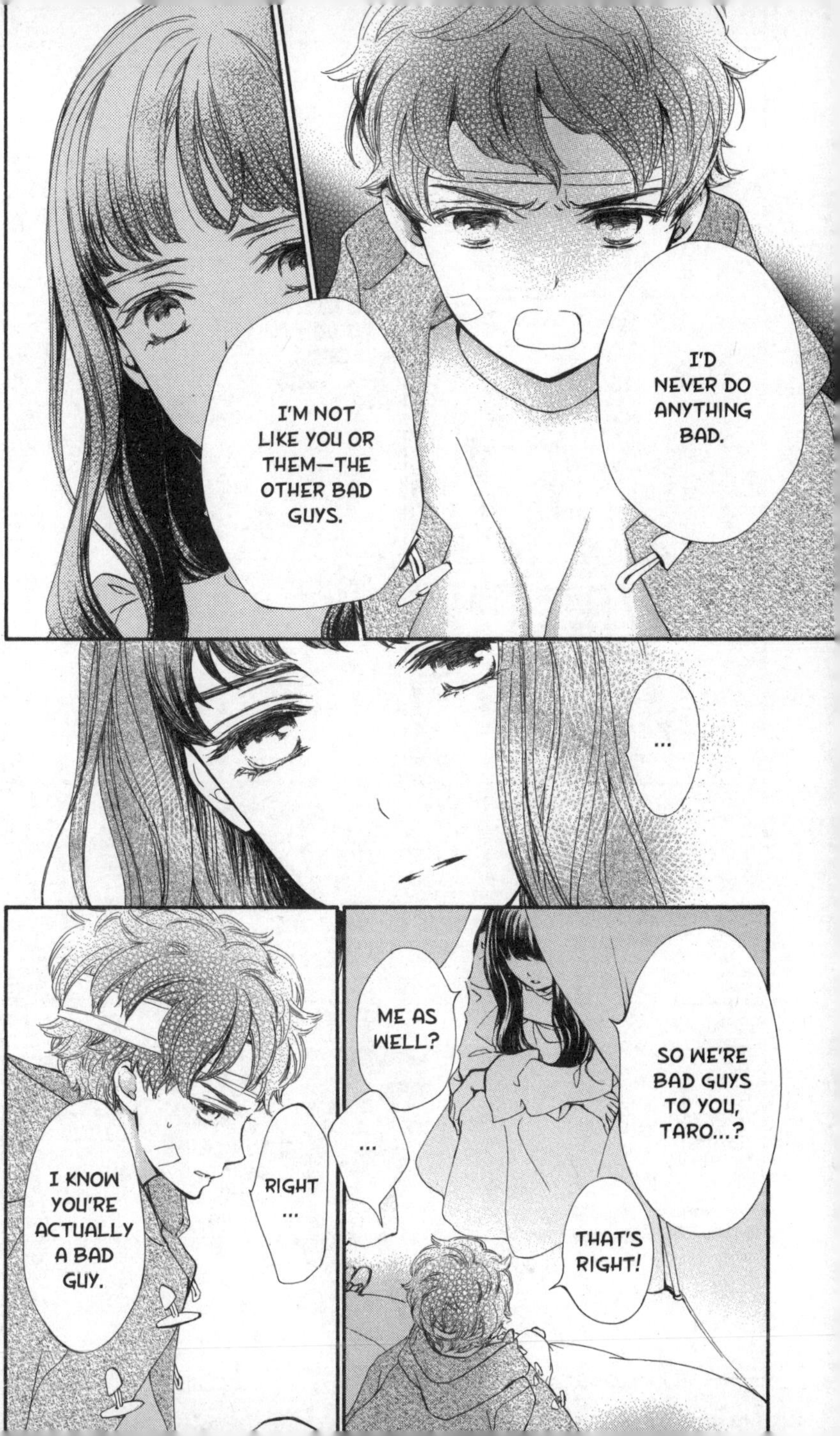
I'D NEVER DO ANYTHING BAD.
I'M NOT LIKE YOU OR THEM—THE OTHER BAD GUYS.
...
SO WE'RE BAD GUYS TO YOU, TARO...?
ME AS WELL?
THAT'S RIGHT!
...
RIGHT...
I KNOW YOU'RE ACTUALLY A BAD GUY.

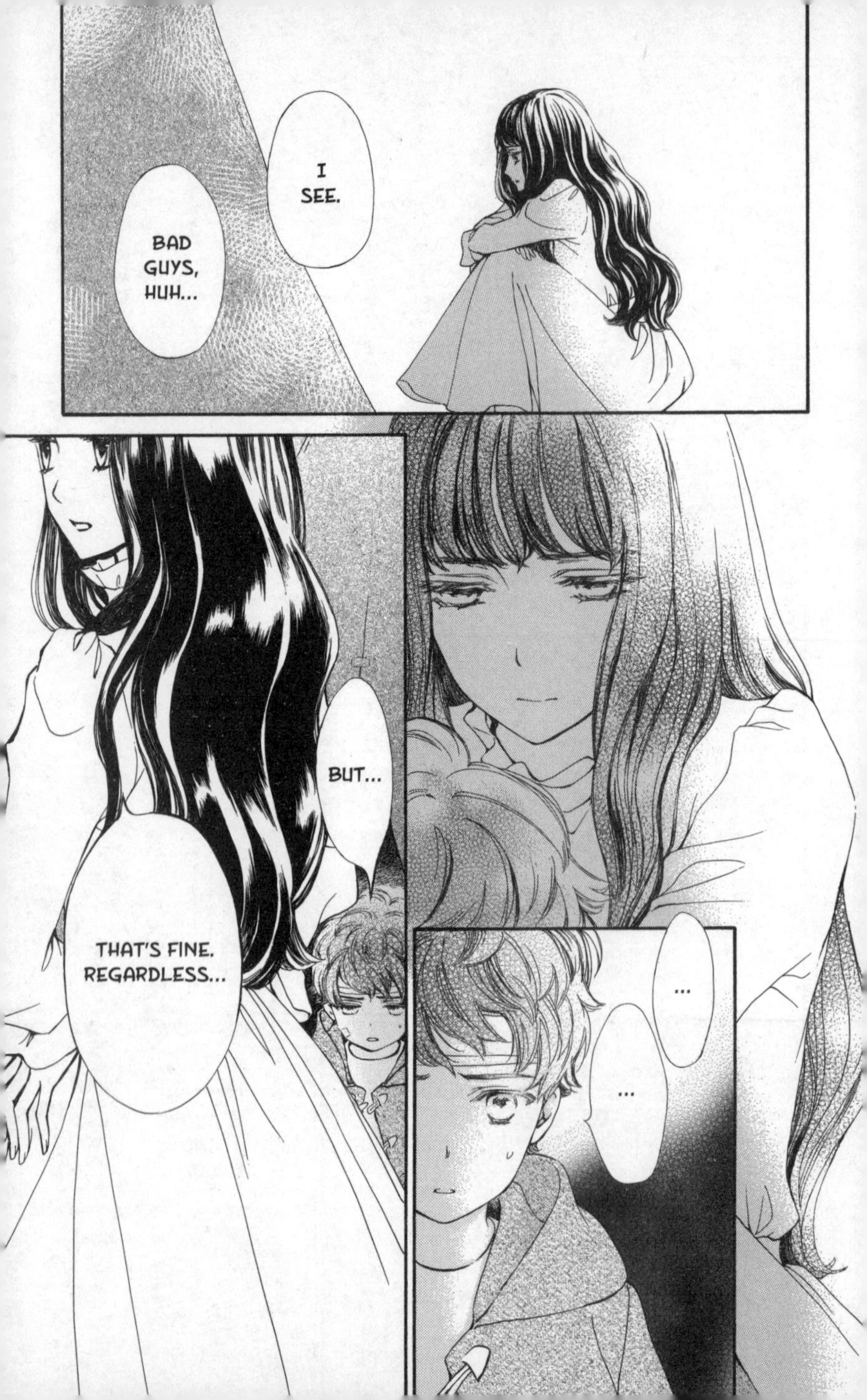
I SEE.
BAD GUYS, HUH...
...
...
BUT...
THAT'S FINE. REGARDLESS...

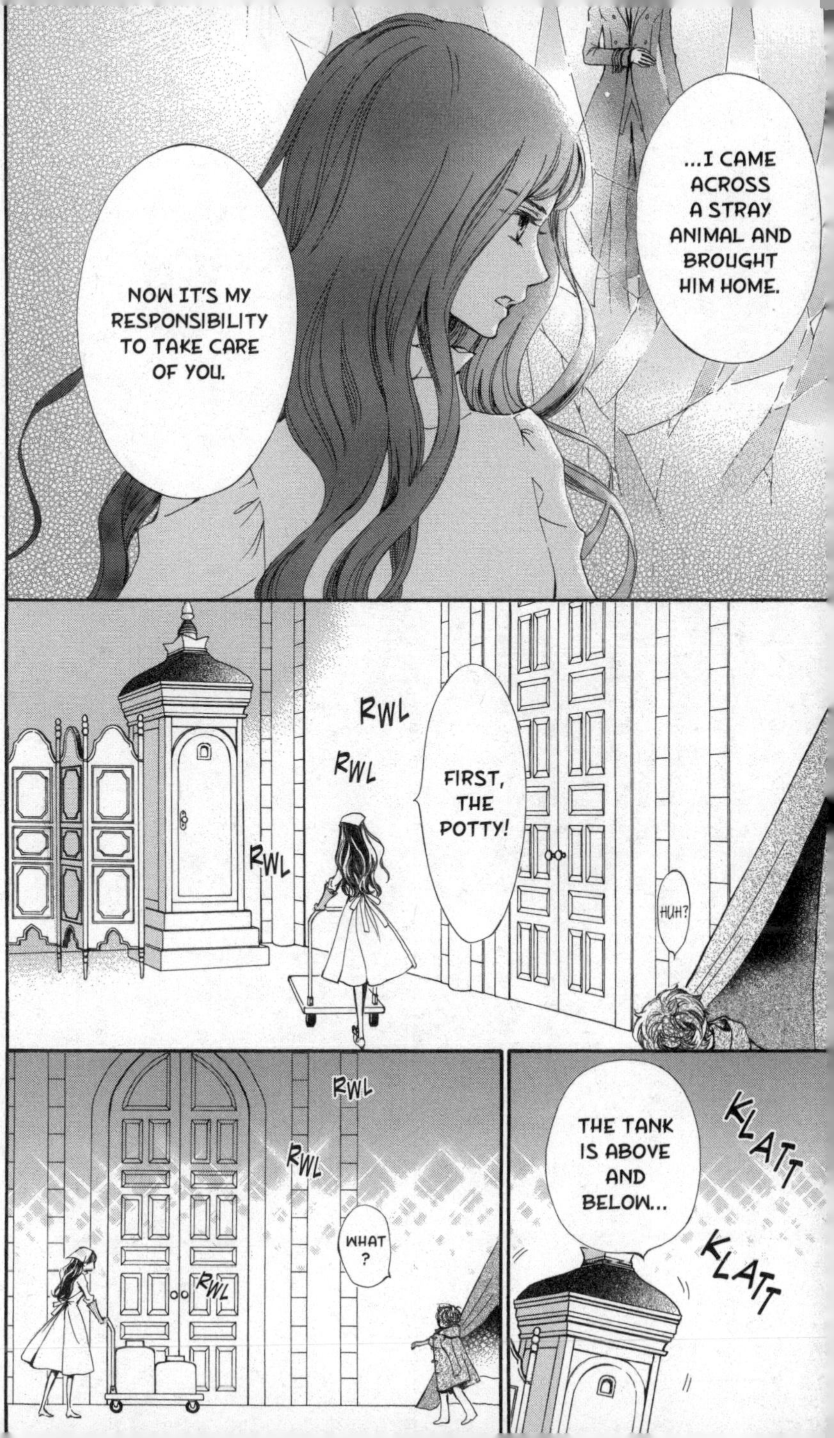
...I CAME ACROSS A STRAY ANIMAL AND BROUGHT HIM HOME.
NOW IT'S MY RESPONSIBILITY TO TAKE CARE OF YOU.
FIRST, THE POTTY!
RWL
RWL
RWL
HUH?
KLATT
KLATT
THE TANK IS ABOVE AND BELOW...
RWL
RWL
WHAT?
RWL

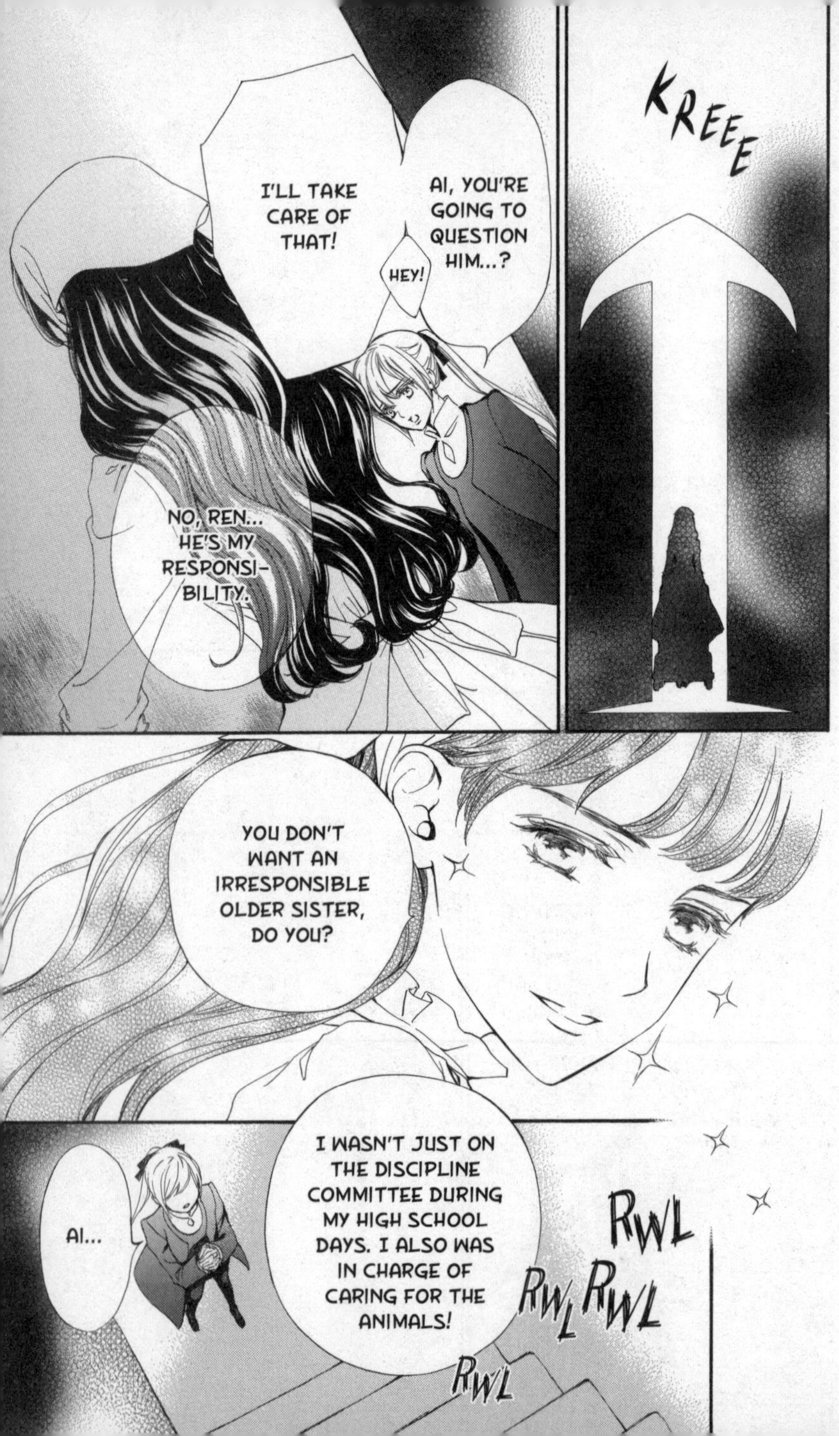
KREEE
AI, YOU'RE GOING TO QUESTION HIM...?
HEY!
I'LL TAKE CARE OF THAT!
NO, REN... HE'S MY RESPONSI-BILITY.
YOU DON'T WANT AN IRRESPONSIBLE OLDER SISTER, DO YOU?
RWL
RWL RWL
I WASN'T JUST ON THE DISCIPLINE COMMITTEE DURING MY HIGH SCHOOL DAYS. I ALSO WAS IN CHARGE OF CARING FOR THE ANIMALS!
AI...
RWL

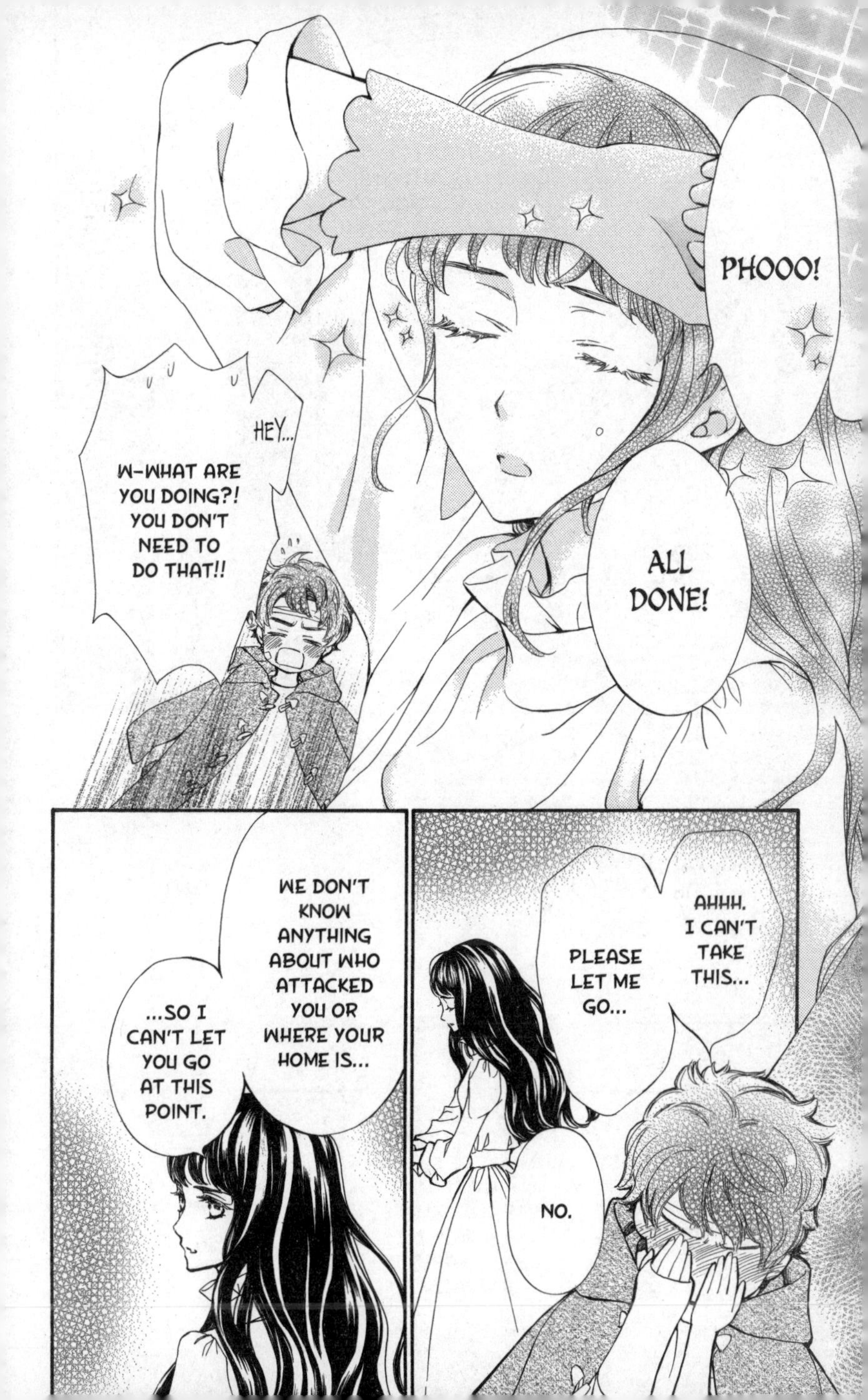
PHOOO!
ALL DONE!
HEY...
W-WHAT ARE YOU DOING?! YOU DON'T NEED TO DO THAT!!
AHHH. I CAN'T TAKE THIS...
PLEASE LET ME GO...
NO.
WE DON'T KNOW ANYTHING ABOUT WHO ATTACKED YOU OR WHERE YOUR HOME IS...
...SO I CAN'T LET YOU GO AT THIS POINT.

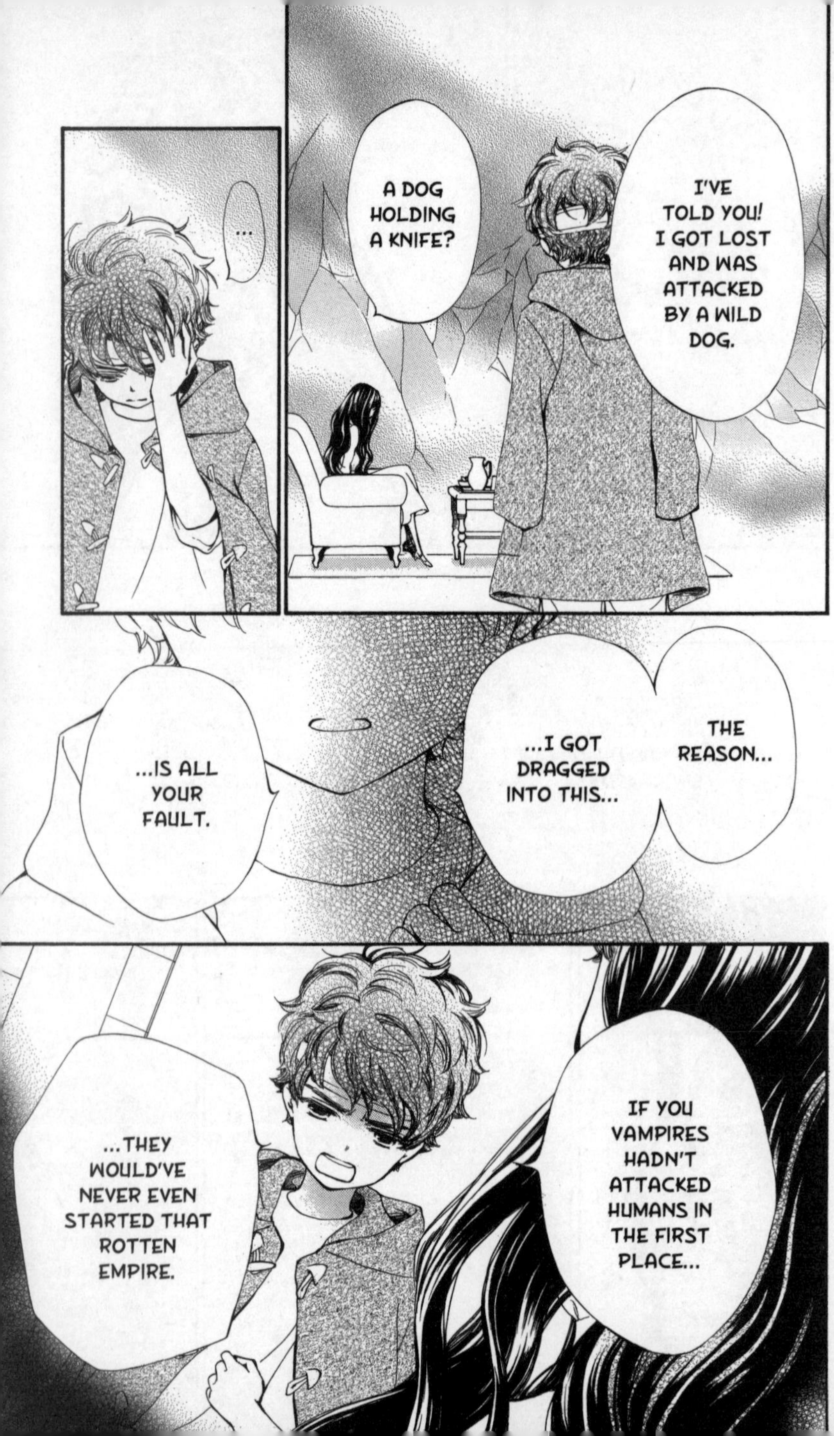
I'VE TOLD YOU! I GOT LOST AND WAS ATTACKED BY A WILD DOG.
A DOG HOLDING A KNIFE?
...
THE REASON...
...I GOT DRAGGED INTO THIS...
...IS ALL YOUR FAULT.
IF YOU VAMPIRES HADN'T ATTACKED HUMANS IN THE FIRST PLACE...
...THEY WOULD'VE NEVER EVEN STARTED THAT ROTTEN EMPIRE.

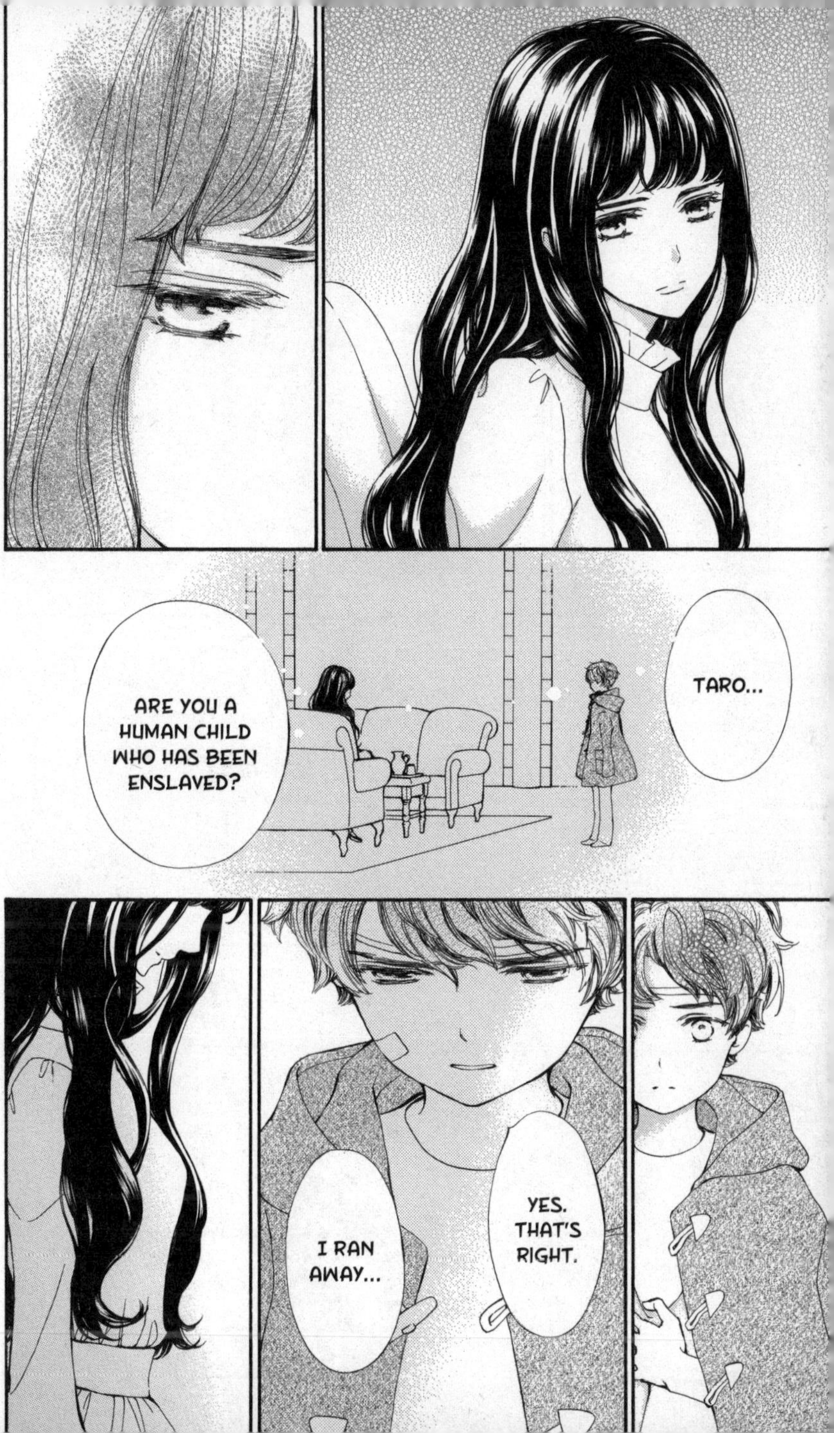
TARO...
ARE YOU A HUMAN CHILD WHO HAS BEEN ENSLAVED?
YES. THAT'S RIGHT.
I RAN AWAY...

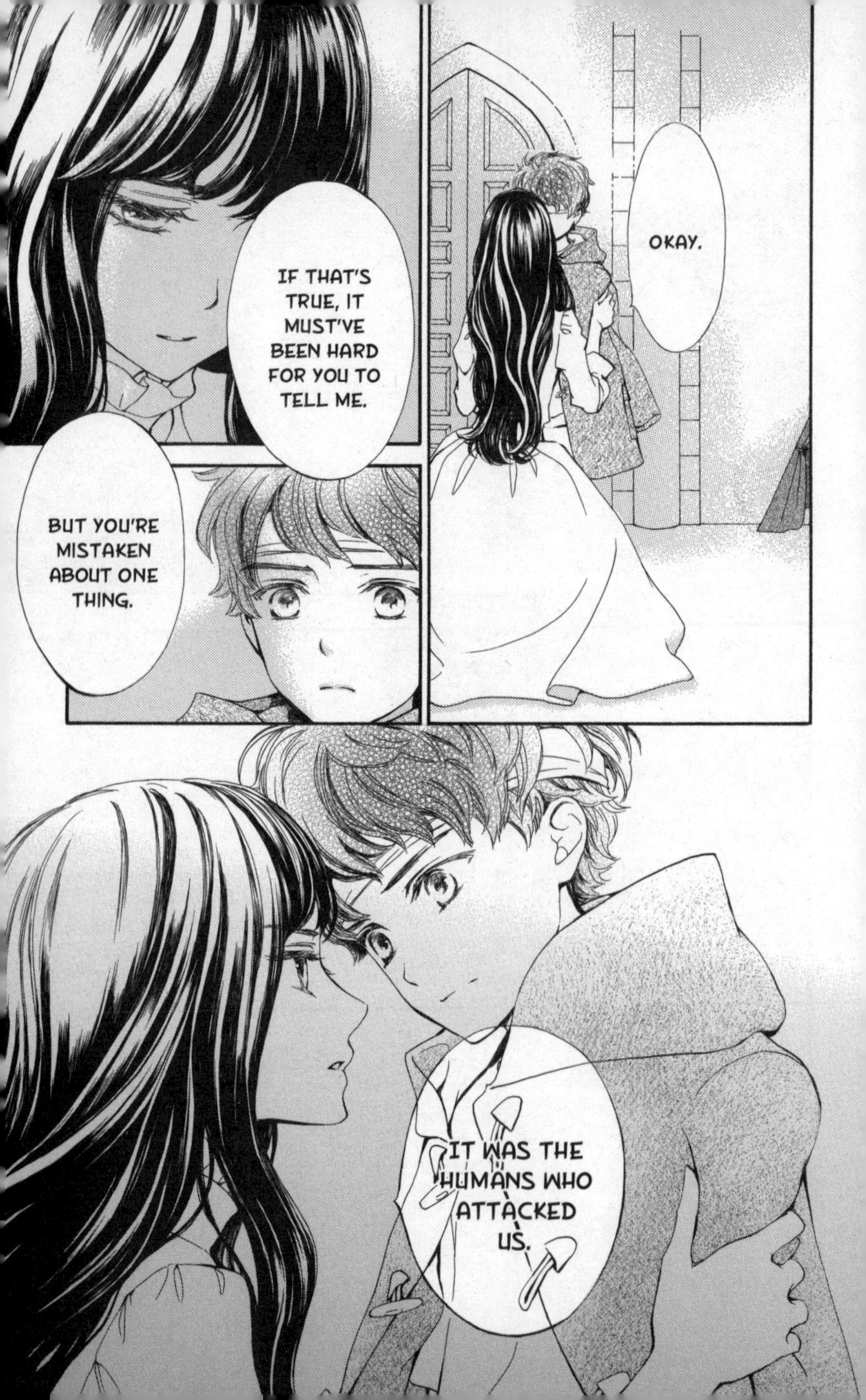
OKAY.
IF THAT'S TRUE, IT MUST'VE BEEN HARD FOR YOU TO TELL ME.
BUT YOU'RE MISTAKEN ABOUT ONE THING.
IT WAS THE HUMANS WHO ATTACKED US.

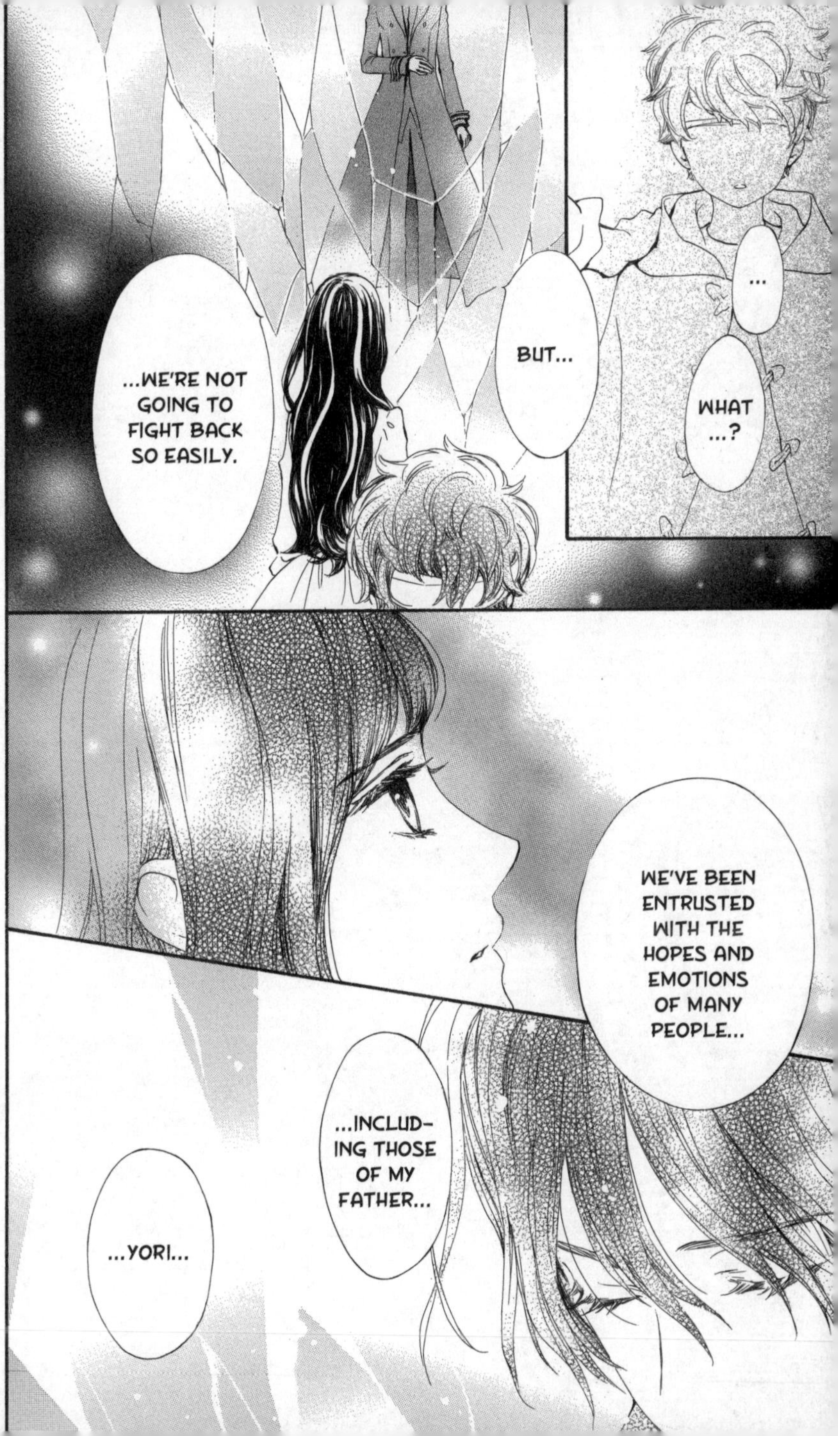
...
WHAT ...?
BUT...
...WE'RE NOT GOING TO FIGHT BACK SO EASILY.
WE'VE BEEN ENTRUSTED WITH THE HOPES AND EMOTIONS OF MANY PEOPLE...
...INCLUD-ING THOSE OF MY FATHER...
...YORI...

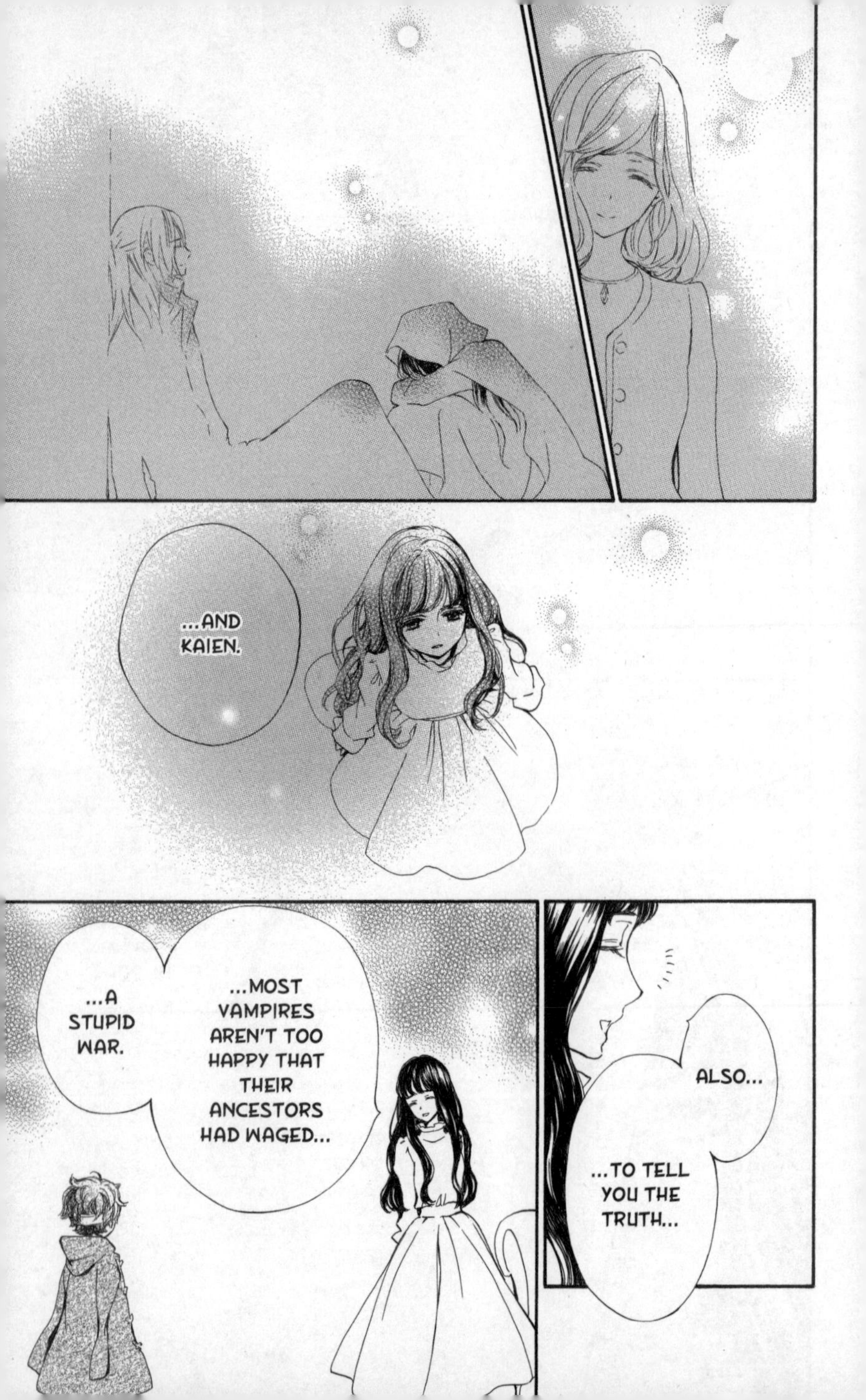
...AND KAIEN.
ALSO...
...TO TELL YOU THE TRUTH...
...MOST VAMPIRES AREN'T TOO HAPPY THAT THEIR ANCESTORS HAD WAGED...
...A STUPID WAR.

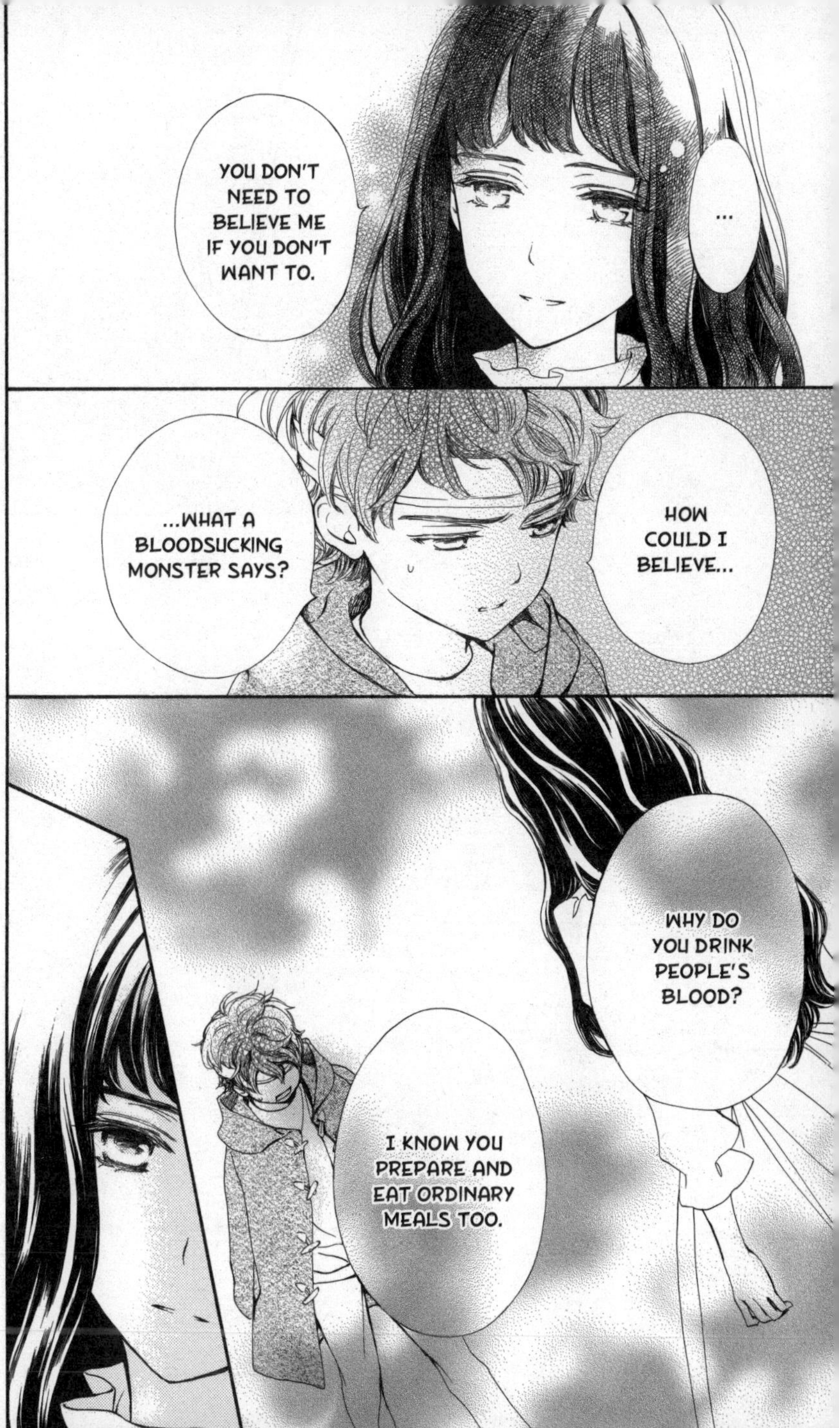
...
YOU DON'T NEED TO BELIEVE ME IF YOU DON'T WANT TO.
HOW COULD I BELIEVE...
...WHAT A BLOODSUCKING MONSTER SAYS?
WHY DO YOU DRINK PEOPLE'S BLOOD?
I KNOW YOU PREPARE AND EAT ORDINARY MEALS TOO.

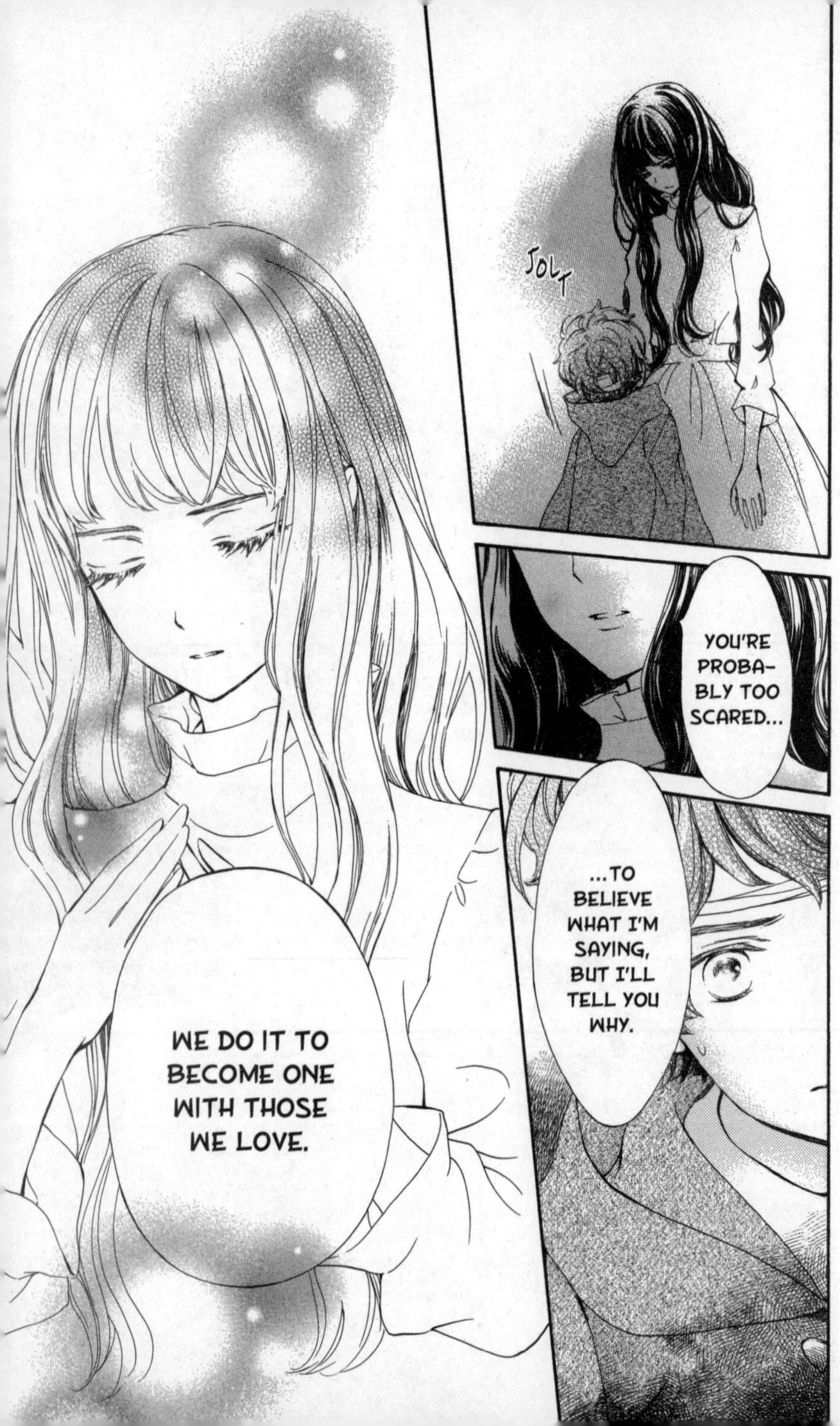
JOLT
YOU'RE PROBABLY TOO SCARED...
...TO BELIEVE WHAT I'M SAYING, BUT I'LL TELL YOU WHY.
WE DO IT TO BECOME ONE WITH THOSE WE LOVE.

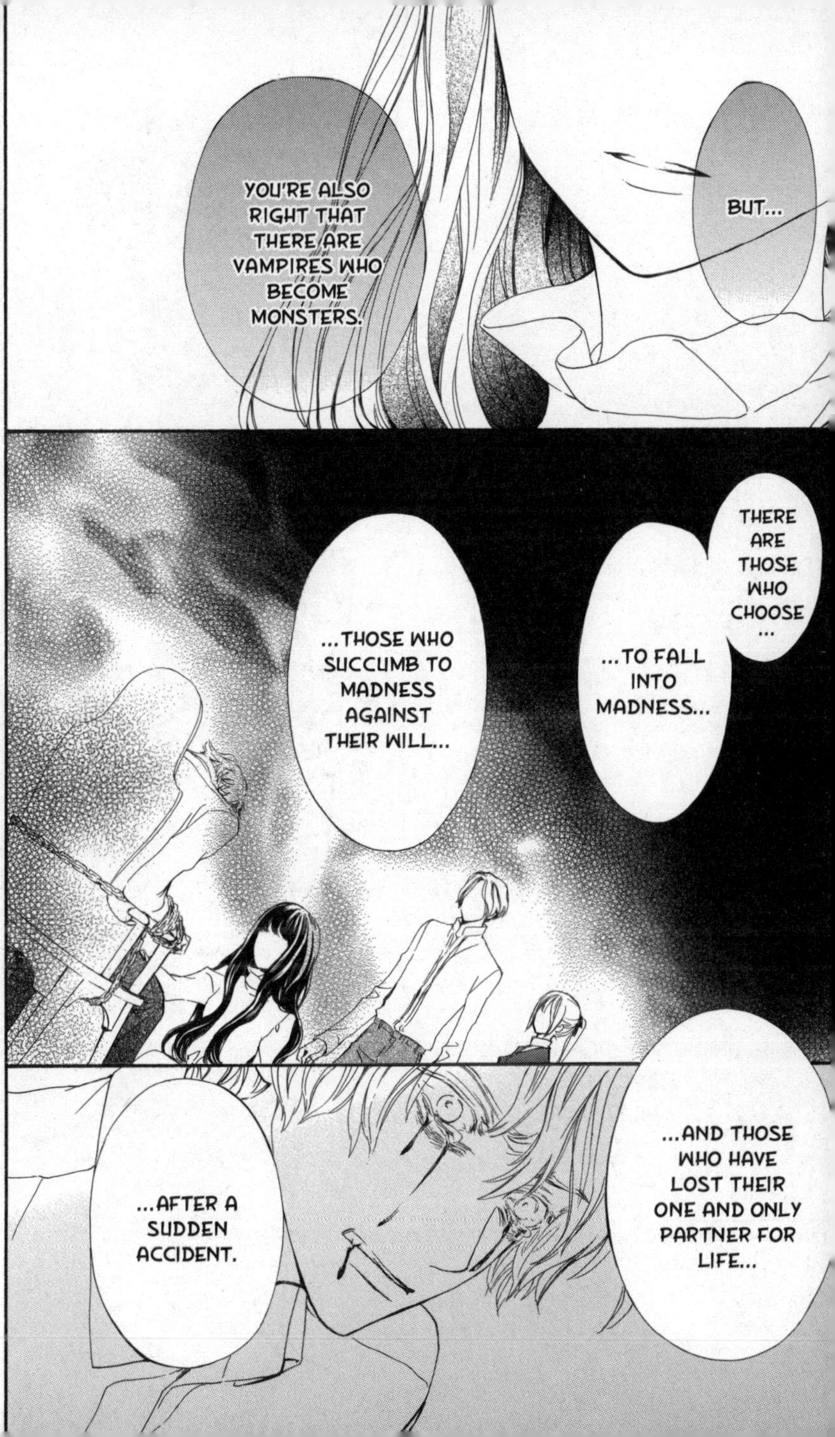
YOU'RE ALSO RIGHT THAT THERE ARE VAMPIRES WHO BECOME MONSTERS.
BUT...
THERE ARE THOSE WHO CHOOSE...
...TO FALL INTO MADNESS...
...THOSE WHO SUCCUMB TO MADNESS AGAINST THEIR WILL...
...AND THOSE WHO HAVE LOST THEIR ONE AND ONLY PARTNER FOR LIFE...
...AFTER A SUDDEN ACCIDENT.

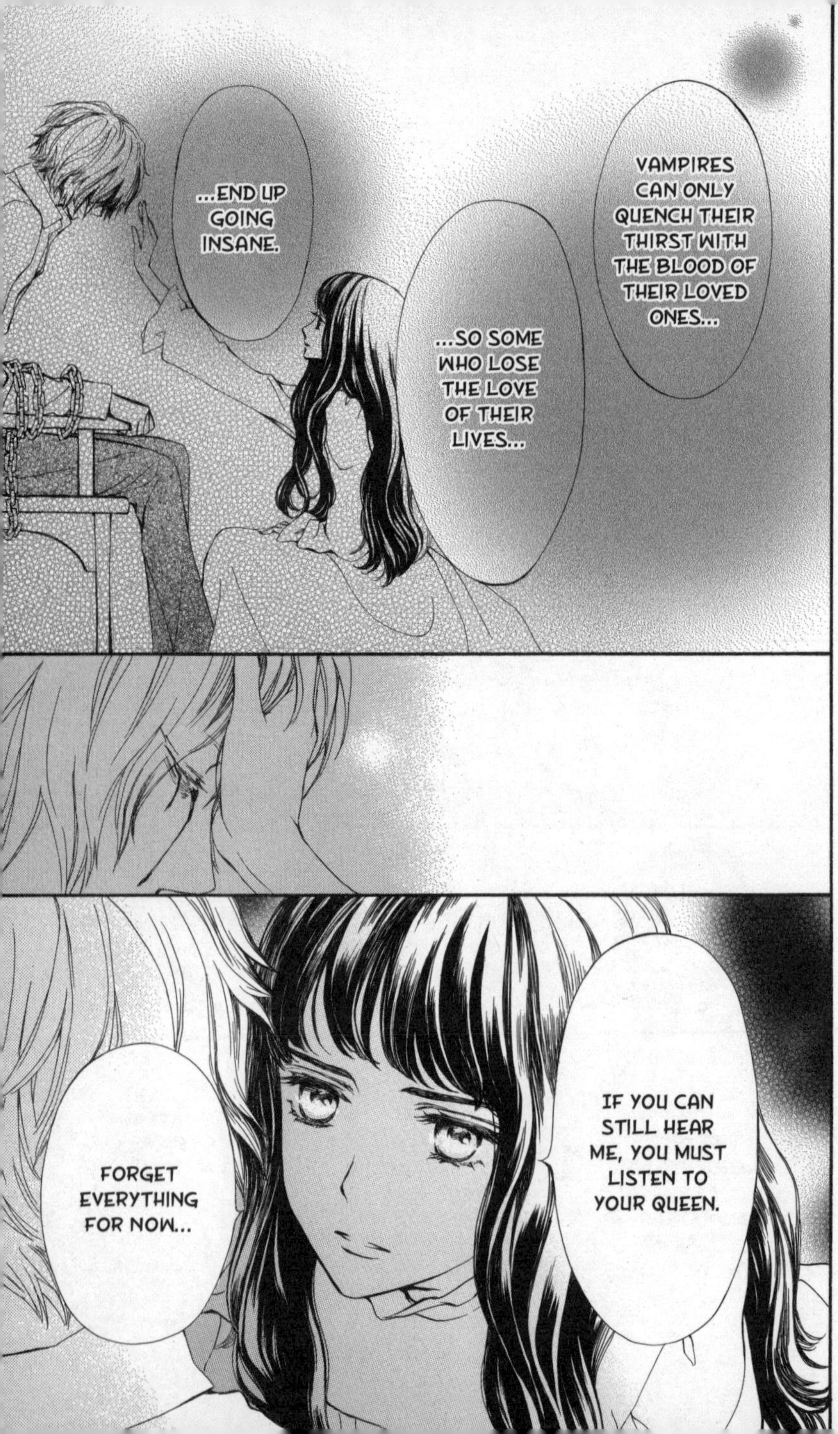
VAMPIRES CAN ONLY QUENCH THEIR THIRST WITH THE BLOOD OF THEIR LOVED ONES...
...SO SOME WHO LOSE THE LOVE OF THEIR LIVES...
...END UP GOING INSANE.
IF YOU CAN STILL HEAR ME, YOU MUST LISTEN TO YOUR QUEEN.
FORGET EVERYTHING FOR NOW...

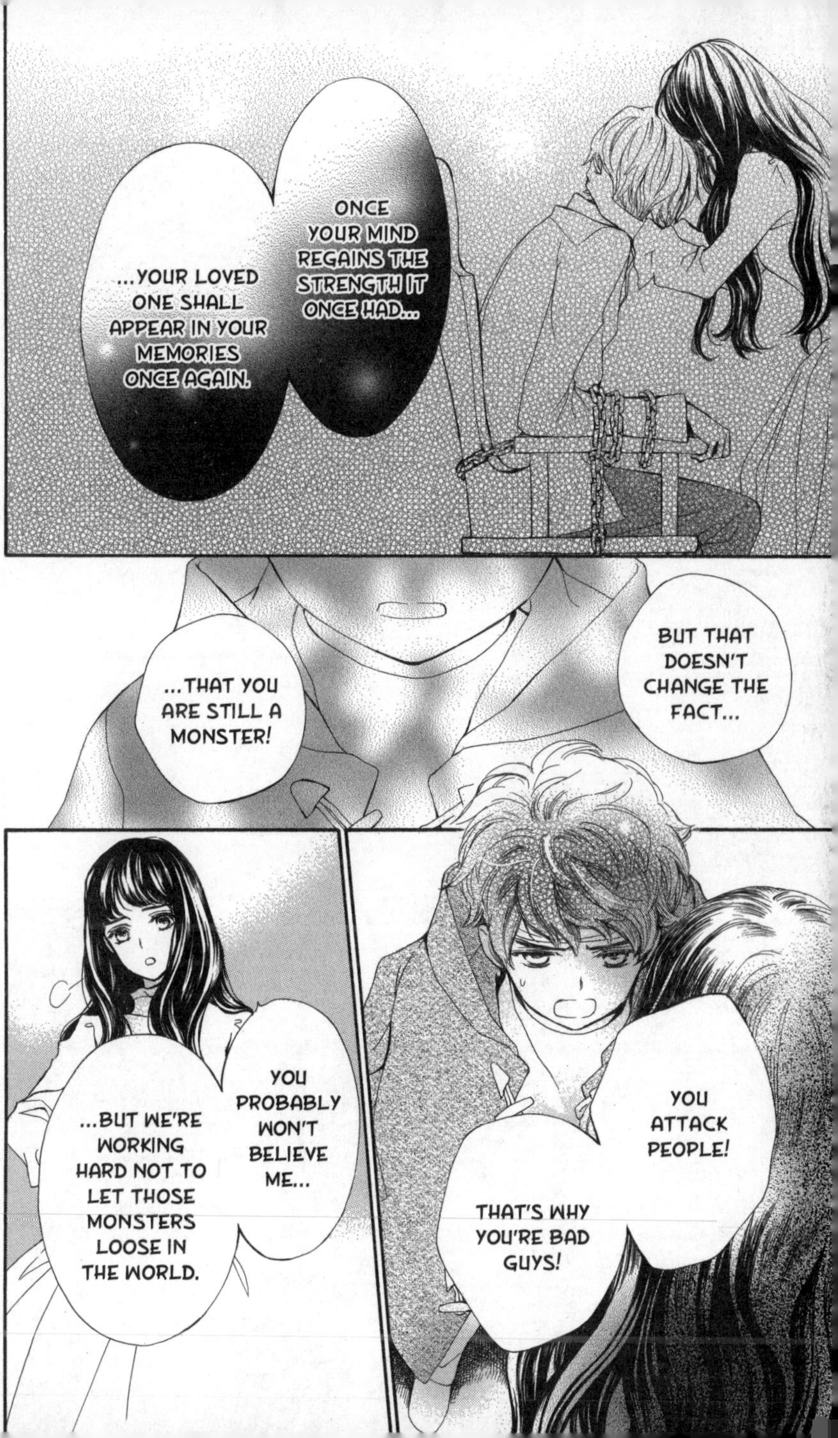
ONCE YOUR MIND REGAINS THE STRENGTH IT ONCE HAD...
...YOUR LOVED ONE SHALL APPEAR IN YOUR MEMORIES ONCE AGAIN.
BUT THAT DOESN'T CHANGE THE FACT...
...THAT YOU ARE STILL A MONSTER!
YOU ATTACK PEOPLE!
THAT'S WHY YOU'RE BAD GUYS!
YOU PROBABLY WON'T BELIEVE ME...
...BUT WE'RE WORKING HARD NOT TO LET THOSE MONSTERS LOOSE IN THE WORLD.

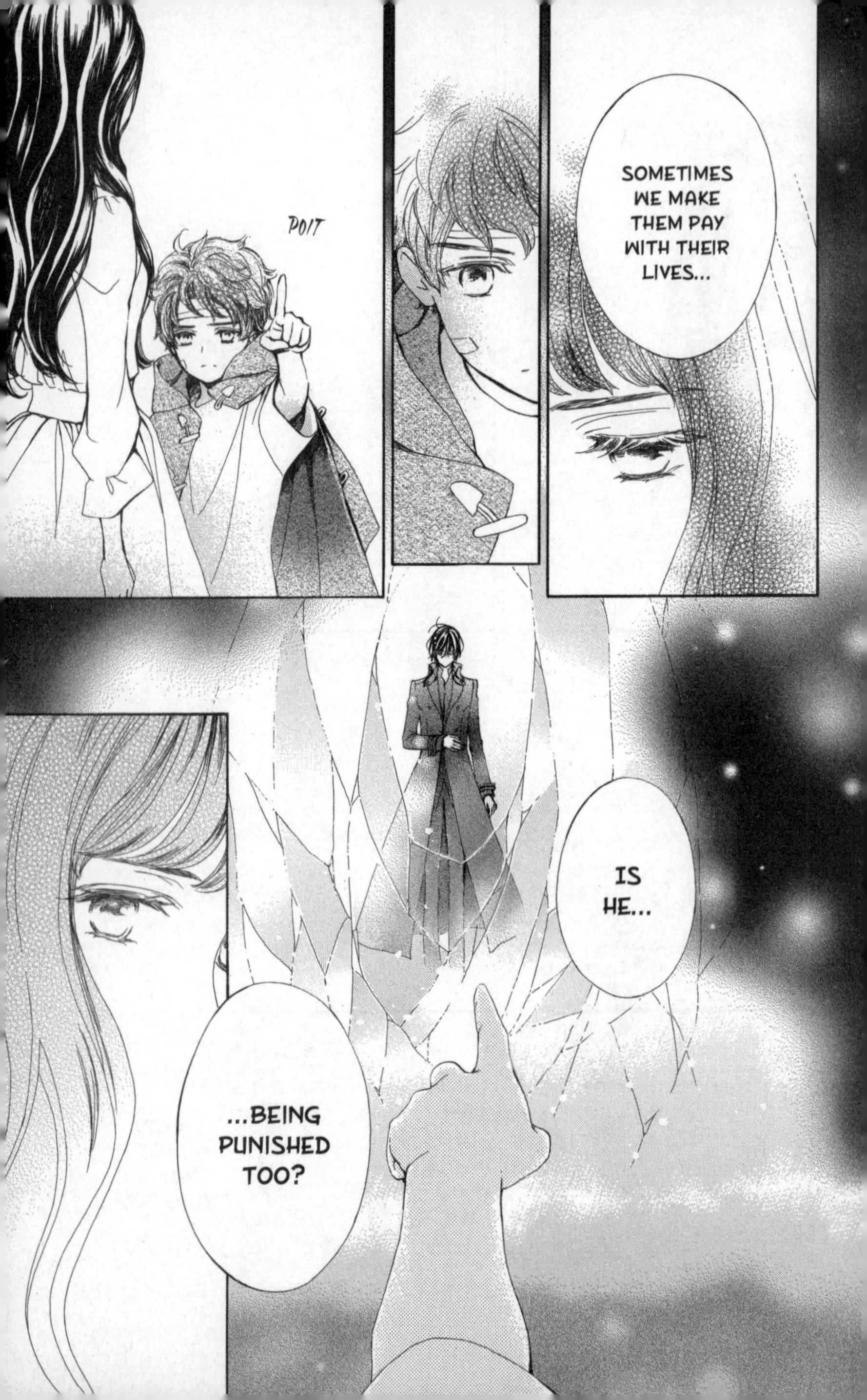
SOMETIMES WE MAKE THEM PAY WITH THEIR LIVES...
POIT
IS HE...
...BEING PUNISHED TOO?

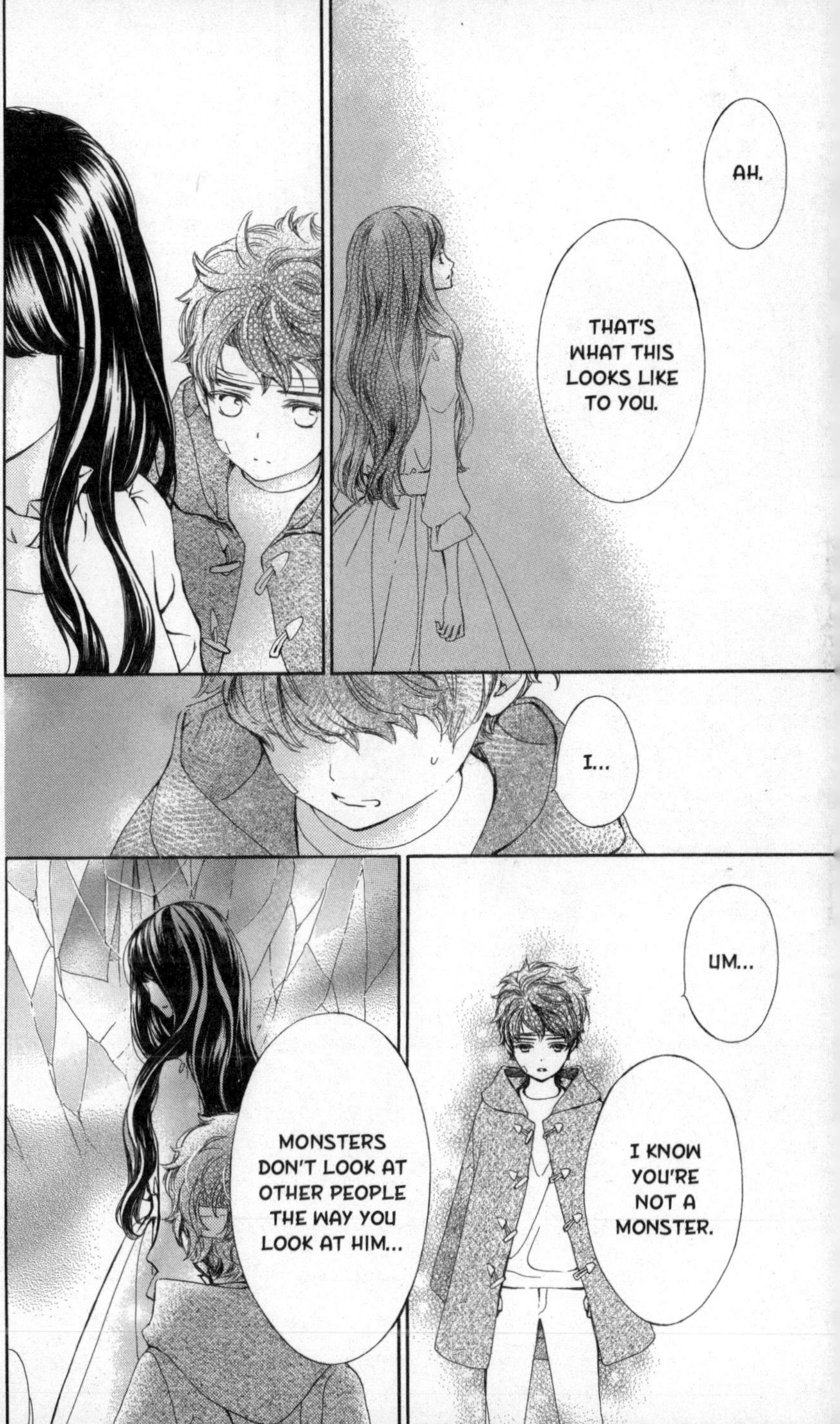
AH.
THAT'S WHAT THIS LOOKS LIKE TO YOU.
I...
UM...
I KNOW YOU'RE NOT A MONSTER.
MONSTERS DON'T LOOK AT OTHER PEOPLE THE WAY YOU LOOK AT HIM...

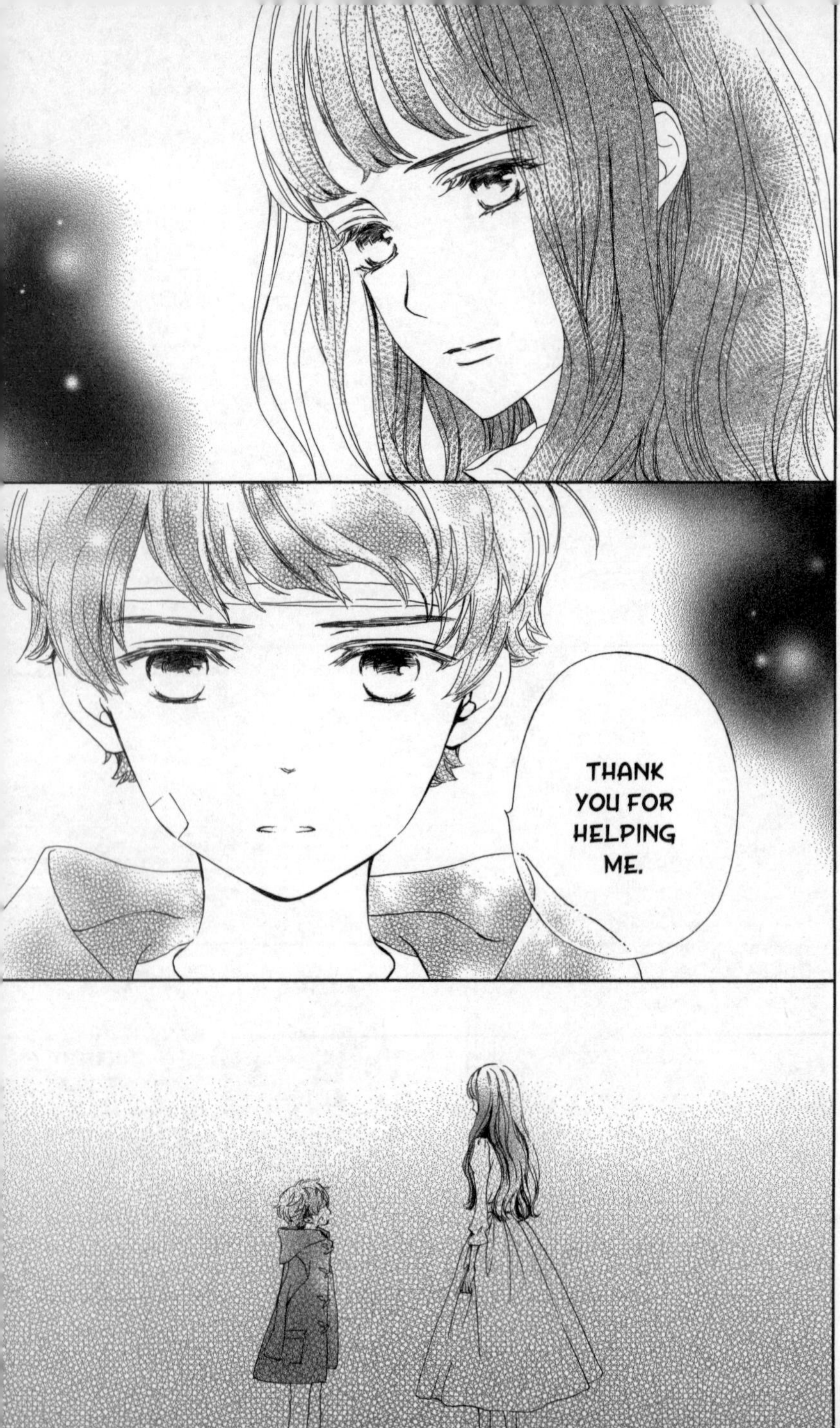
THANK YOU FOR HELPING ME.

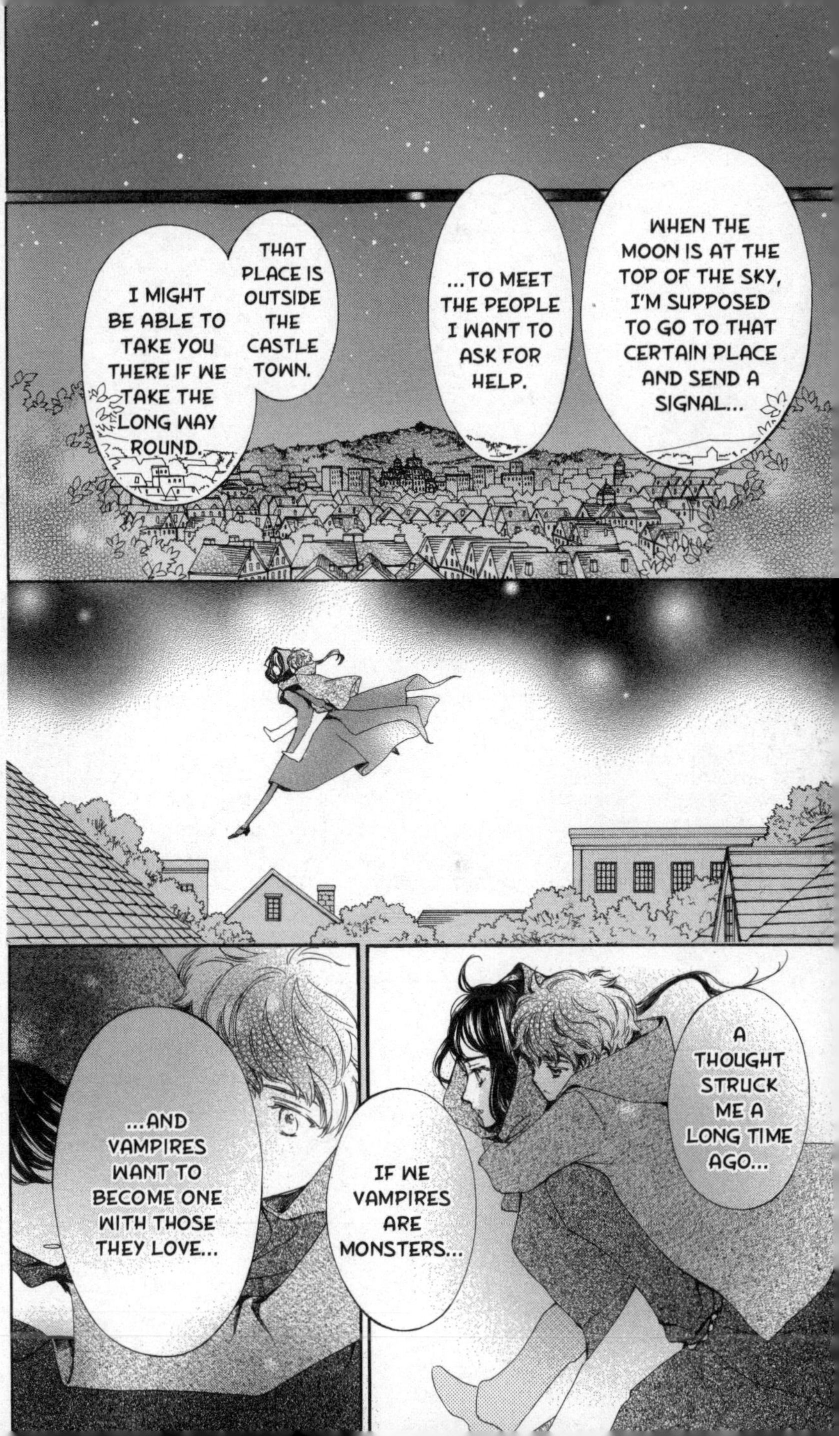
WHEN THE MOON IS AT THE TOP OF THE SKY, I'M SUPPOSED TO GO TO THAT CERTAIN PLACE AND SEND A SIGNAL...
...TO MEET THE PEOPLE I WANT TO ASK FOR HELP.
THAT PLACE IS OUTSIDE THE CASTLE TOWN.
I MIGHT BE ABLE TO TAKE YOU THERE IF WE TAKE THE LONG WAY ROUND.
A THOUGHT STRUCK ME A LONG TIME AGO...
IF WE VAMPIRES ARE MONSTERS...
...AND VAMPIRES WANT TO BECOME ONE WITH THOSE THEY LOVE...

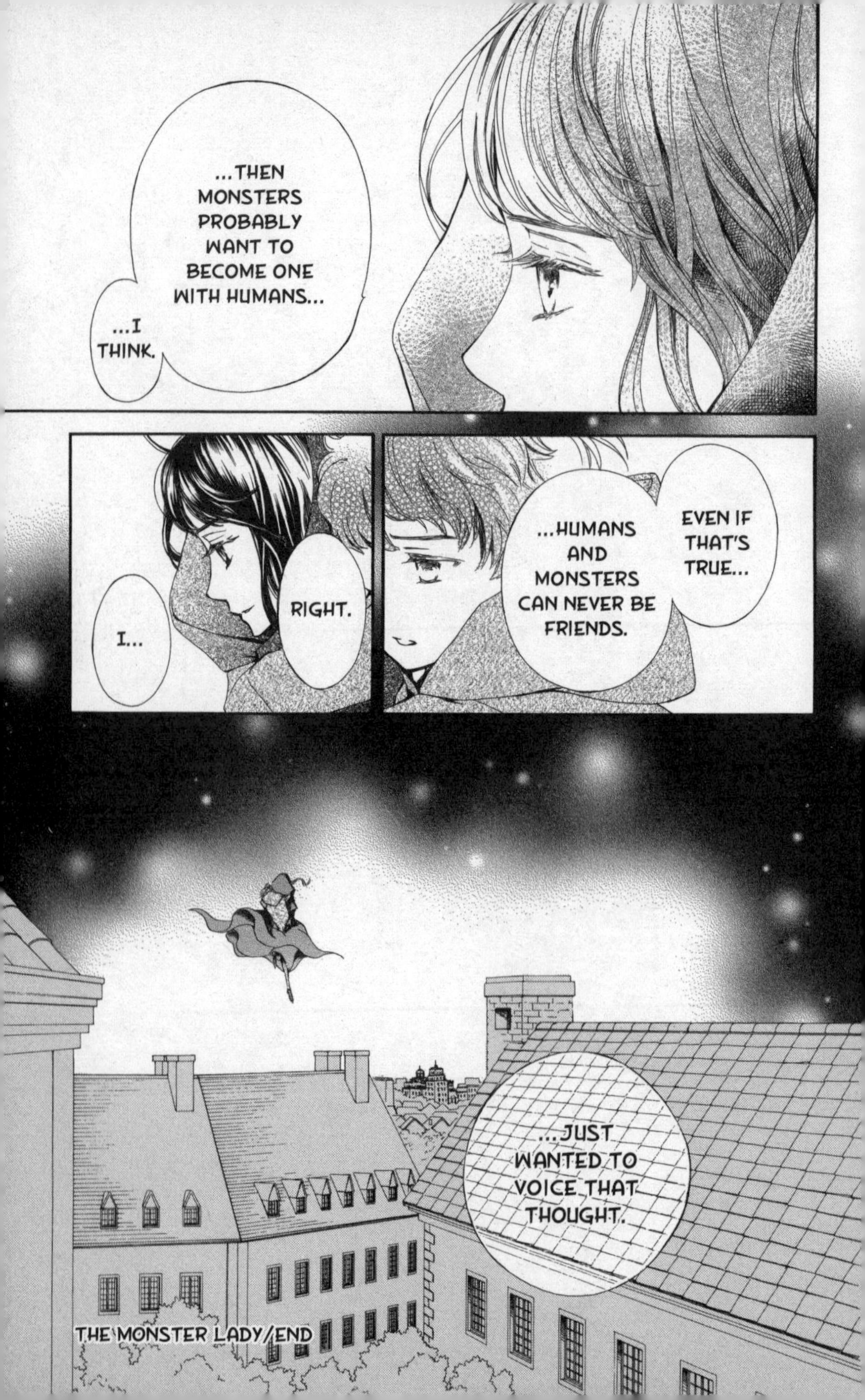
...THEN MONSTERS PROBABLY WANT TO BECOME ONE WITH HUMANS...
...I THINK.
EVEN IF THAT'S TRUE...
...HUMANS AND MONSTERS CAN NEVER BE FRIENDS.
RIGHT.
I...
...JUST WANTED TO VOICE THAT THOUGHT.
THE MONSTER LADY/END

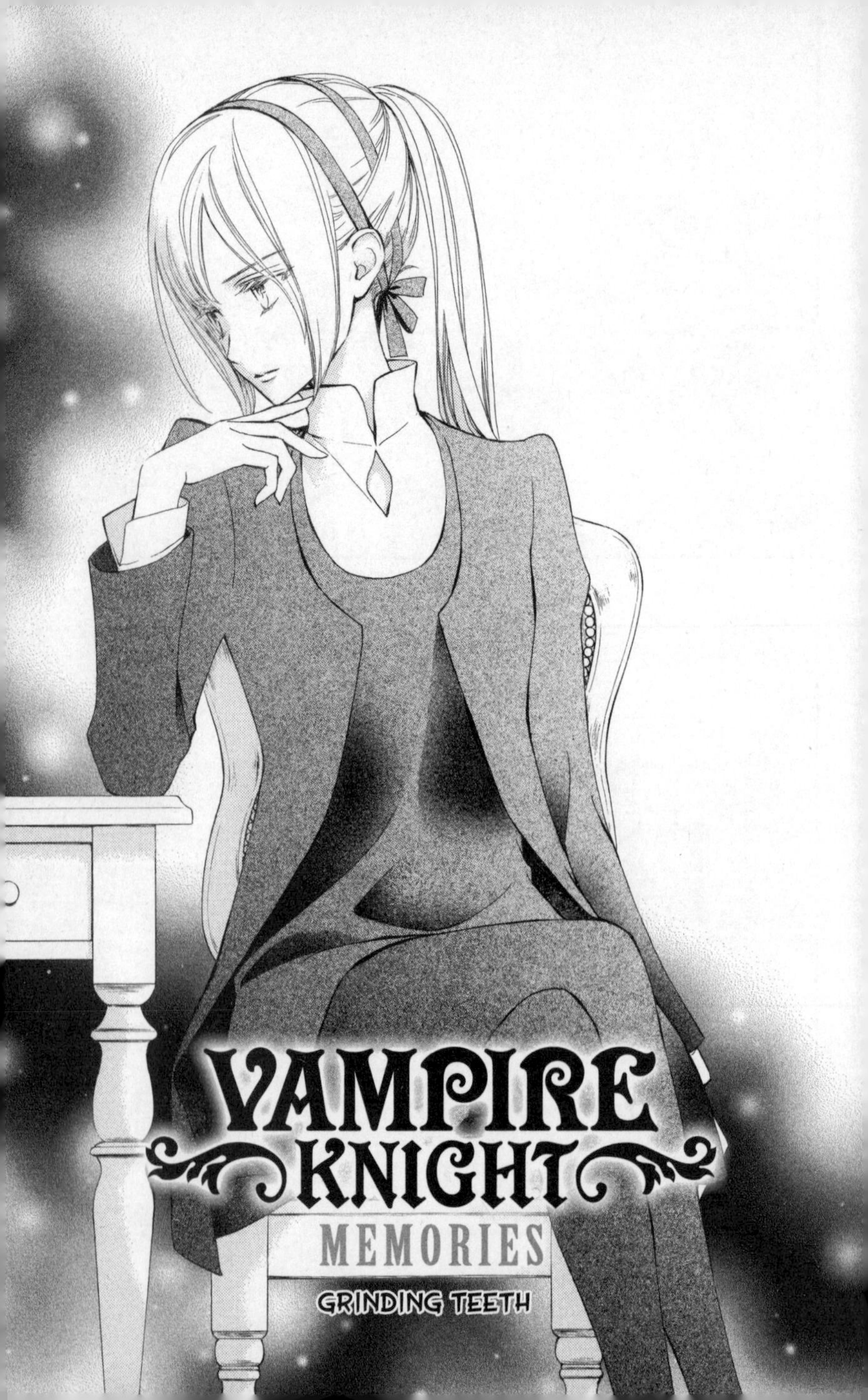
VAMPIRE KNIGHT
MEMORIES
GRINDING TEETH

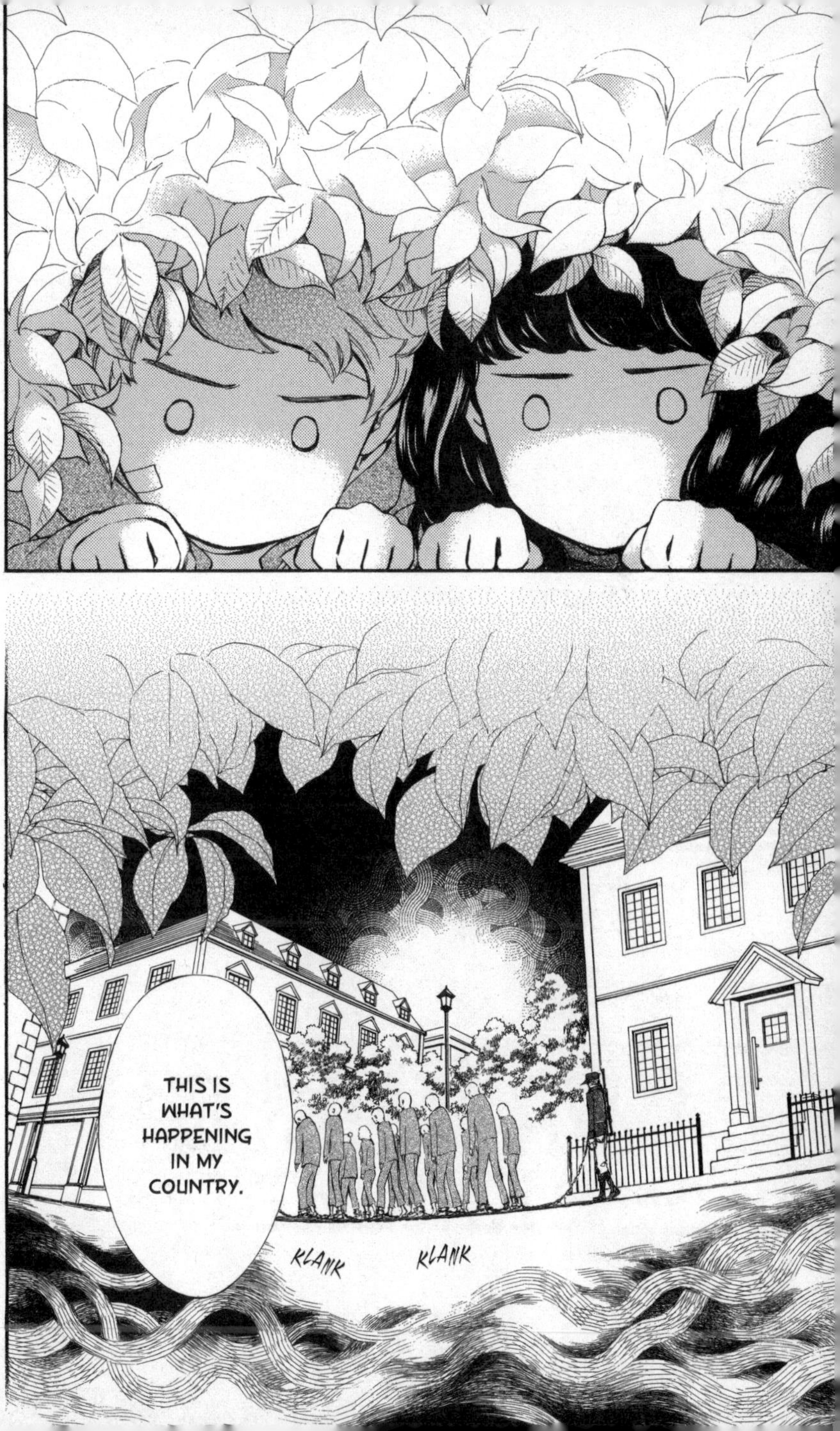
THIS IS WHAT'S HAPPENING IN MY COUNTRY.
KLANK
KLANK

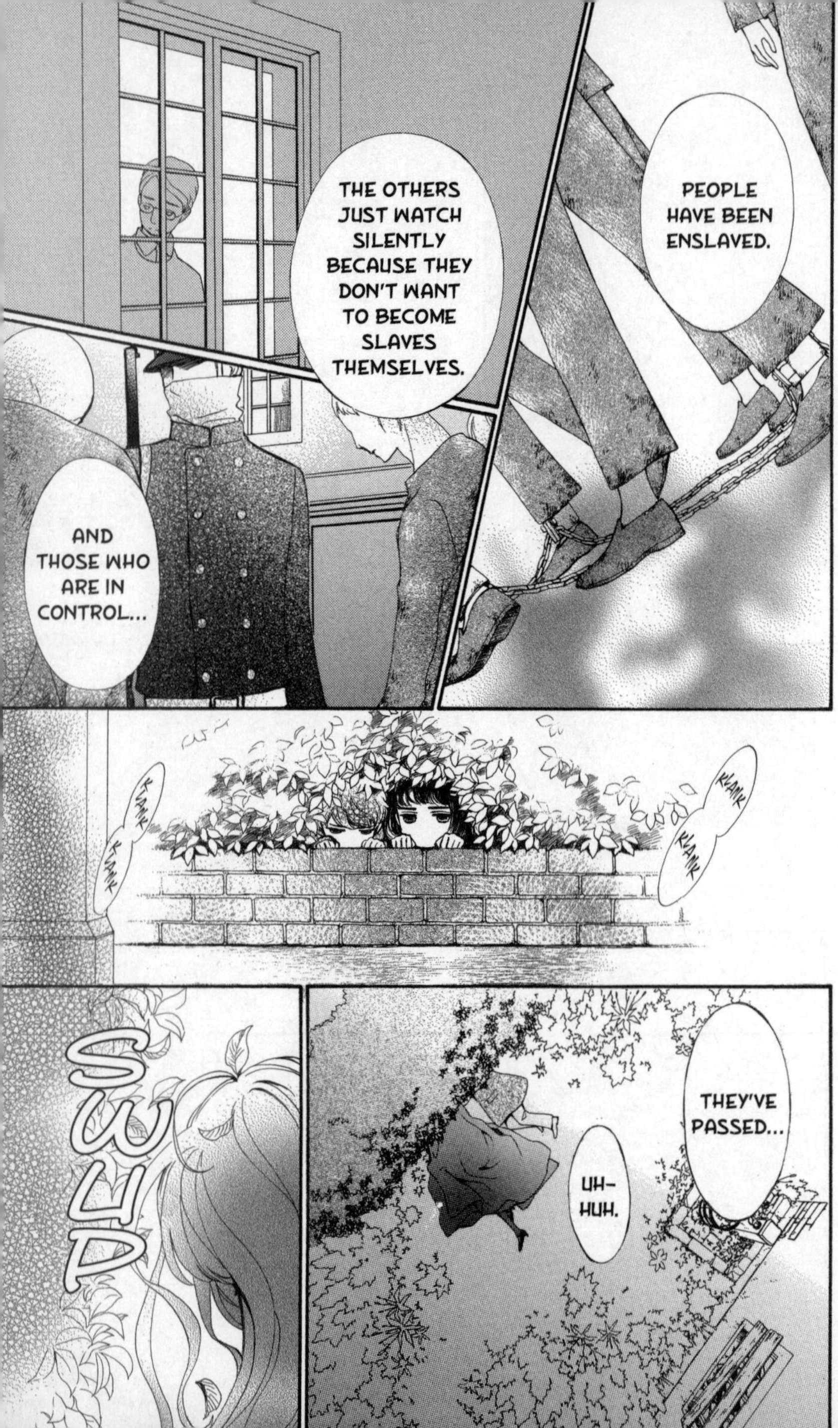
PEOPLE HAVE BEEN ENSLAVED.
THE OTHERS JUST WATCH SILENTLY BECAUSE THEY DON'T WANT TO BECOME SLAVES THEMSELVES.
AND THOSE WHO ARE IN CONTROL...
KLANK
KLANK
KLANK
KLANK
THEY'VE PASSED...
UH-HUH.
SWUP

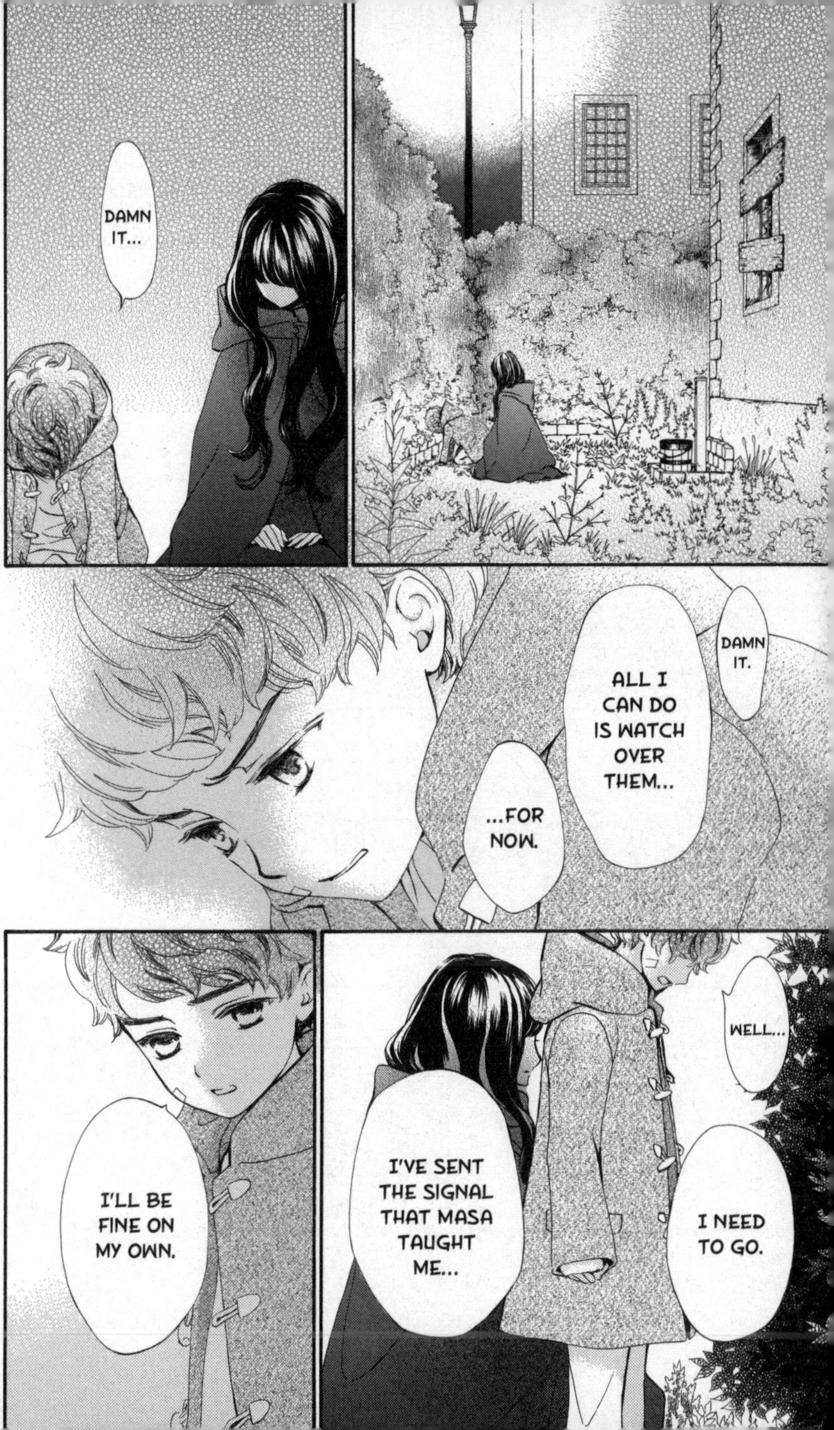
DAMN IT...
DAMN IT.
ALL I CAN DO IS WATCH OVER THEM...
...FOR NOW.
WELL...
I NEED TO GO.
I'VE SENT THE SIGNAL THAT MASA TAUGHT ME...
I'LL BE FINE ON MY OWN.

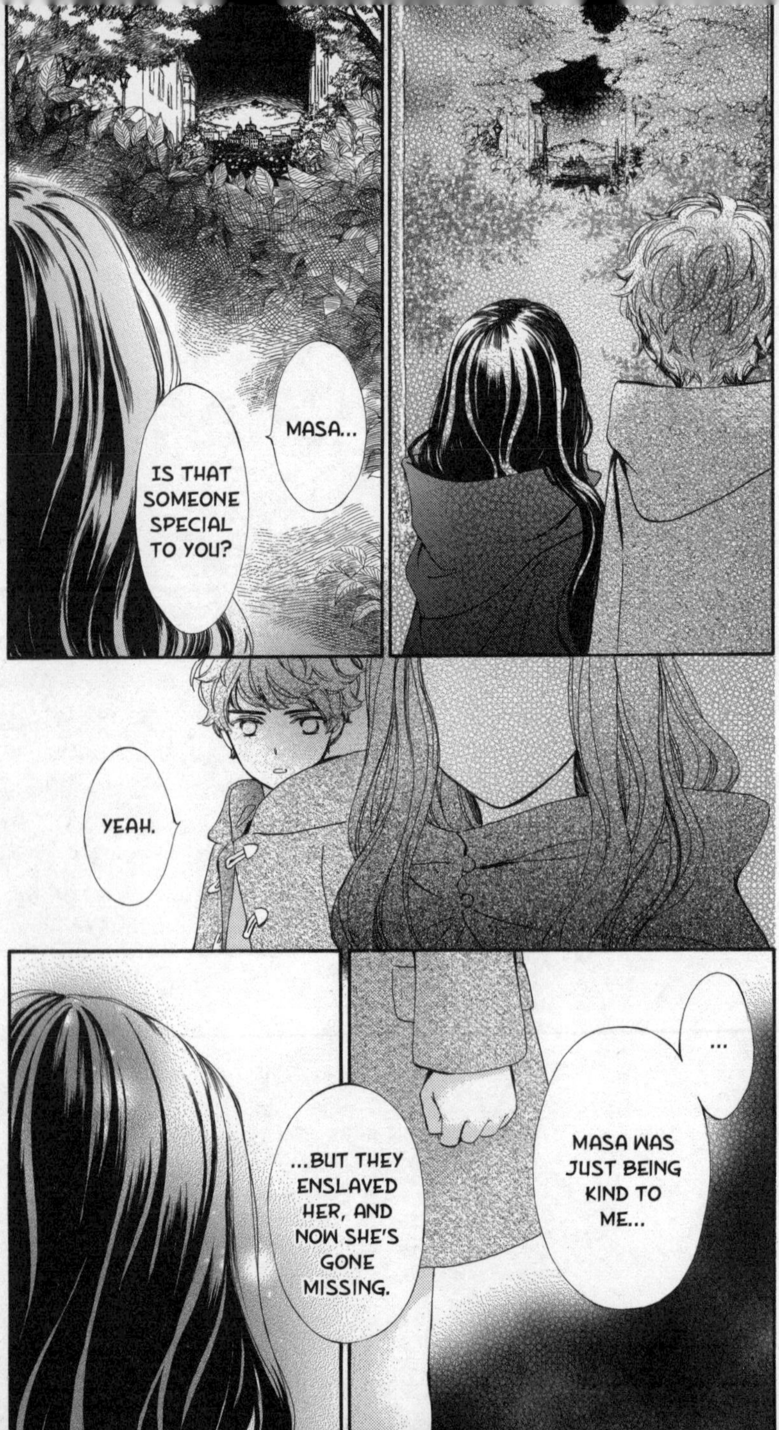
MASA...
IS THAT SOMEONE SPECIAL TO YOU?
YEAH.
...
MASA WAS JUST BEING KIND TO ME...
...BUT THEY ENSLAVED HER, AND NOW SHE'S GONE MISSING.

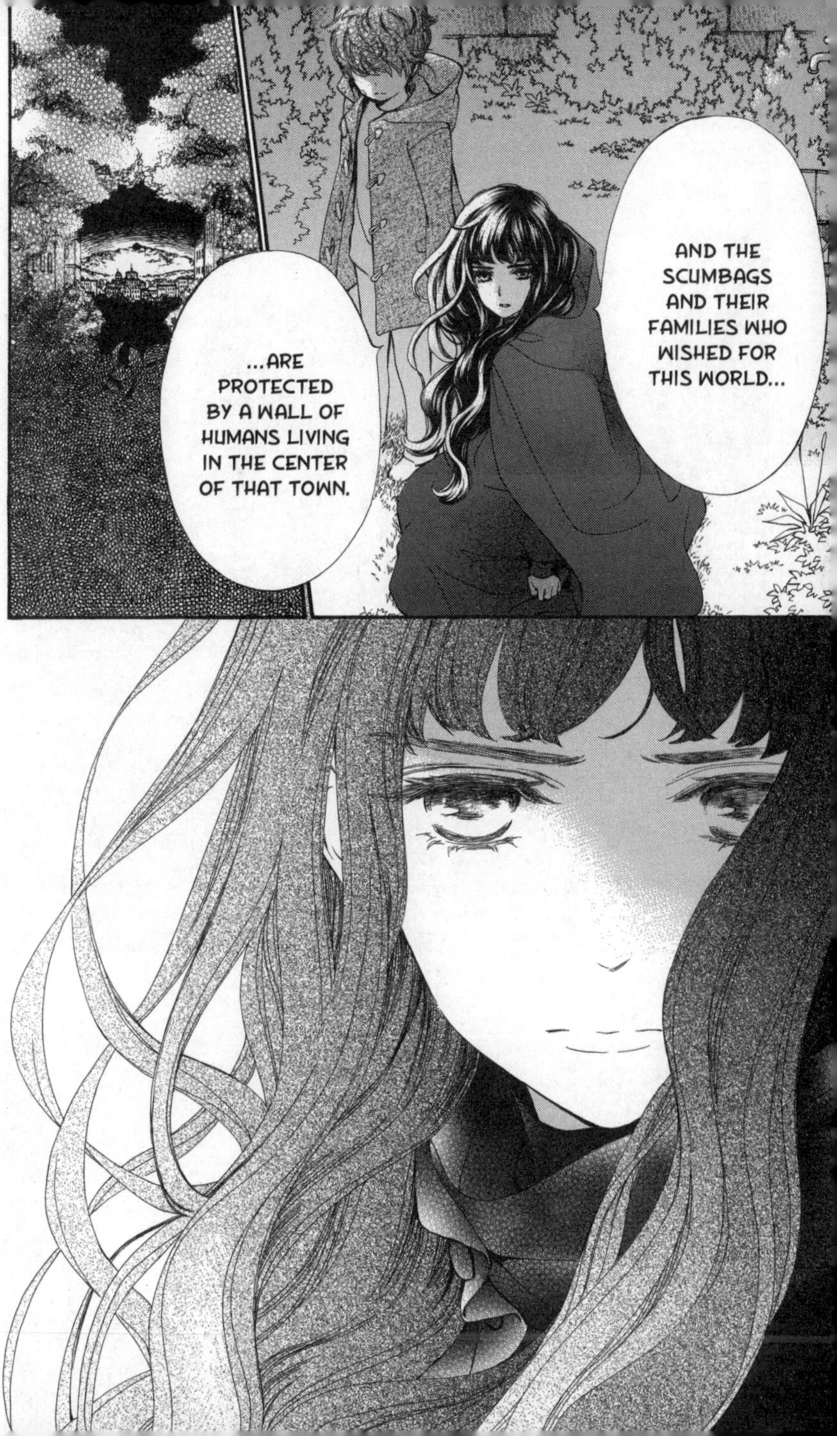
AND THE SCUMBAGS AND THEIR FAMILIES WHO WISHED FOR THIS WORLD...
...ARE PROTECTED BY A WALL OF HUMANS LIVING IN THE CENTER OF THAT TOWN.

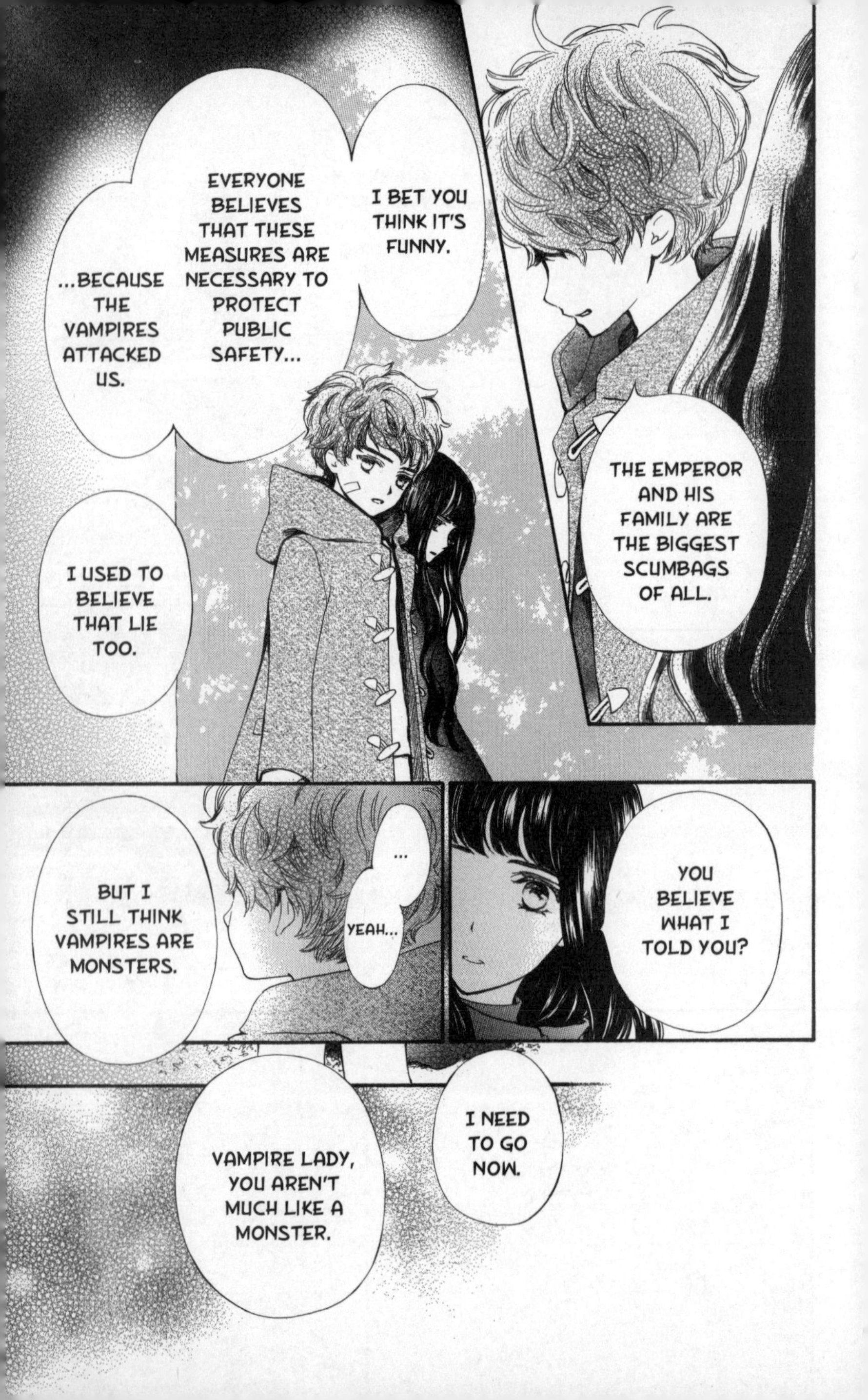
THE EMPEROR AND HIS FAMILY ARE THE BIGGEST SCUMBAGS OF ALL.
I BET YOU THINK IT'S FUNNY.
EVERYONE BELIEVES THAT THESE MEASURES ARE NECESSARY TO PROTECT PUBLIC SAFETY...
...BECAUSE THE VAMPIRES ATTACKED US.
I USED TO BELIEVE THAT LIE TOO.
YOU BELIEVE WHAT I TOLD YOU?
...
YEAH...
BUT I STILL THINK VAMPIRES ARE MONSTERS.
I NEED TO GO NOW.
VAMPIRE LADY, YOU AREN'T MUCH LIKE A MONSTER.

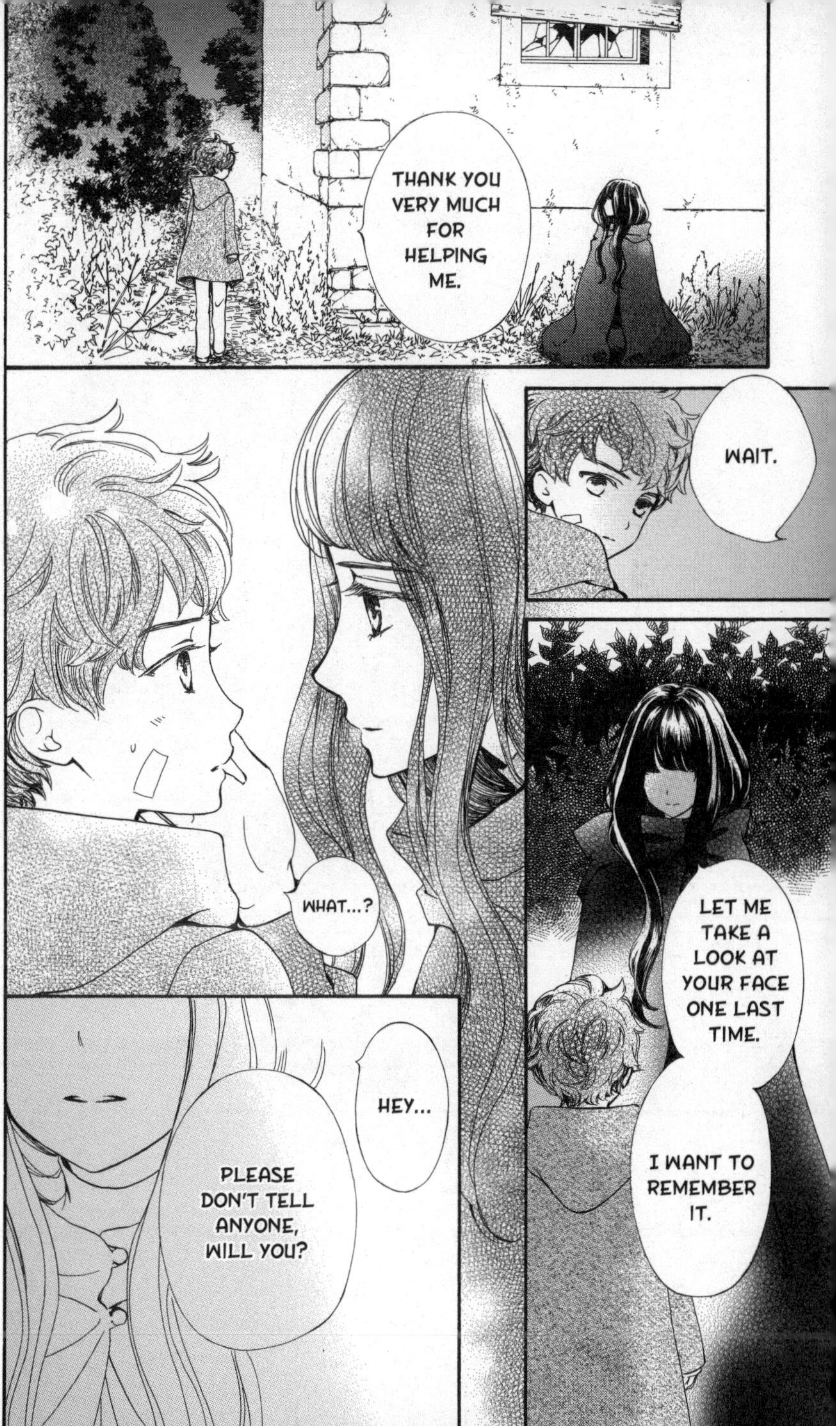
THANK YOU VERY MUCH FOR HELPING ME.
WAIT.
LET ME TAKE A LOOK AT YOUR FACE ONE LAST TIME.
I WANT TO REMEMBER IT.
WHAT...?
HEY...
PLEASE DON'T TELL ANYONE, WILL YOU?

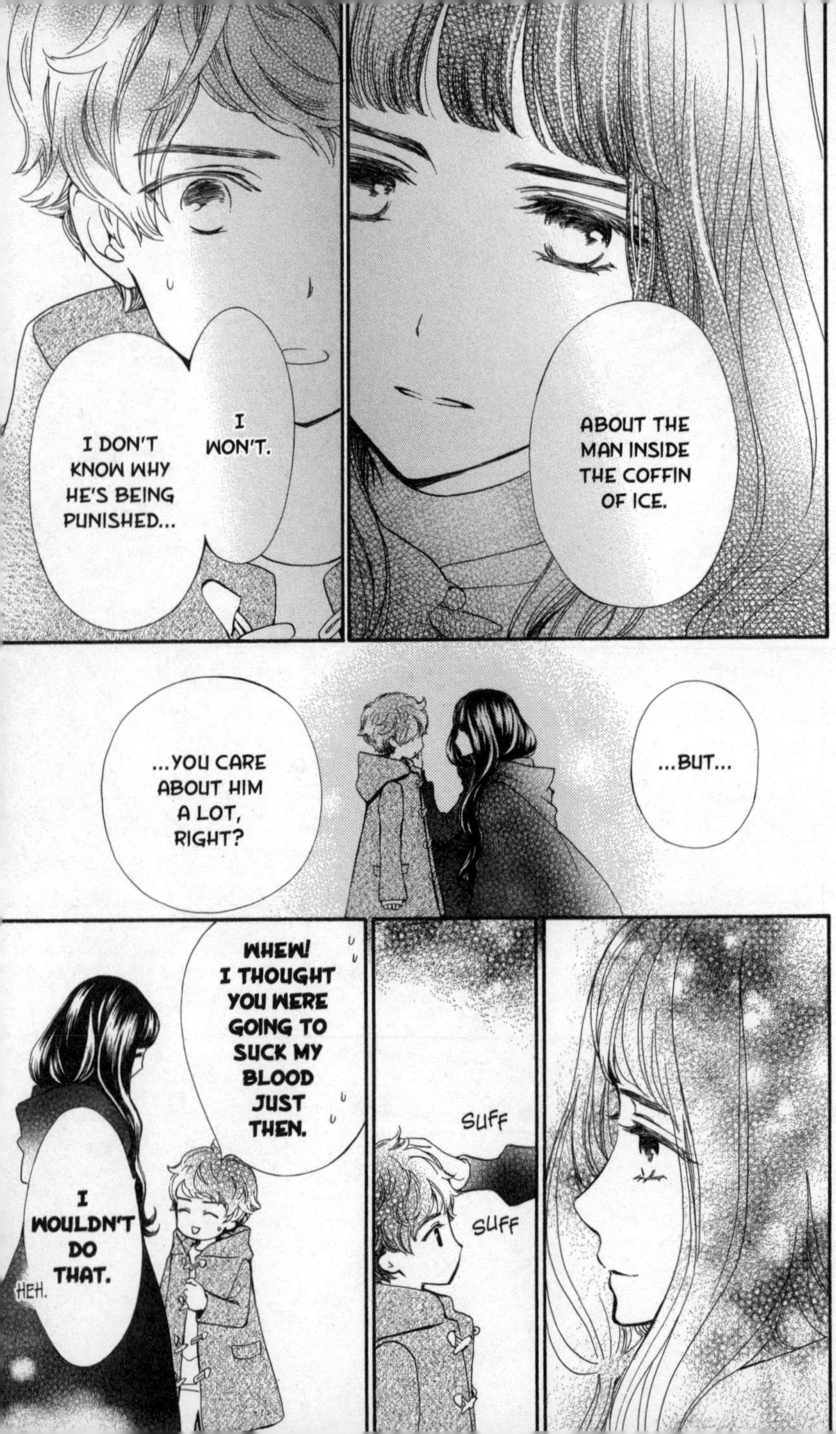
ABOUT THE MAN INSIDE THE COFFIN OF ICE.
I WON'T.
I DON'T KNOW WHY HE'S BEING PUNISHED...
...BUT...
...YOU CARE ABOUT HIM A LOT, RIGHT?
SUFF
SUFF
WHEW! I THOUGHT YOU WERE GOING TO SUCK MY BLOOD JUST THEN.
I WOULDN'T DO THAT.
HEH.

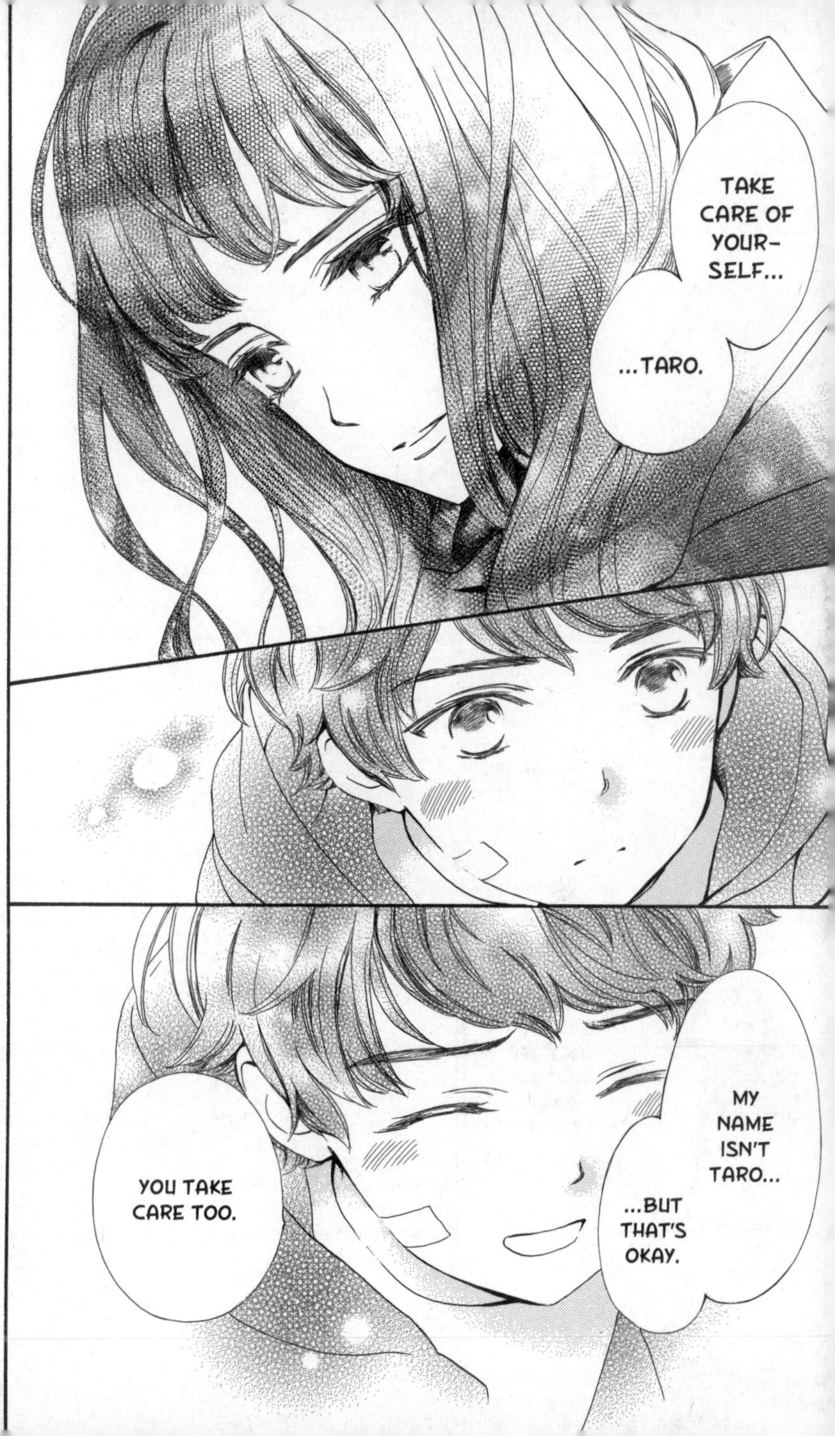
TAKE CARE OF YOUR-SELF...
...TARO.
MY NAME ISN'T TARO...
...BUT THAT'S OKAY.
YOU TAKE CARE TOO.

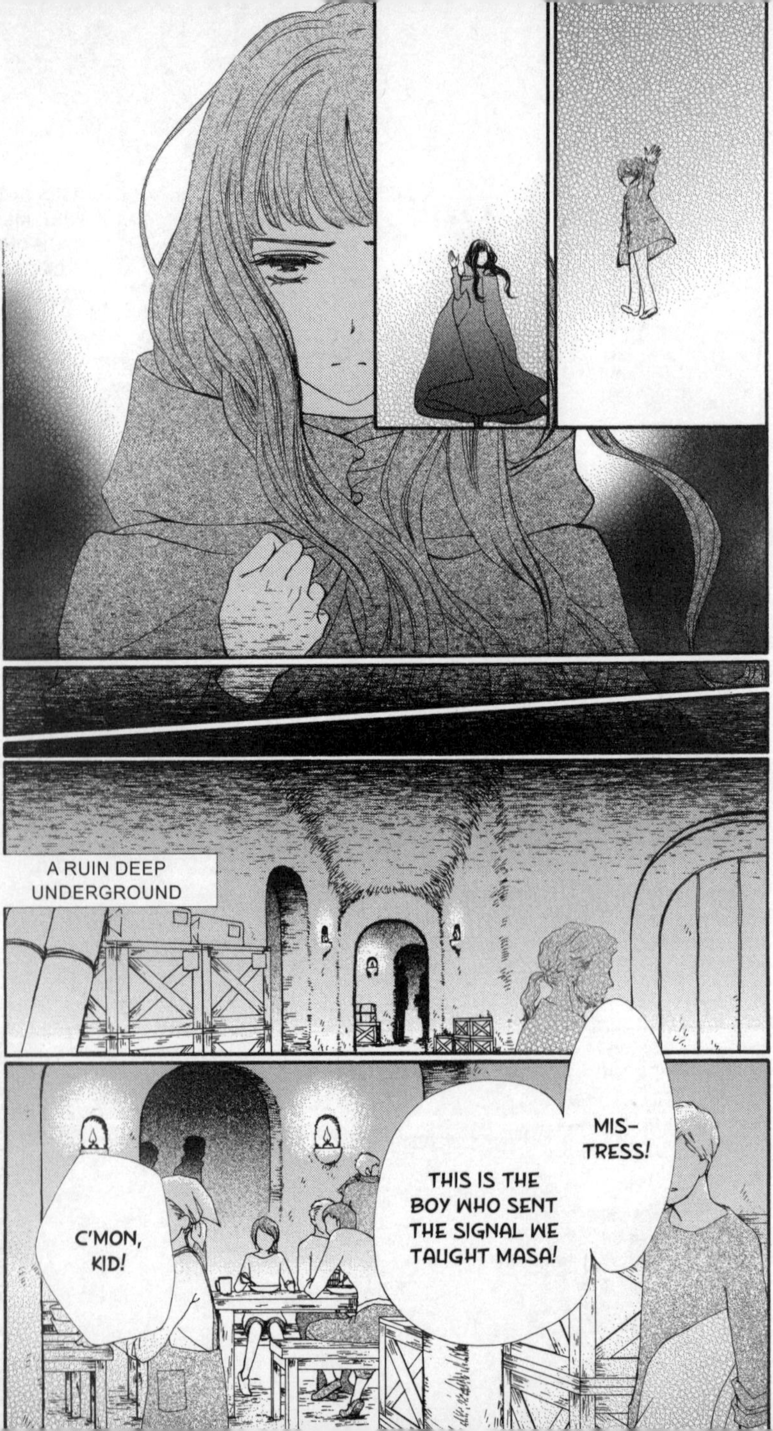
A RUIN DEEP UNDERGROUND
MIS-TRESS!
THIS IS THE BOY WHO SENT THE SIGNAL WE TAUGHT MASA!
C'MON, KID!

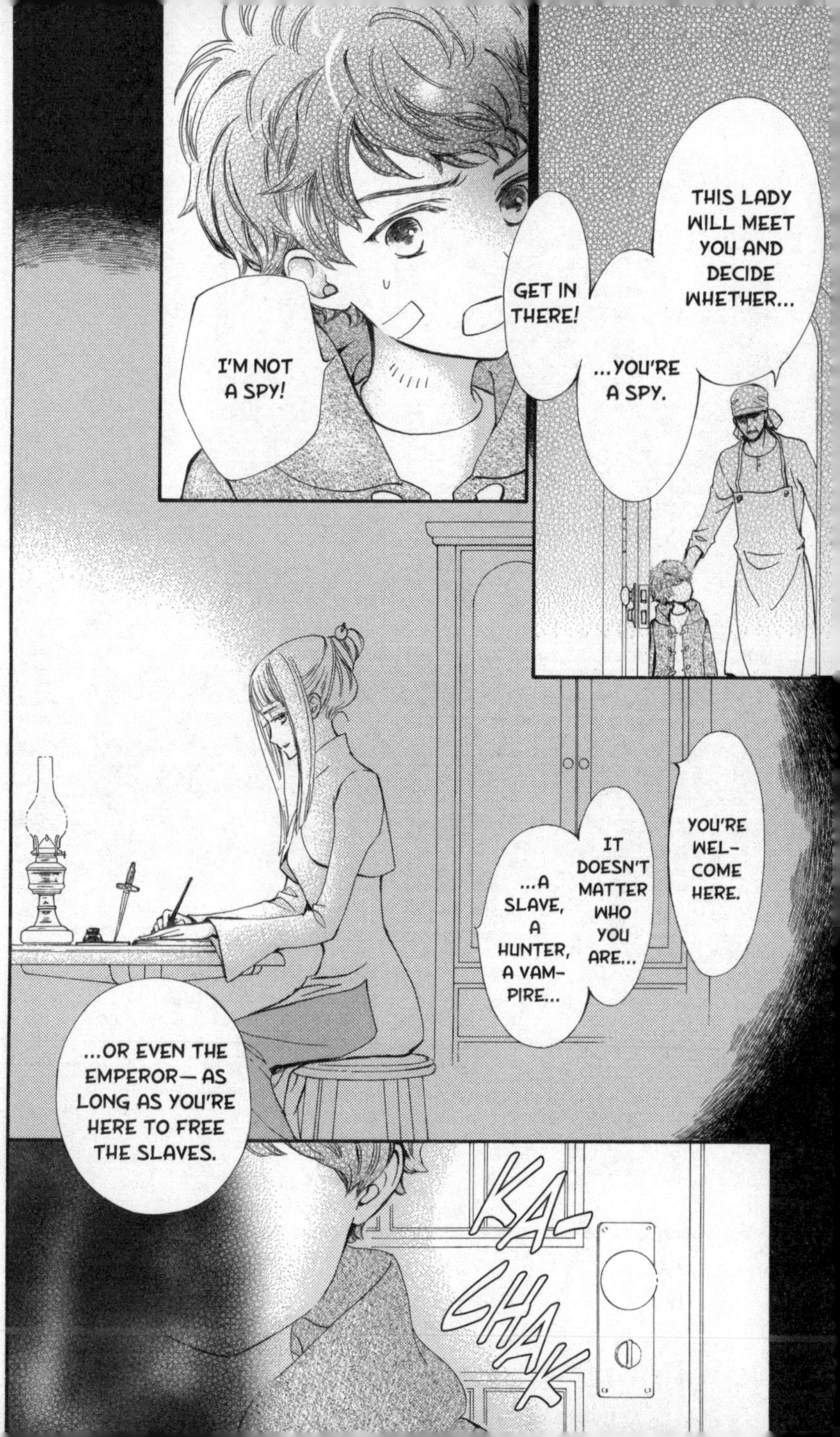
THIS LADY WILL MEET YOU AND DECIDE WHETHER...
...YOU'RE A SPY.
GET IN THERE!
I'M NOT A SPY!
YOU'RE WEL-COME HERE.
IT DOESN'T MATTER WHO YOU ARE...
...A SLAVE, A HUNTER, A VAM-PIRE...
...OR EVEN THE EMPEROR— AS LONG AS YOU'RE HERE TO FREE THE SLAVES.
KA-CHAK

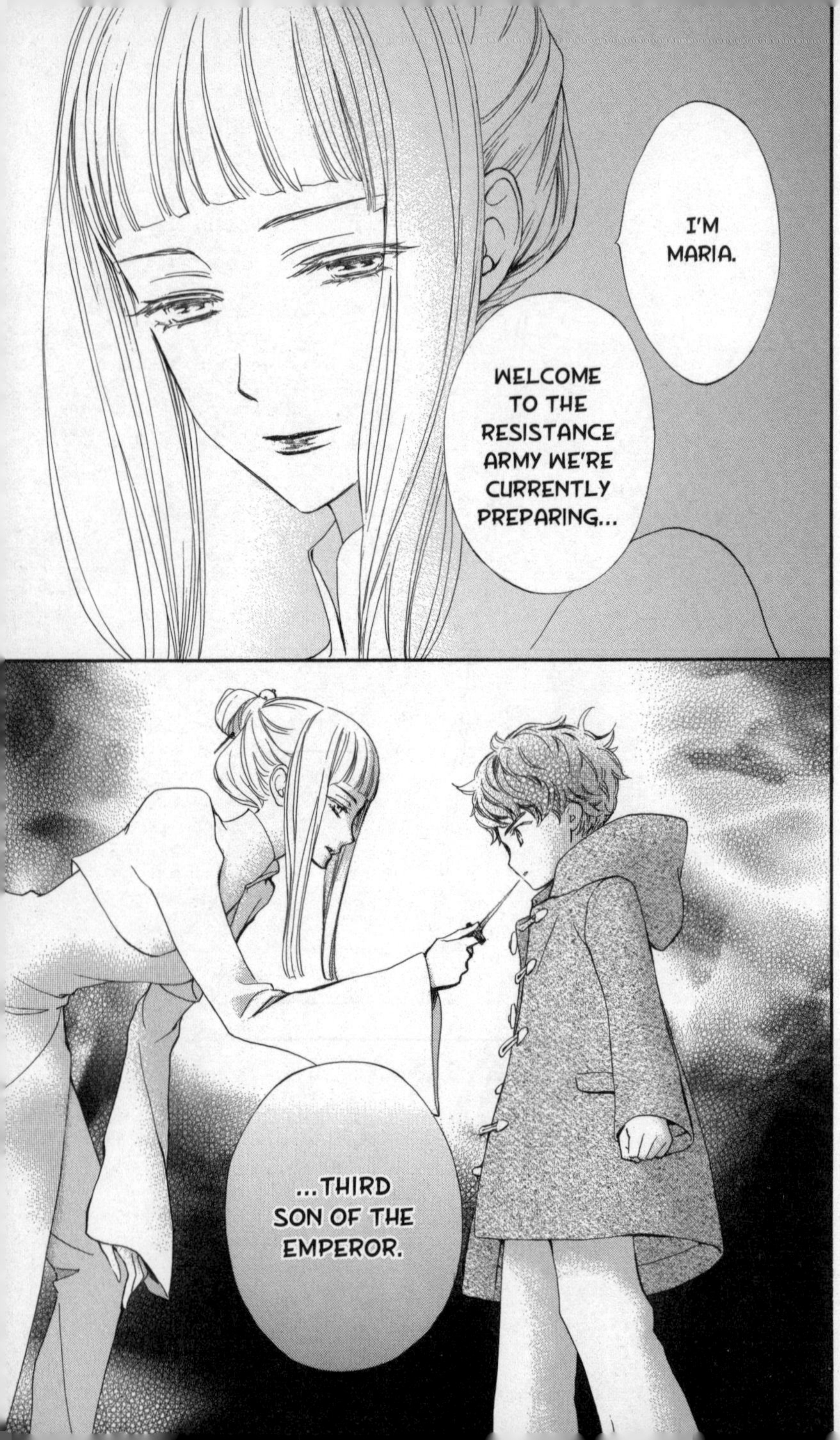
I'M MARIA.
WELCOME TO THE RESISTANCE ARMY WE'RE CURRENTLY PREPARING...
...THIRD SON OF THE EMPEROR.

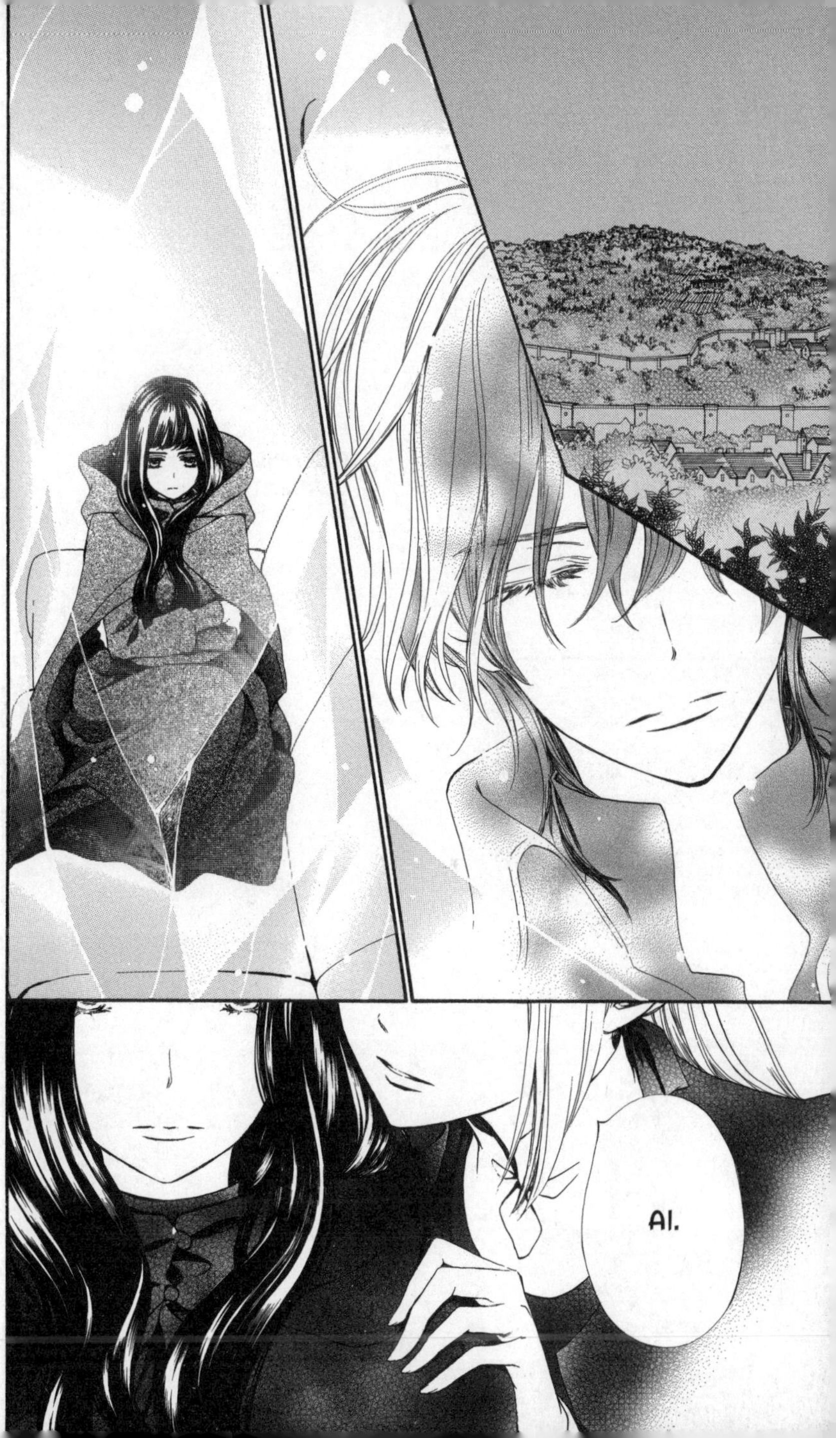
AI.

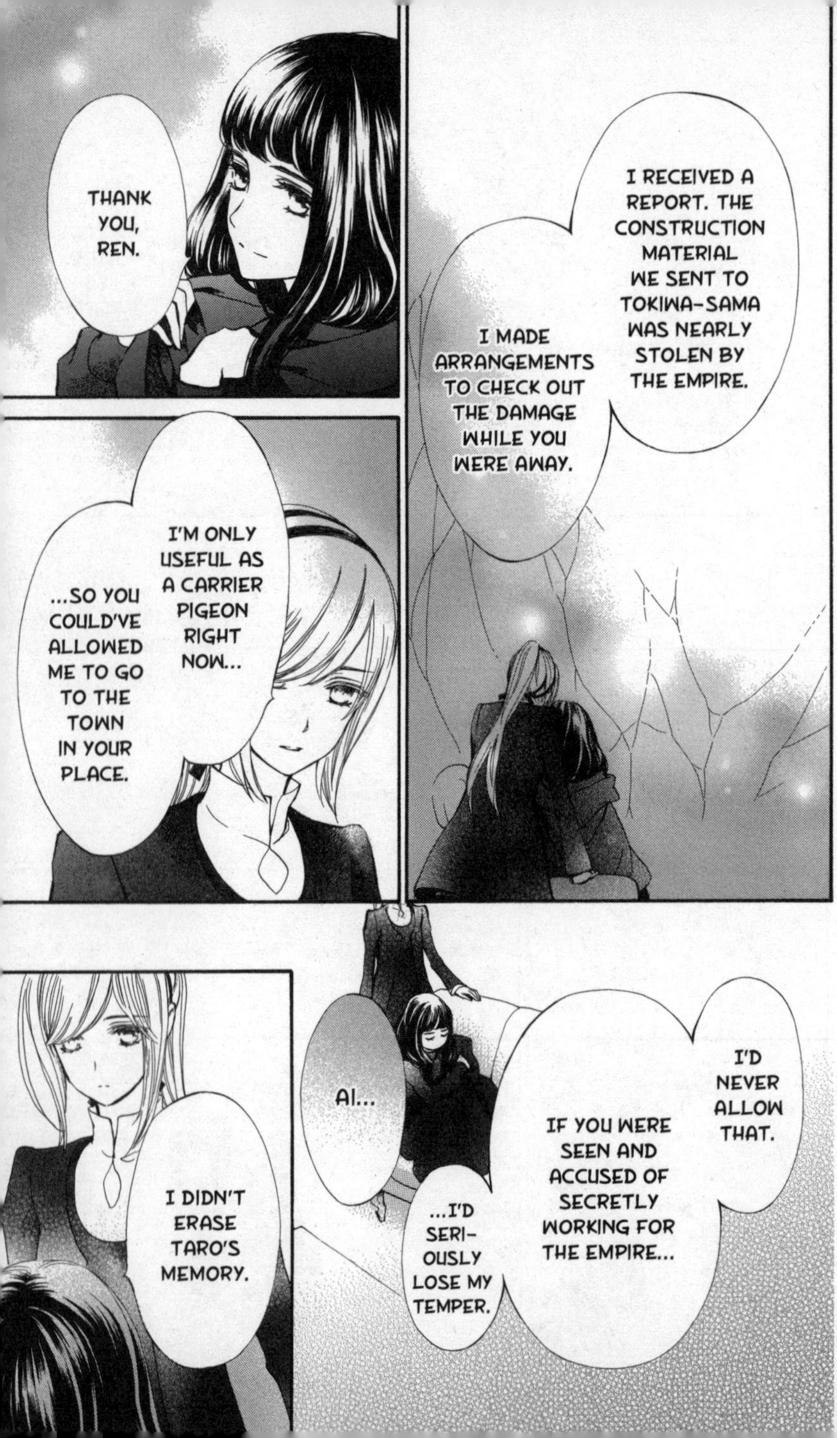
I RECEIVED A REPORT. THE CONSTRUCTION MATERIAL WE SENT TO TOKIWA-SAMA WAS NEARLY STOLEN BY THE EMPIRE.
I MADE ARRANGEMENTS TO CHECK OUT THE DAMAGE WHILE YOU WERE AWAY.
THANK YOU, REN.
I'M ONLY USEFUL AS A CARRIER PIGEON RIGHT NOW...
...SO YOU COULD'VE ALLOWED ME TO GO TO THE TOWN IN YOUR PLACE.
I'D NEVER ALLOW THAT.
IF YOU WERE SEEN AND ACCUSED OF SECRETLY WORKING FOR THE EMPIRE...
...I'D SERI-OUSLY LOSE MY TEMPER.
AI...
I DIDN'T ERASE TARO'S MEMORY.

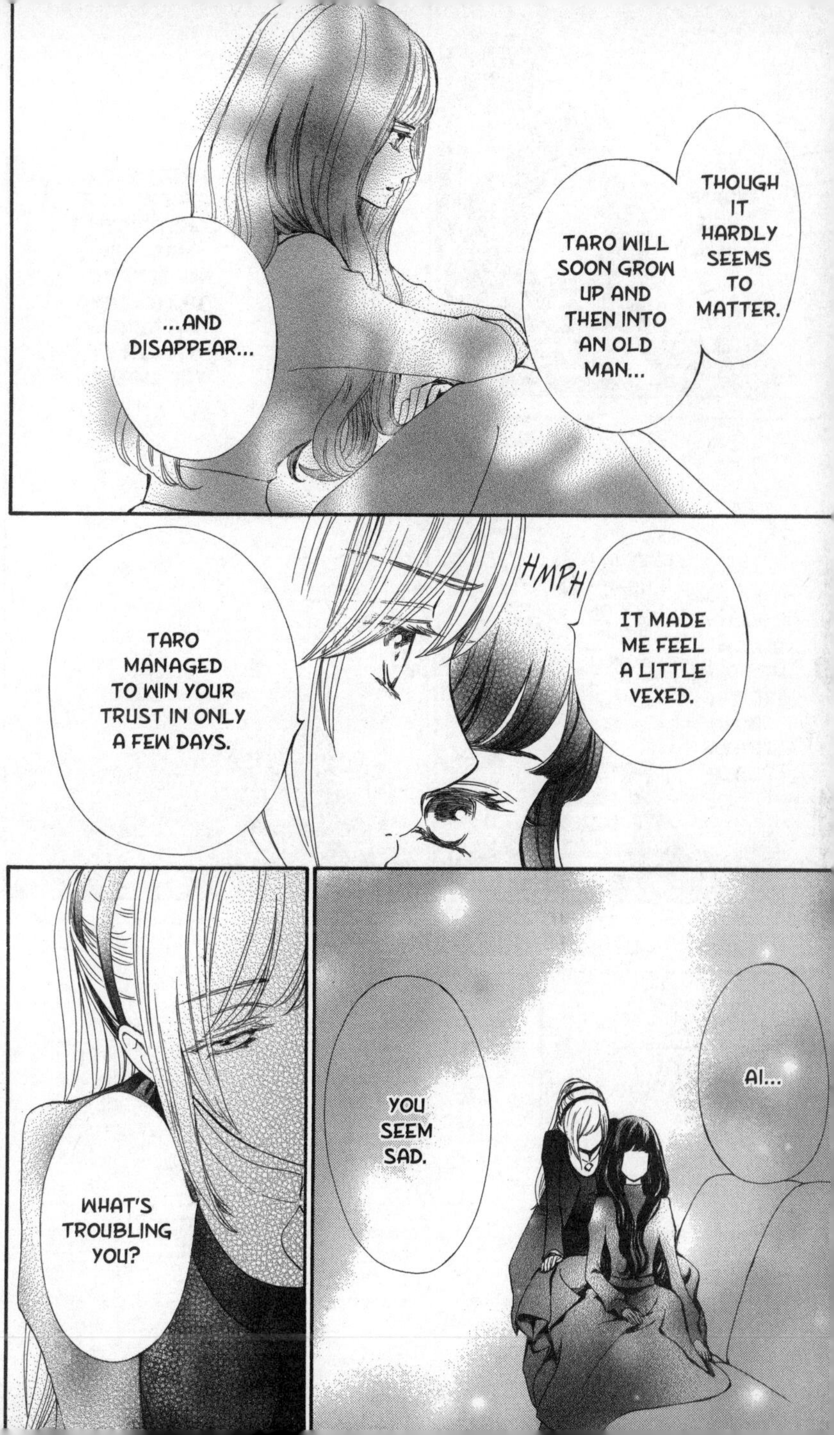
THOUGH IT HARDLY SEEMS TO MATTER.
TARO WILL SOON GROW UP AND THEN INTO AN OLD MAN...
...AND DISAPPEAR...
HMPH
IT MADE ME FEEL A LITTLE VEXED.
TARO MANAGED TO WIN YOUR TRUST IN ONLY A FEW DAYS.
AI...
YOU SEEM SAD.
WHAT'S TROUBLING YOU?

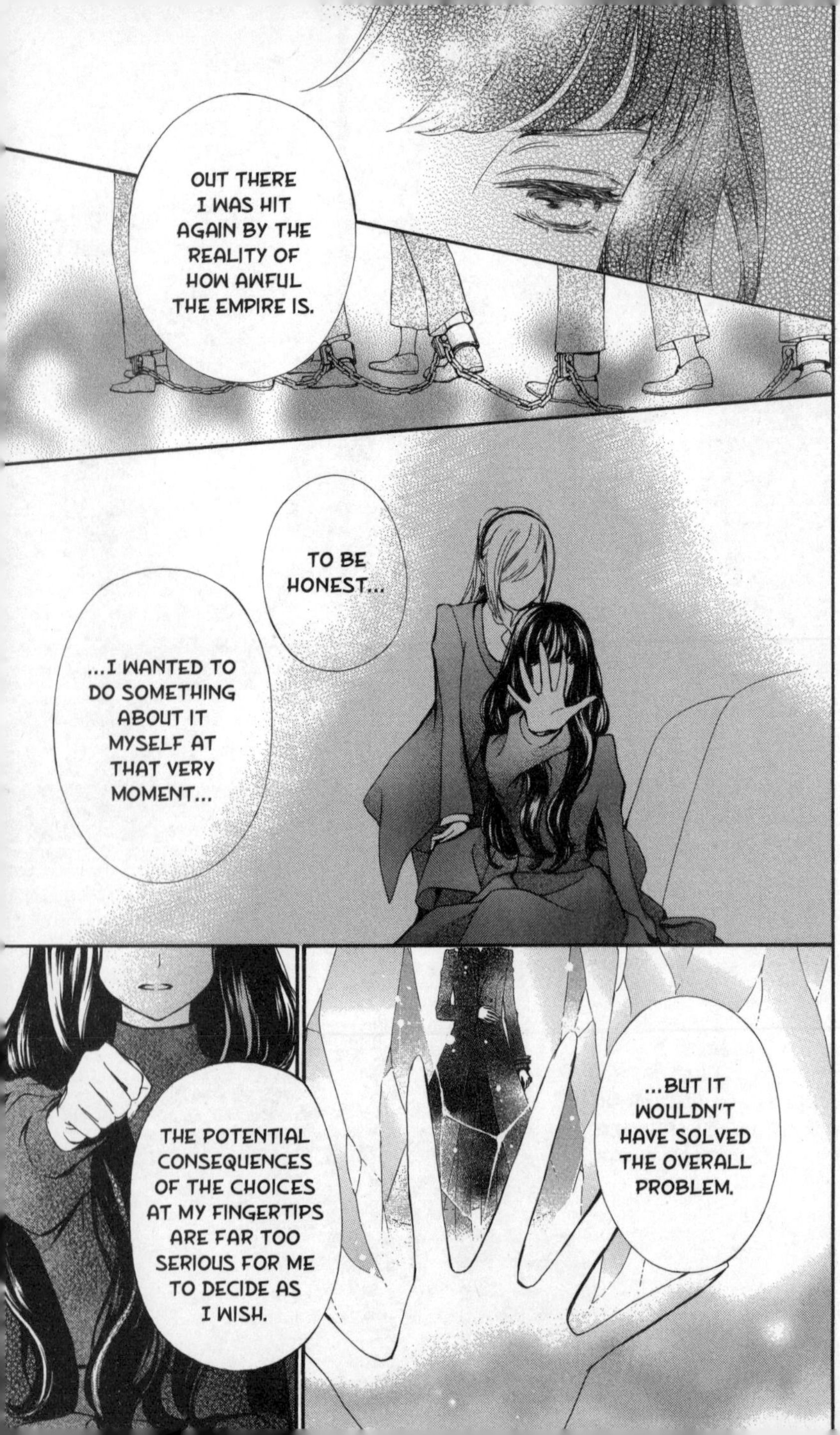
OUT THERE I WAS HIT AGAIN BY THE REALITY OF HOW AWFUL THE EMPIRE IS.
TO BE HONEST...
...I WANTED TO DO SOMETHING ABOUT IT MYSELF AT THAT VERY MOMENT...
...BUT IT WOULDN'T HAVE SOLVED THE OVERALL PROBLEM.
THE POTENTIAL CONSEQUENCES OF THE CHOICES AT MY FINGERTIPS ARE FAR TOO SERIOUS FOR ME TO DECIDE AS I WISH.

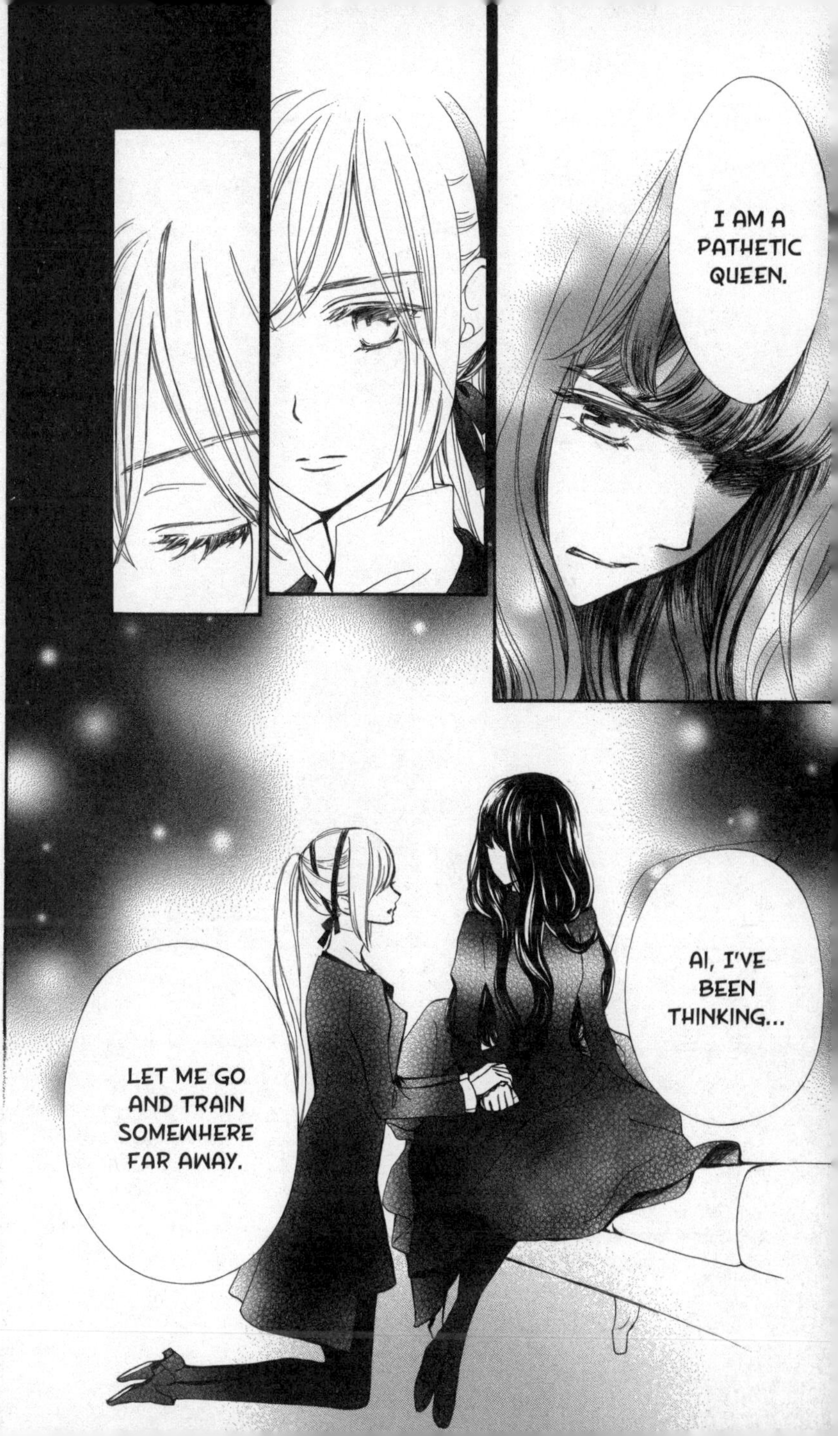
I AM A PATHETIC QUEEN.
AI, I'VE BEEN THINKING...
LET ME GO AND TRAIN SOMEWHERE FAR AWAY.

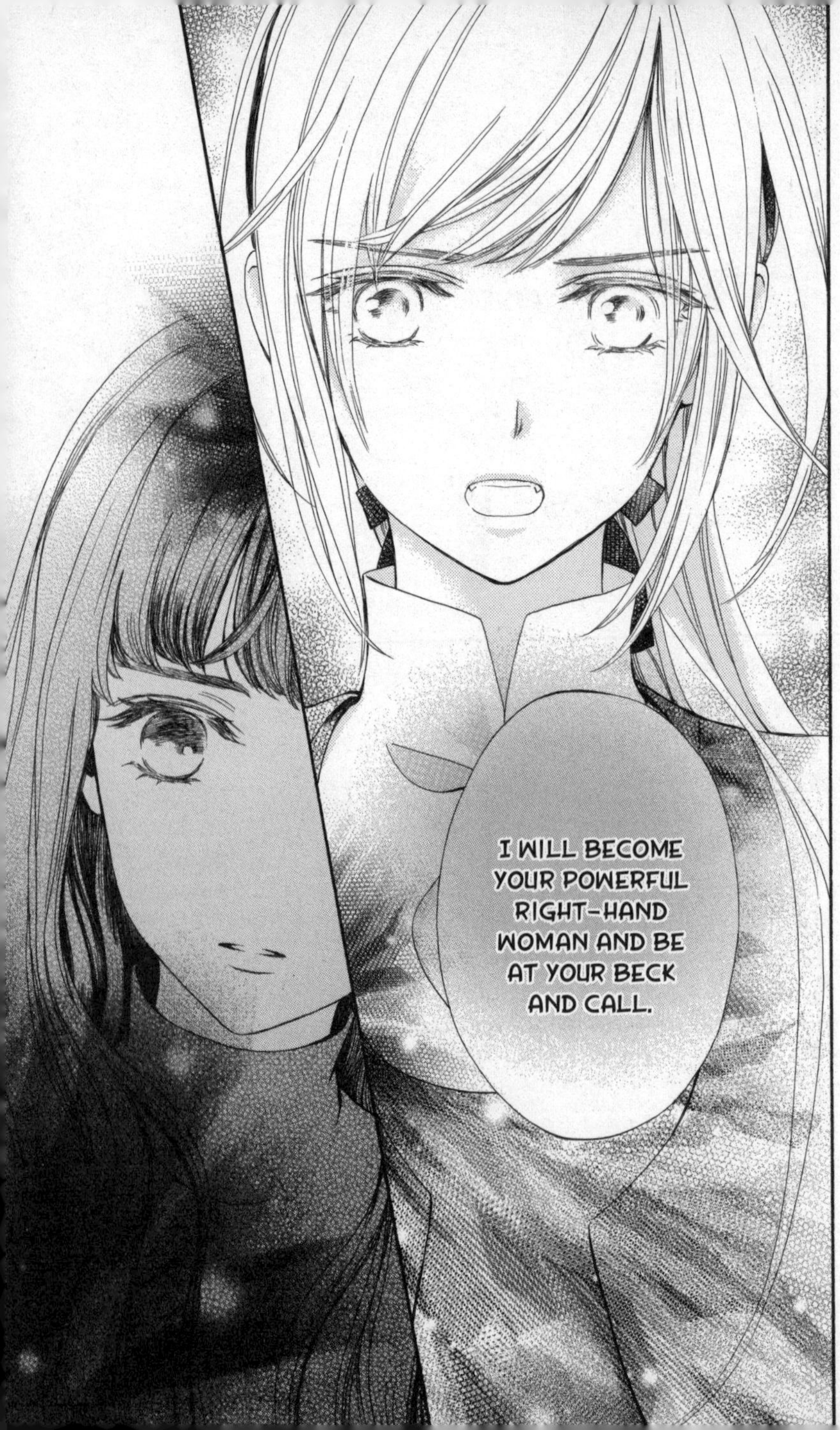
I WILL BECOME YOUR POWERFUL RIGHT-HAND WOMAN AND BE AT YOUR BECK AND CALL.

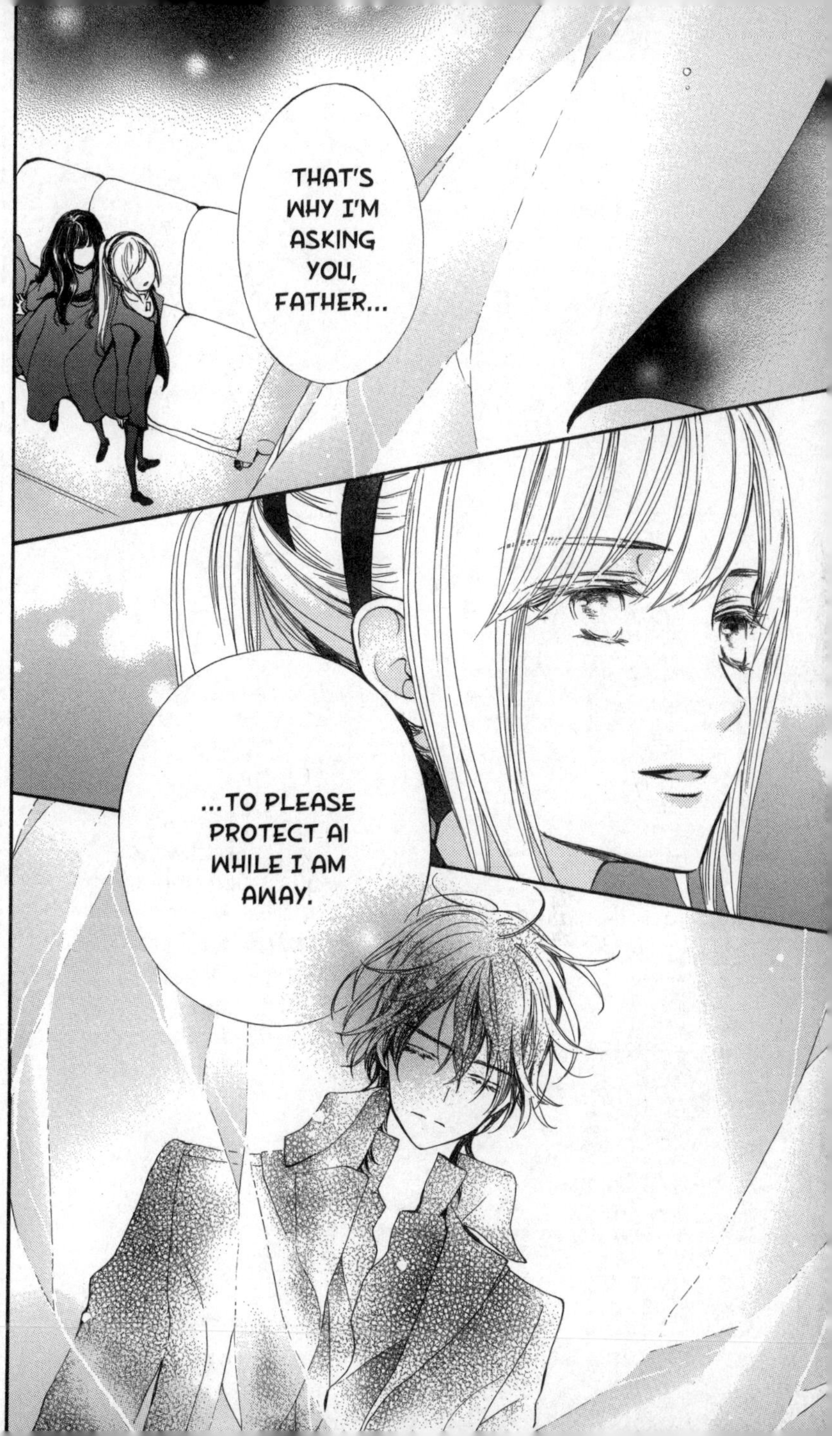
THAT'S WHY I'M ASKING YOU, FATHER...
...TO PLEASE PROTECT AI WHILE I AM AWAY.

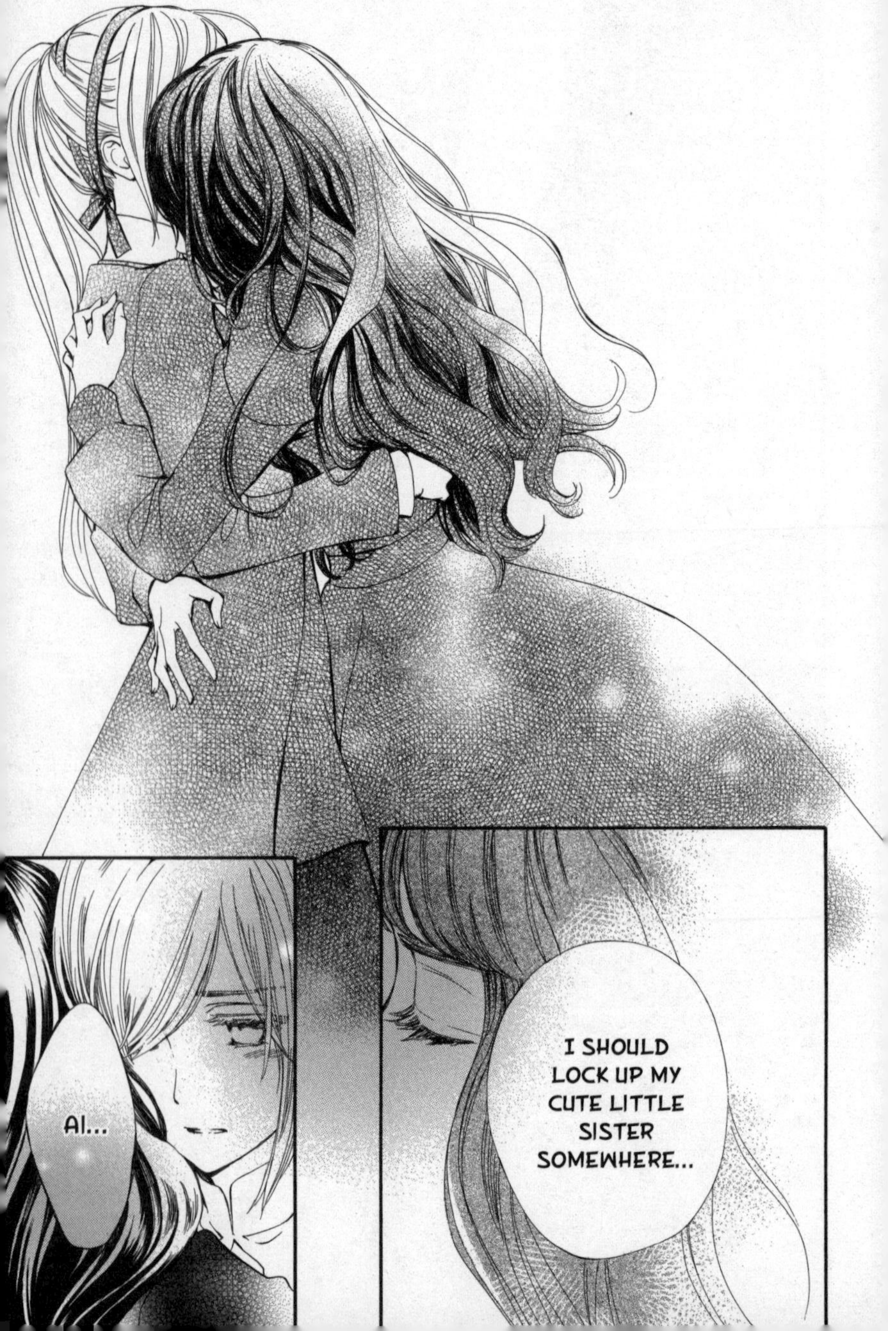
I SHOULD LOCK UP MY CUTE LITTLE SISTER SOMEWHERE...
AI...

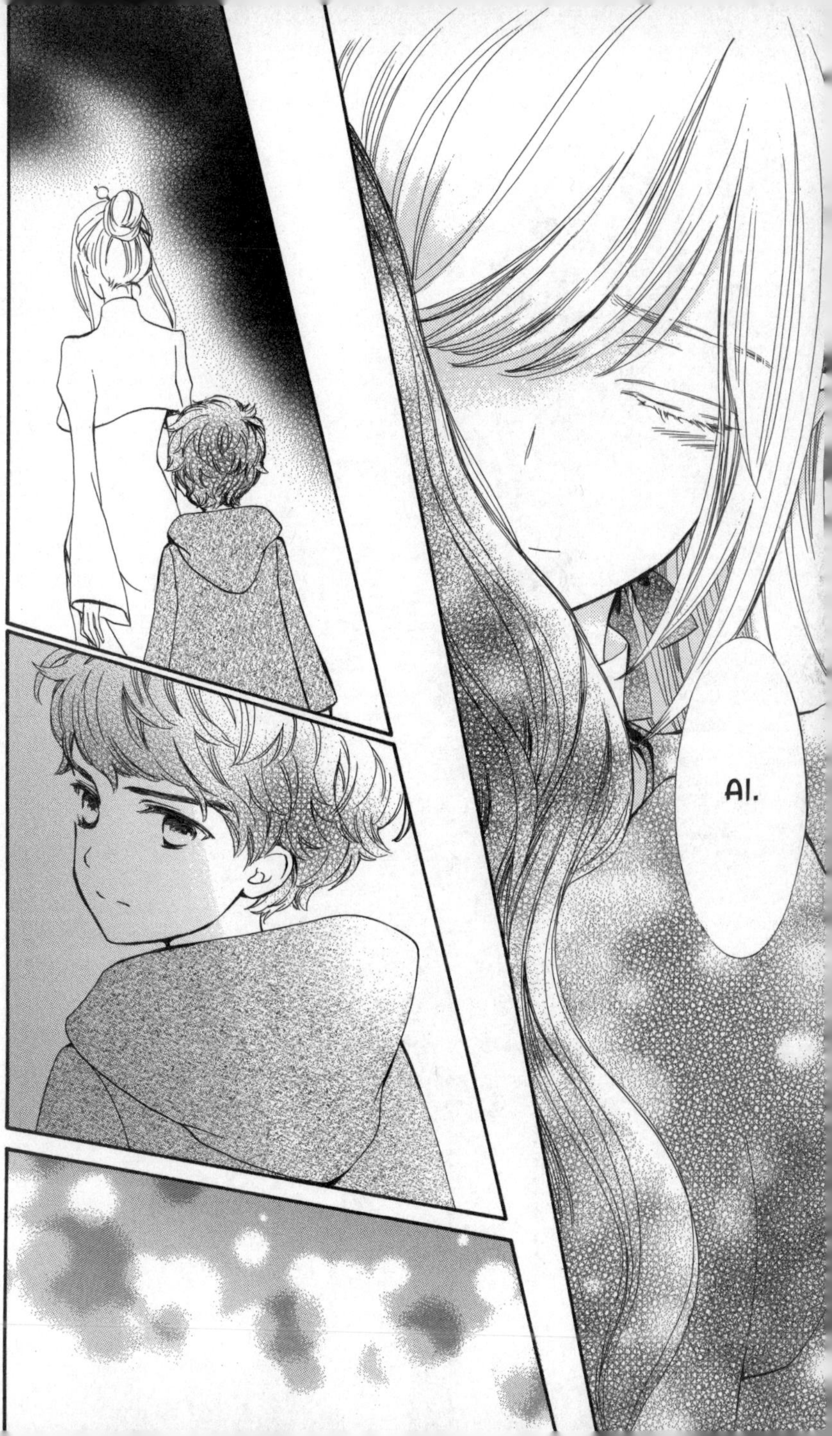
AI.

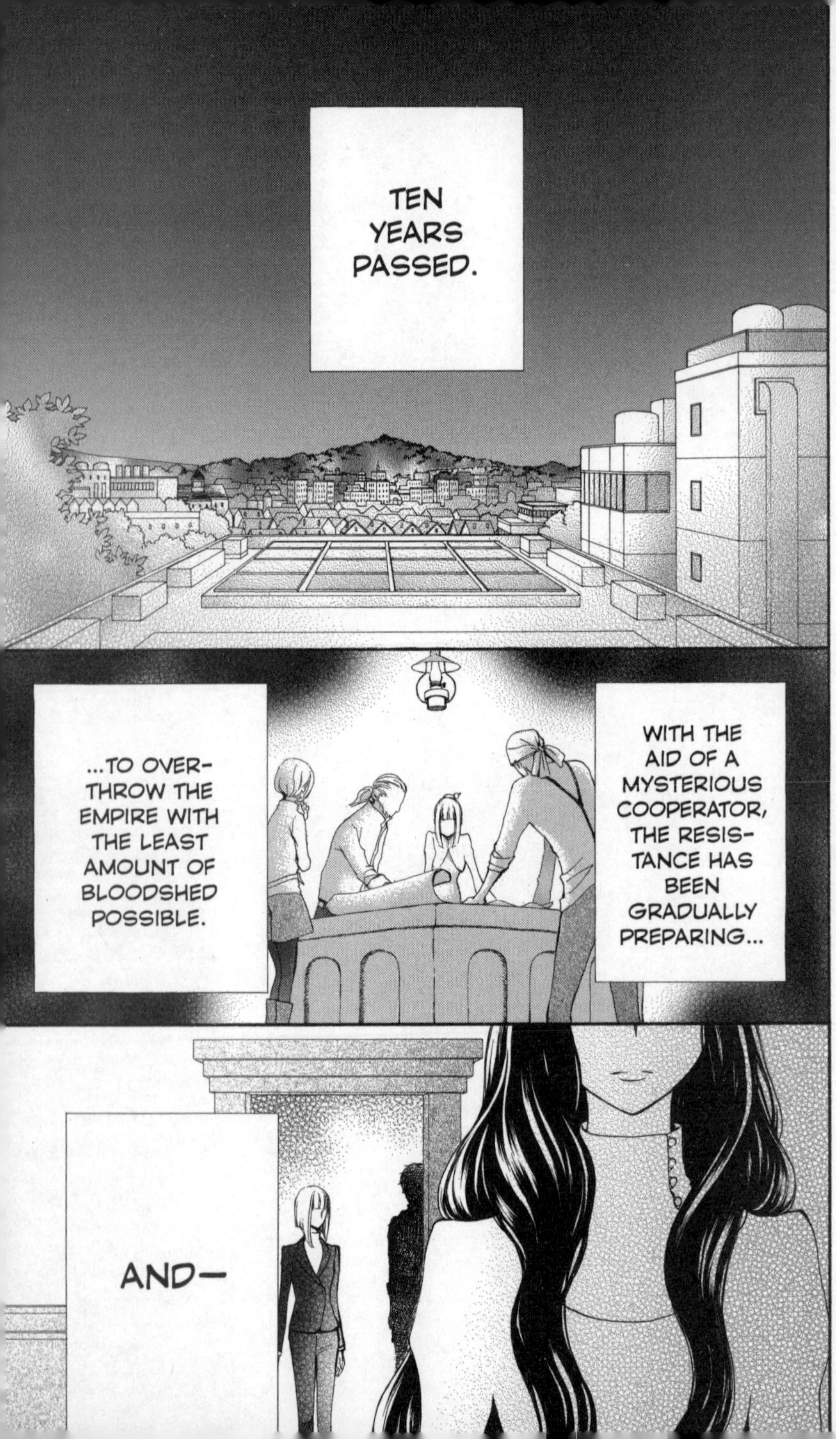
TEN YEARS PASSED.
WITH THE AID OF A MYSTERIOUS COOPERATOR, THE RESIS-TANCE HAS BEEN GRADUALLY PREPARING...
...TO OVER-THROW THE EMPIRE WITH THE LEAST AMOUNT OF BLOODSHED POSSIBLE.
AND—

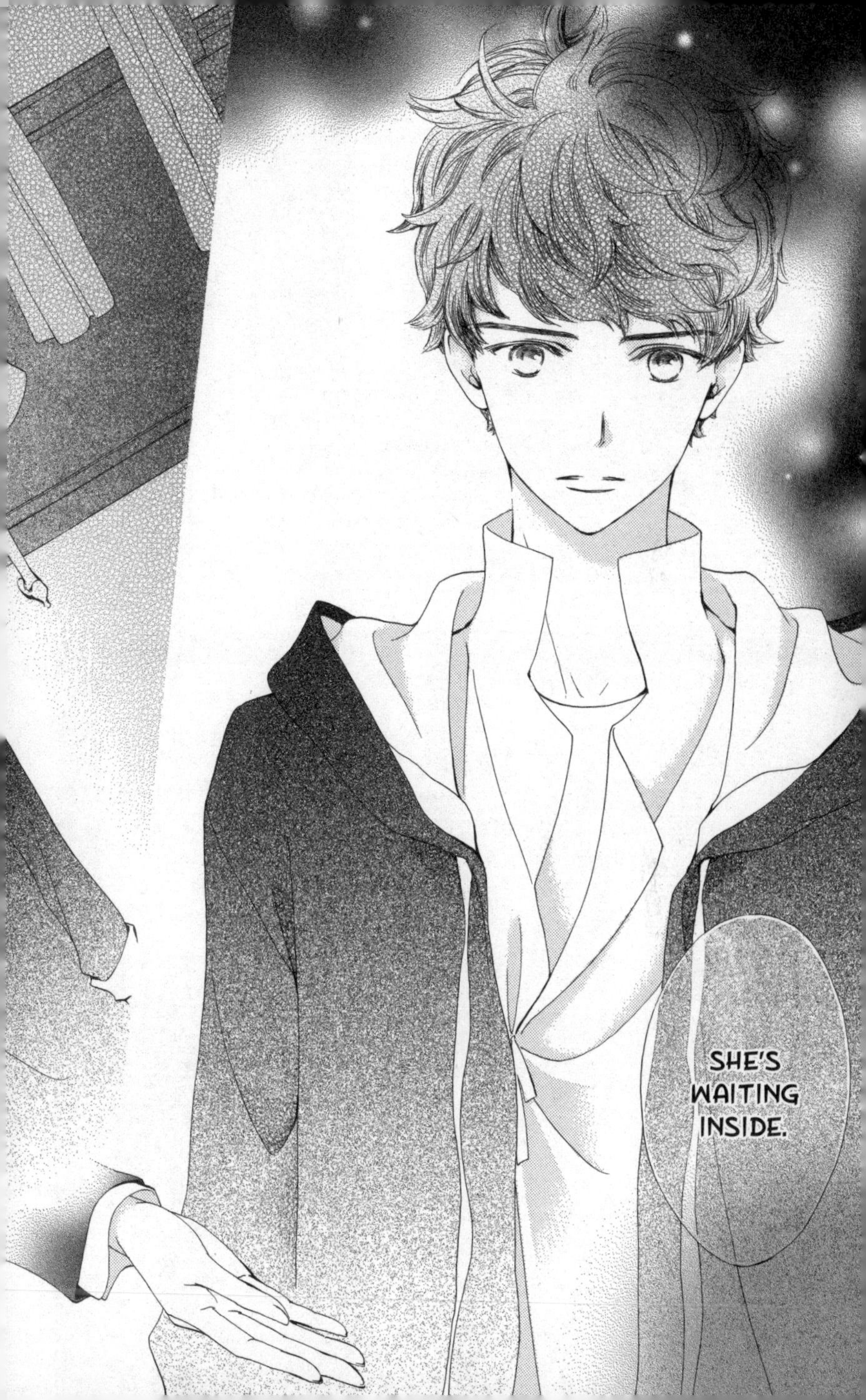
SHE'S WAITING INSIDE.

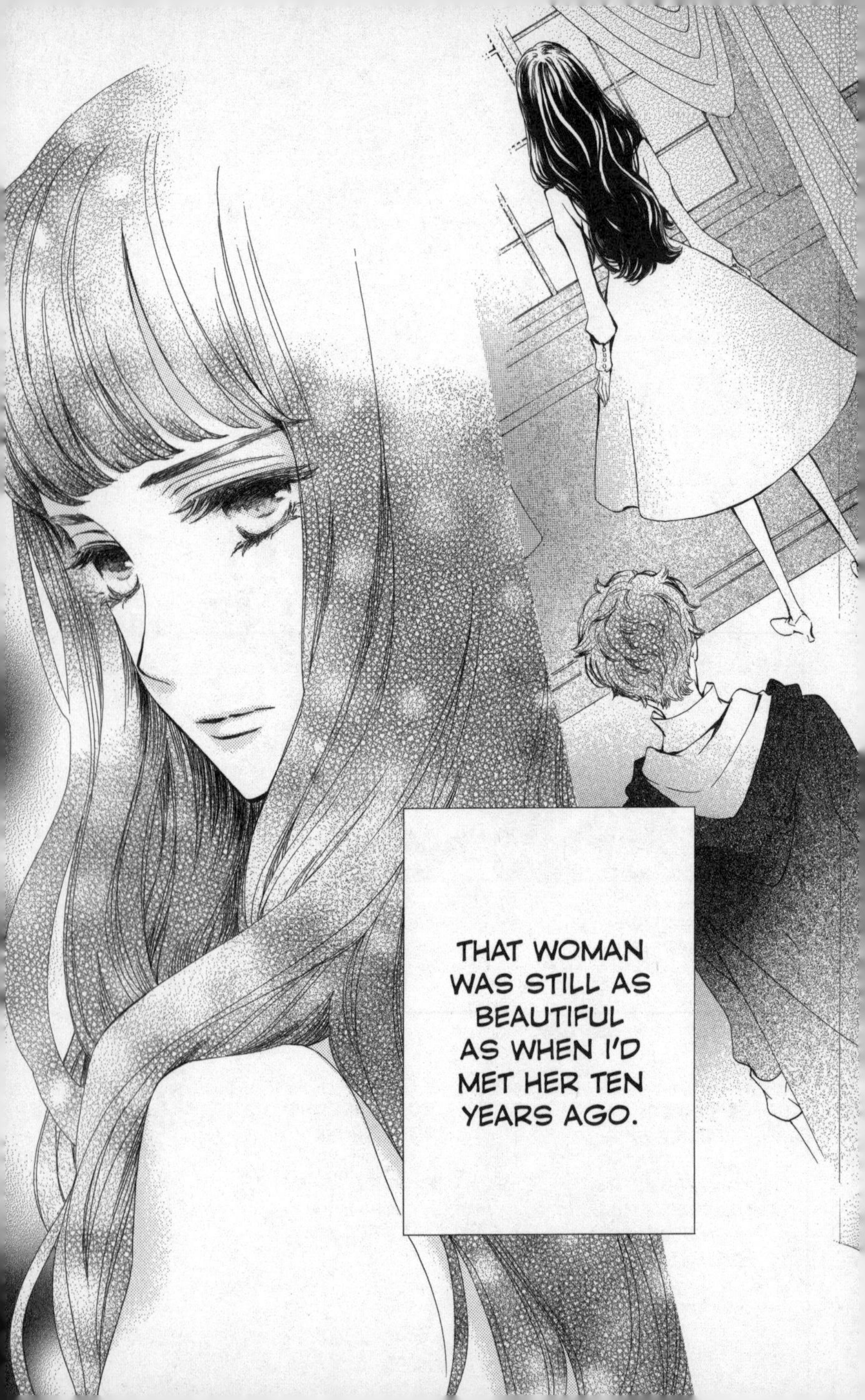
THAT WOMAN WAS STILL AS BEAUTIFUL AS WHEN I'D MET HER TEN YEARS AGO.

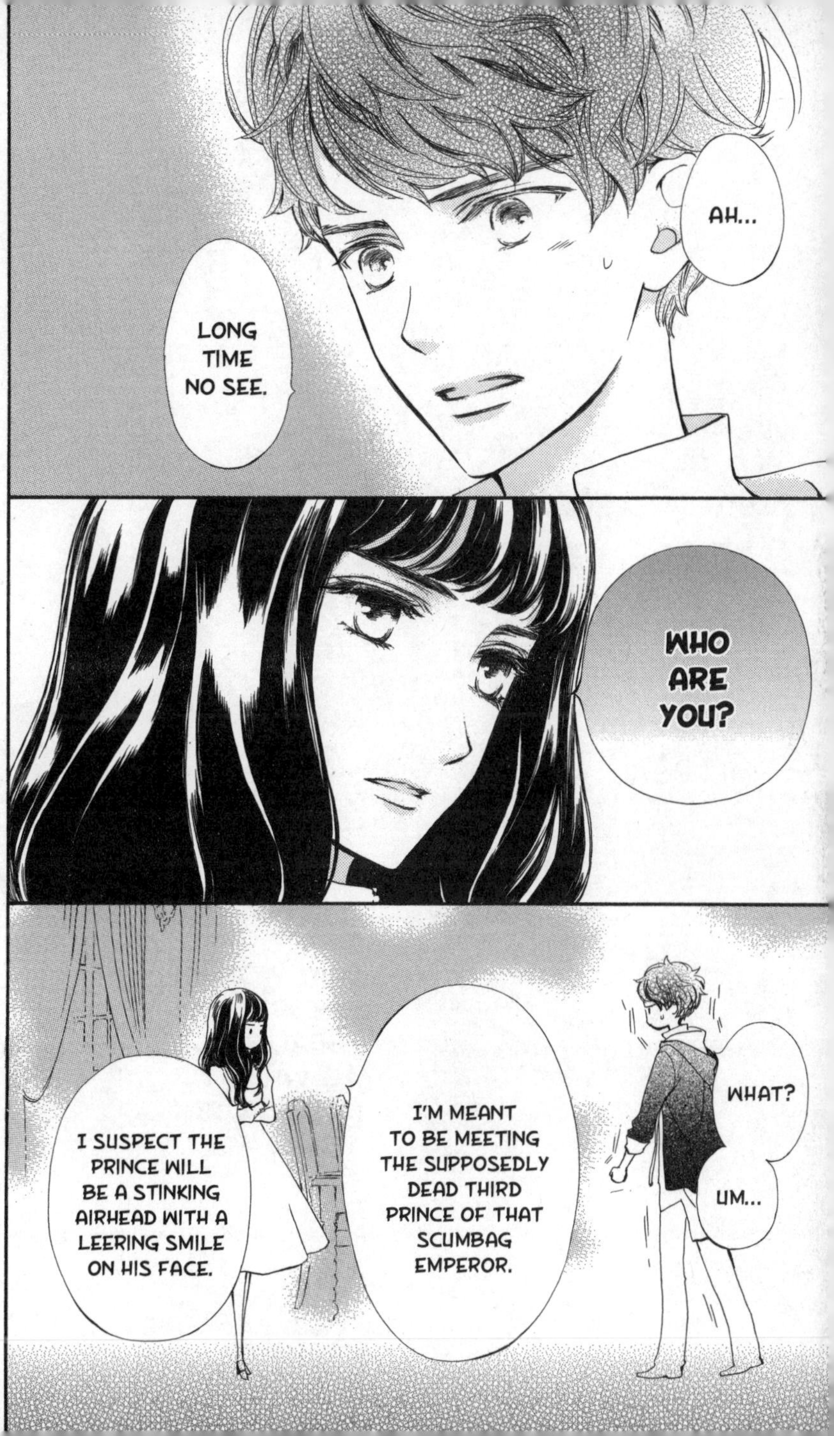
AH...
LONG TIME NO SEE.
WHO ARE YOU?
WHAT?
UM...
I'M MEANT TO BE MEETING THE SUPPOSEDLY DEAD THIRD PRINCE OF THAT SCUMBAG EMPEROR.
I SUSPECT THE PRINCE WILL BE A STINKING AIRHEAD WITH A LEERING SMILE ON HIS FACE.

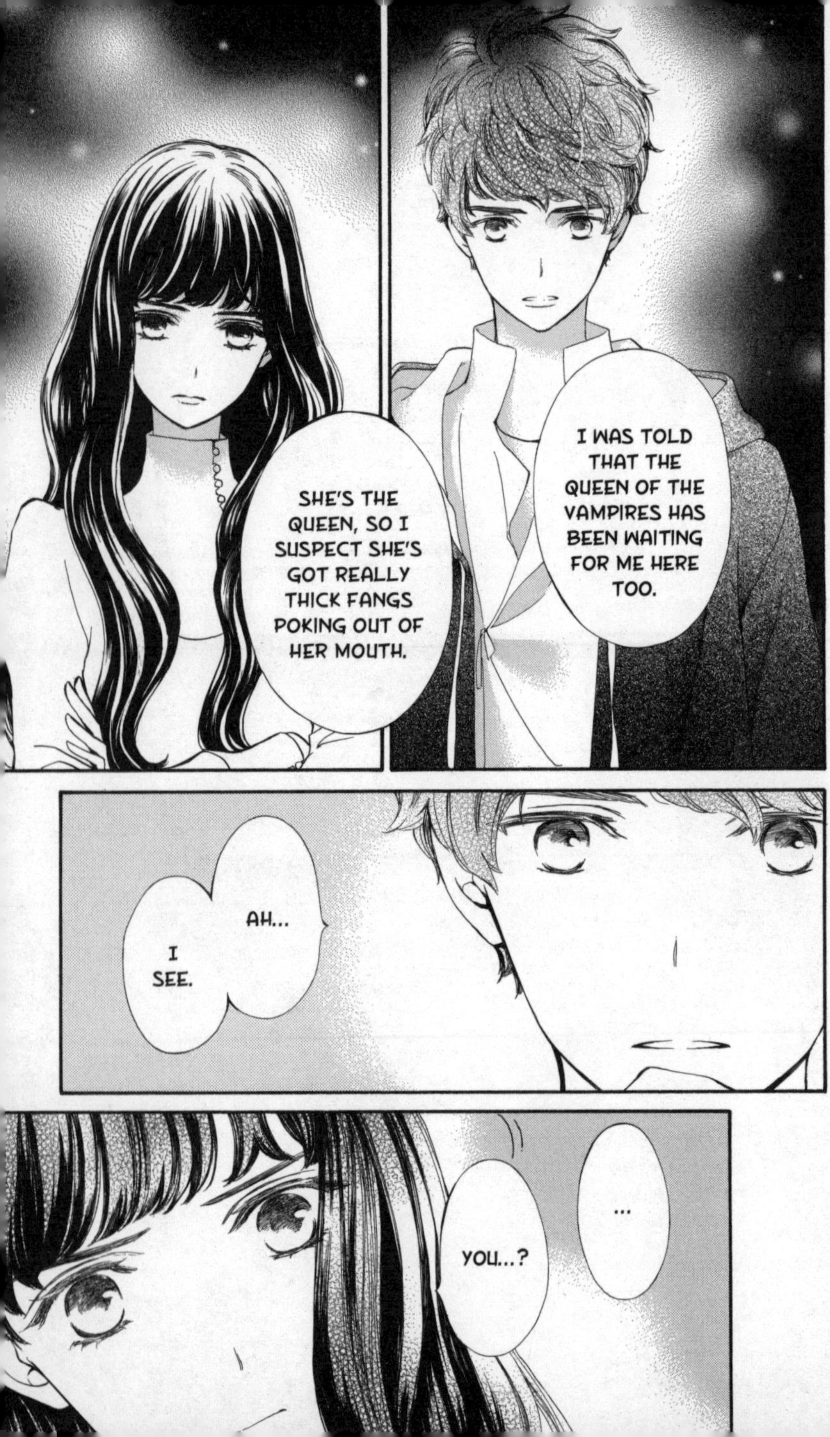
I WAS TOLD THAT THE QUEEN OF THE VAMPIRES HAS BEEN WAITING FOR ME HERE TOO.
SHE'S THE QUEEN, SO I SUSPECT SHE'S GOT REALLY THICK FANGS POKING OUT OF HER MOUTH.
AH...
I SEE.
...
YOU...?

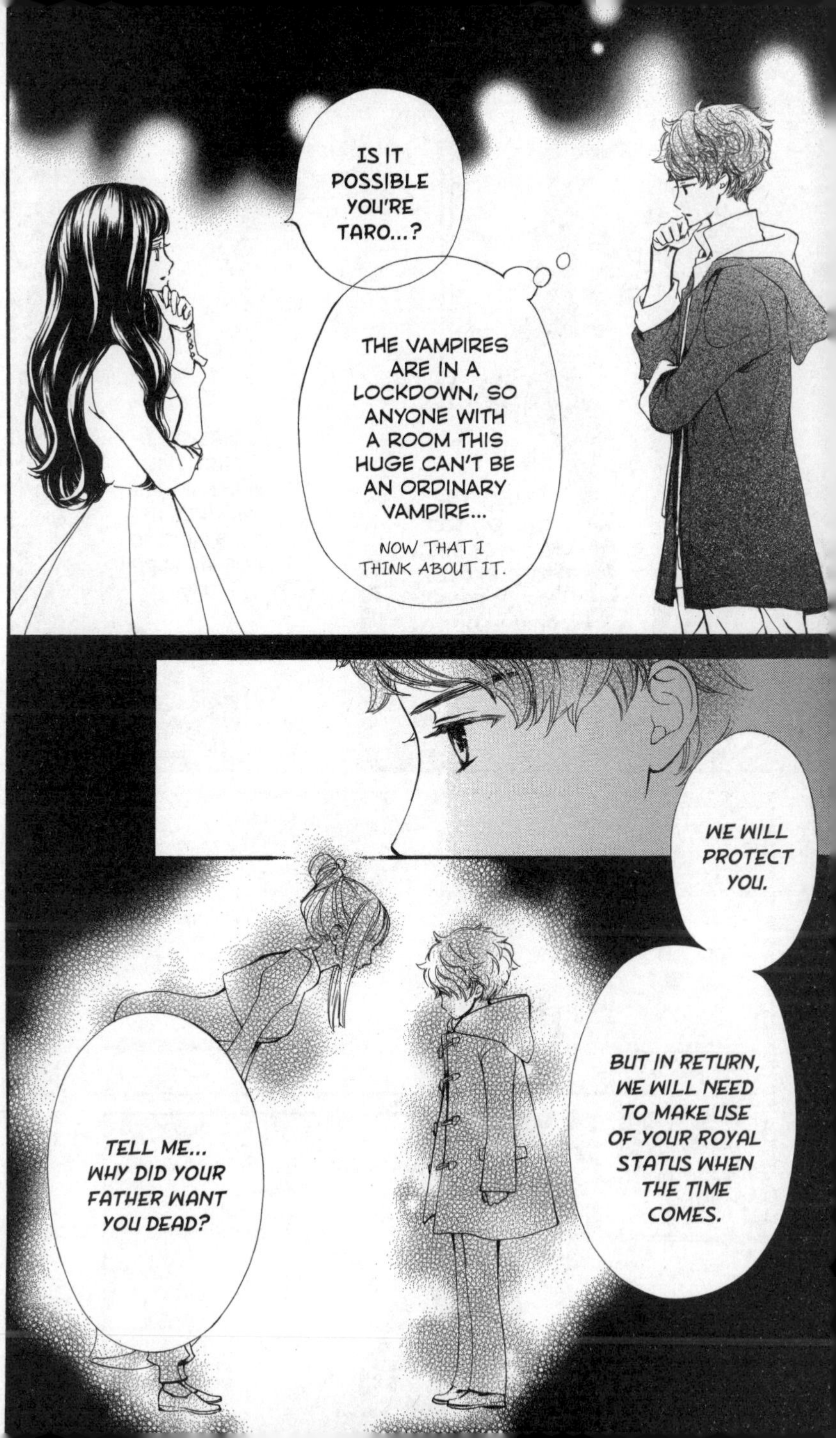
IS IT POSSIBLE YOU'RE TARO...?
THE VAMPIRES ARE IN A LOCKDOWN, SO ANYONE WITH A ROOM THIS HUGE CAN'T BE AN ORDINARY VAMPIRE...
NOW THAT I THINK ABOUT IT.
WE WILL PROTECT YOU.
BUT IN RETURN, WE WILL NEED TO MAKE USE OF YOUR ROYAL STATUS WHEN THE TIME COMES.
TELL ME... WHY DID YOUR FATHER WANT YOU DEAD?

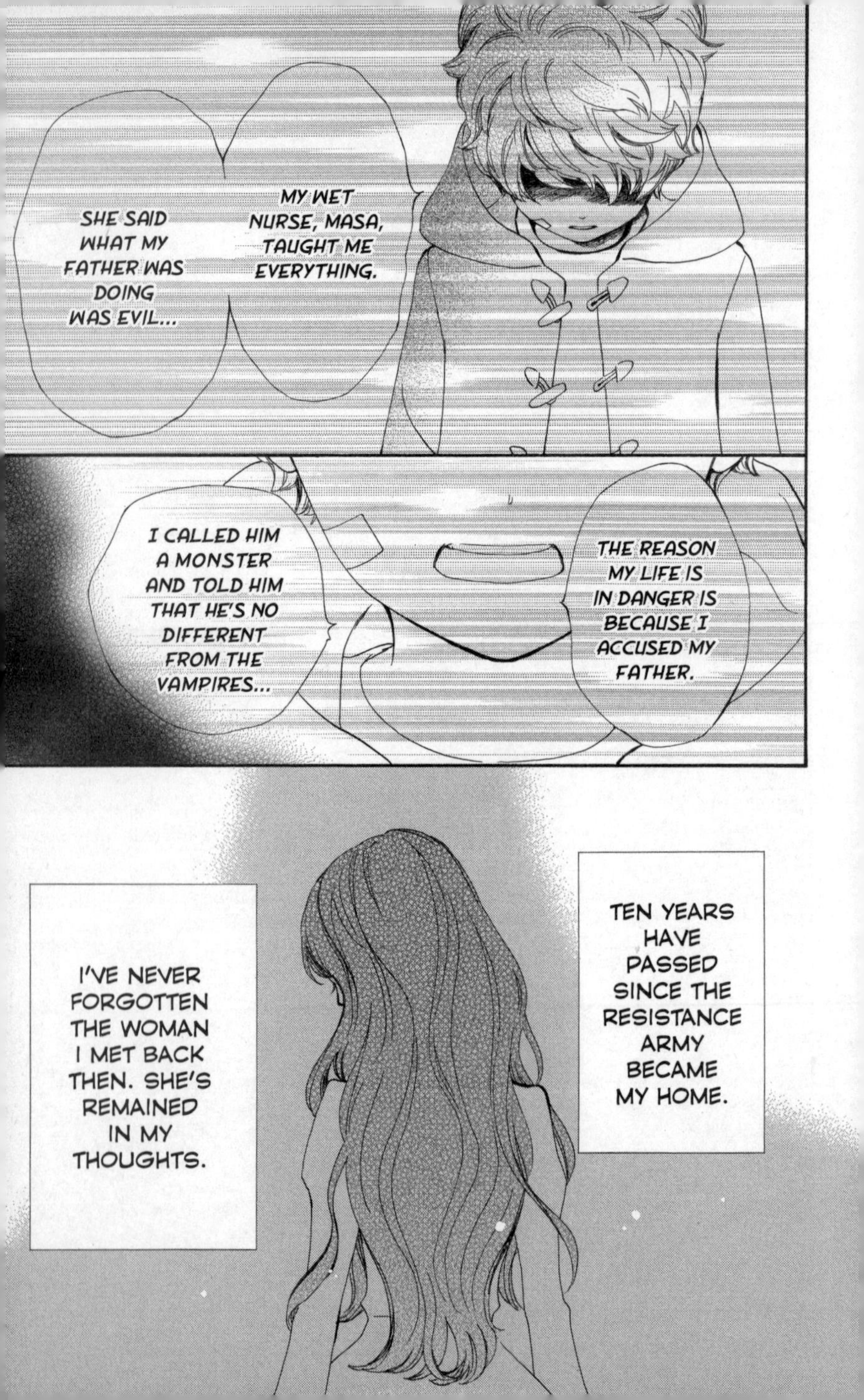
MY WET NURSE, MASA, TAUGHT ME EVERYTHING.
SHE SAID WHAT MY FATHER WAS DOING WAS EVIL...
THE REASON MY LIFE IS IN DANGER IS BECAUSE I ACCUSED MY FATHER.
I CALLED HIM A MONSTER AND TOLD HIM THAT HE'S NO DIFFERENT FROM THE VAMPIRES...
TEN YEARS HAVE PASSED SINCE THE RESISTANCE ARMY BECAME MY HOME.
I'VE NEVER FORGOTTEN THE WOMAN I MET BACK THEN. SHE'S REMAINED IN MY THOUGHTS.

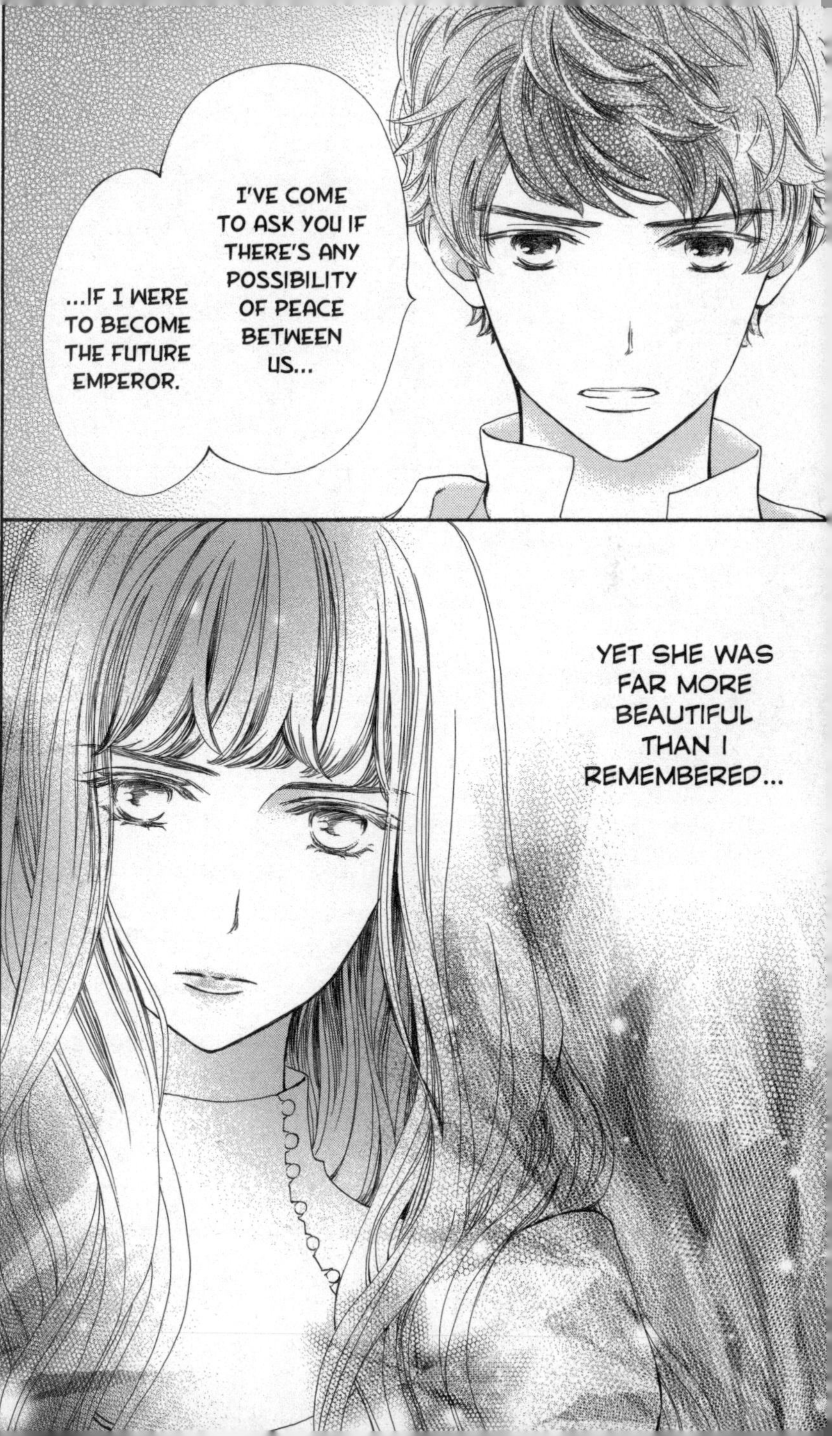
I'VE COME TO ASK YOU IF THERE'S ANY POSSIBILITY OF PEACE BETWEEN US...
...IF I WERE TO BECOME THE FUTURE EMPEROR.
YET SHE WAS FAR MORE BEAUTIFUL THAN I REMEMBERED...

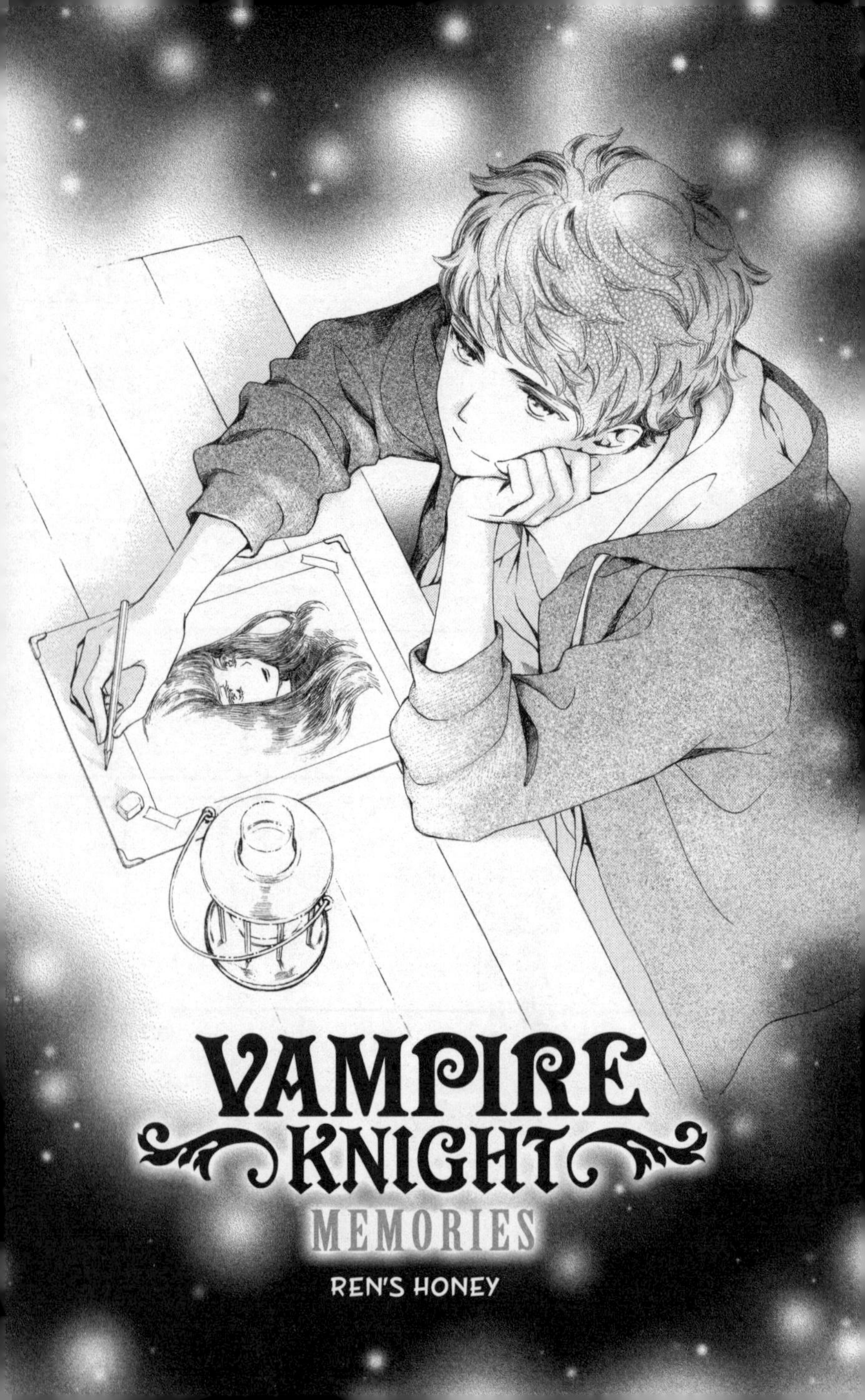
VAMPIRE KNIGHT
MEMORIES
REN'S HONEY

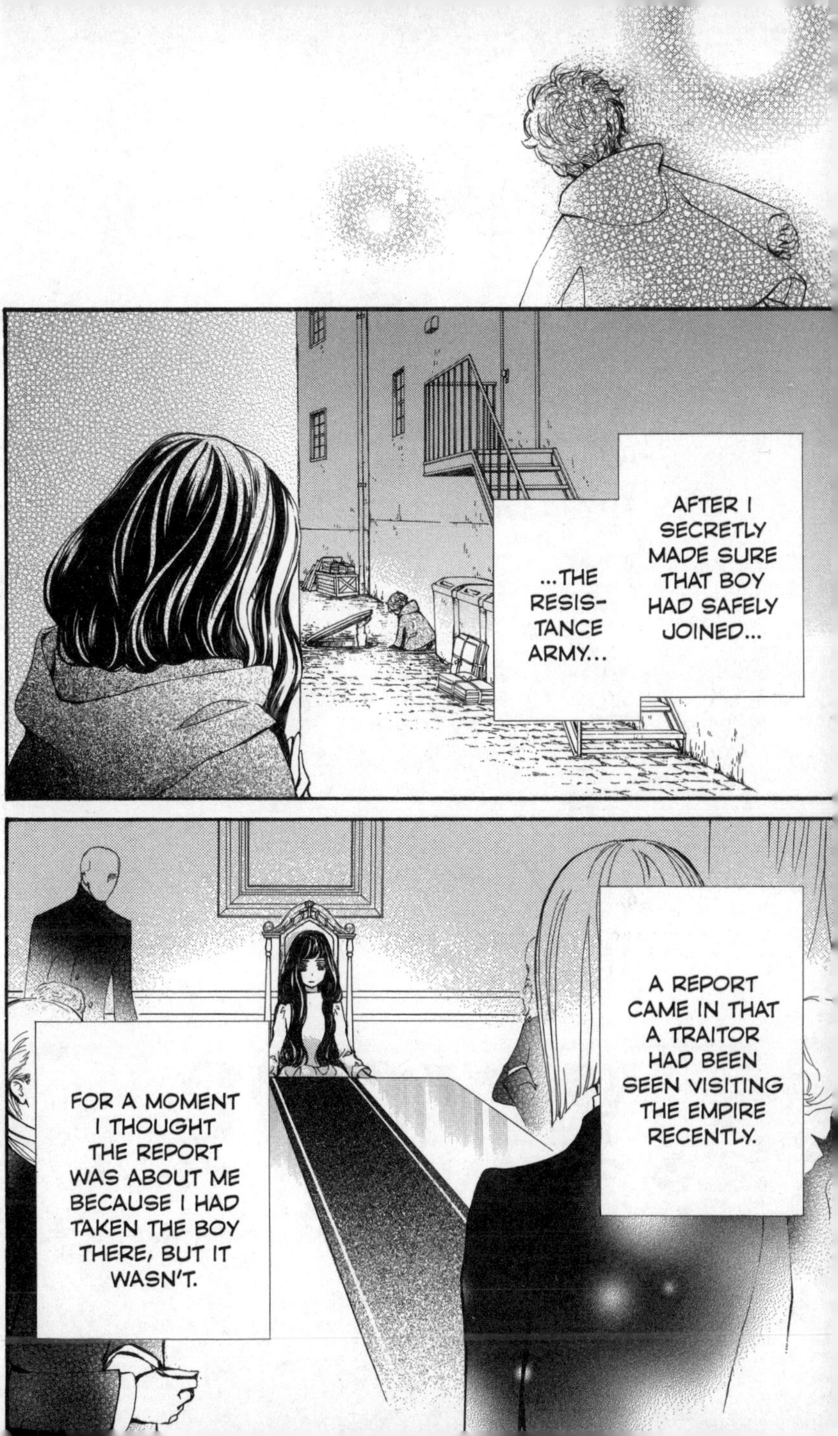
AFTER I SECRETLY MADE SURE THAT BOY HAD SAFELY JOINED...
...THE RESIS-TANCE ARMY...
A REPORT CAME IN THAT A TRAITOR HAD BEEN SEEN VISITING THE EMPIRE RECENTLY.
FOR A MOMENT I THOUGHT THE REPORT WAS ABOUT ME BECAUSE I HAD TAKEN THE BOY THERE, BUT IT WASN'T.

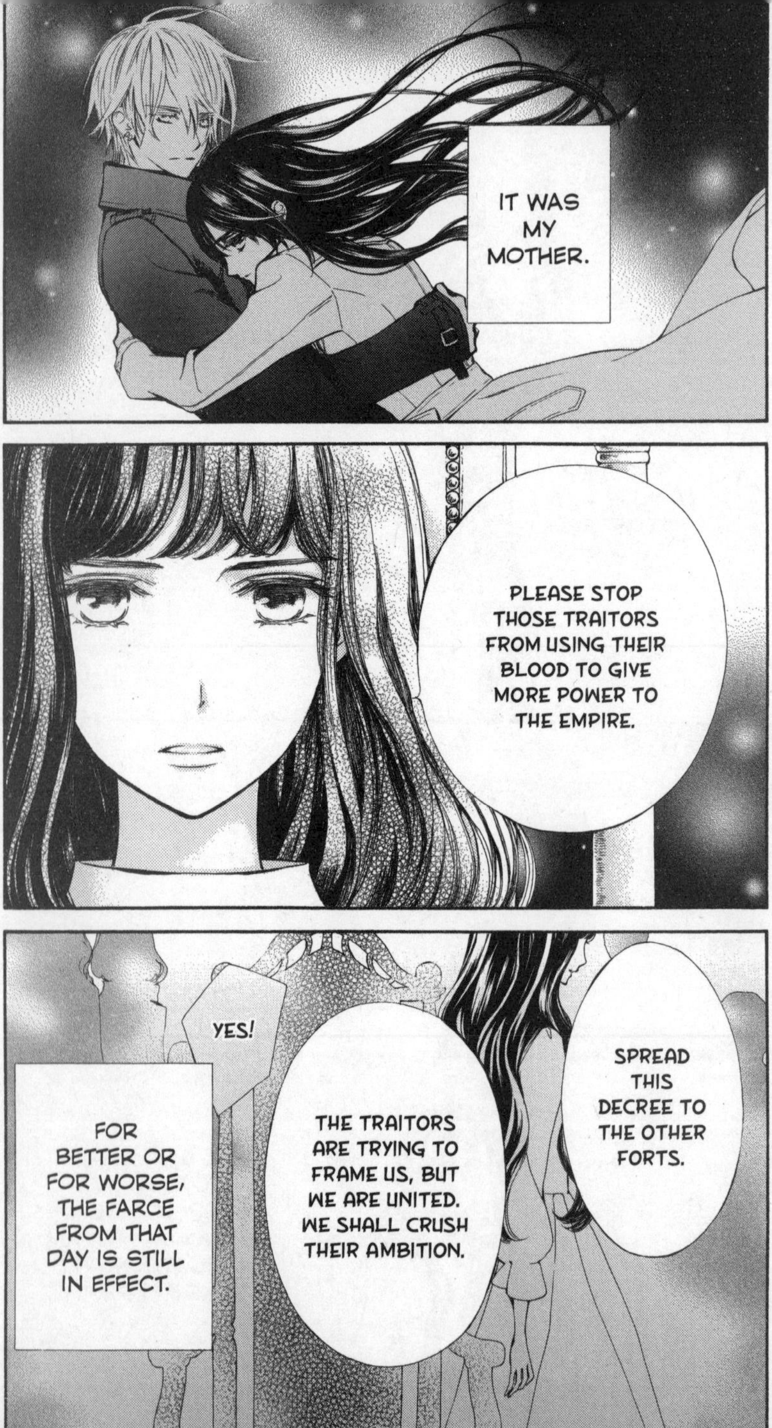
IT WAS MY MOTHER.
PLEASE STOP THOSE TRAITORS FROM USING THEIR BLOOD TO GIVE MORE POWER TO THE EMPIRE.
SPREAD THIS DECREE TO THE OTHER FORTS.
THE TRAITORS ARE TRYING TO FRAME US, BUT WE ARE UNITED. WE SHALL CRUSH THEIR AMBITION.
YES!
FOR BETTER OR FOR WORSE, THE FARCE FROM THAT DAY IS STILL IN EFFECT.

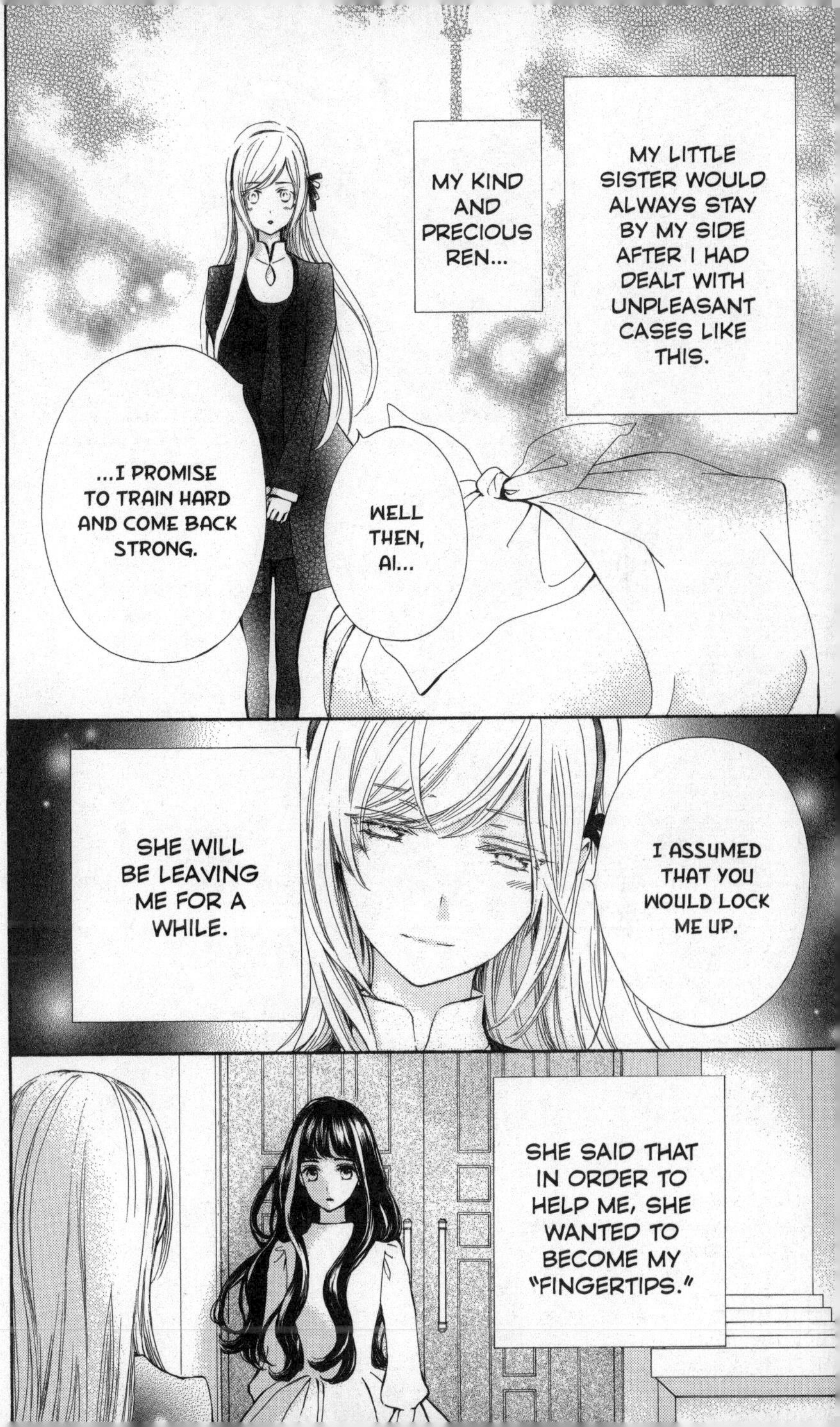
MY LITTLE SISTER WOULD ALWAYS STAY BY MY SIDE AFTER I HAD DEALT WITH UNPLEASANT CASES LIKE THIS.
MY KIND AND PRECIOUS REN...
WELL THEN, AI...
...I PROMISE TO TRAIN HARD AND COME BACK STRONG.
I ASSUMED THAT YOU WOULD LOCK ME UP.
SHE WILL BE LEAVING ME FOR A WHILE.
SHE SAID THAT IN ORDER TO HELP ME, SHE WANTED TO BECOME MY "FINGERTIPS."

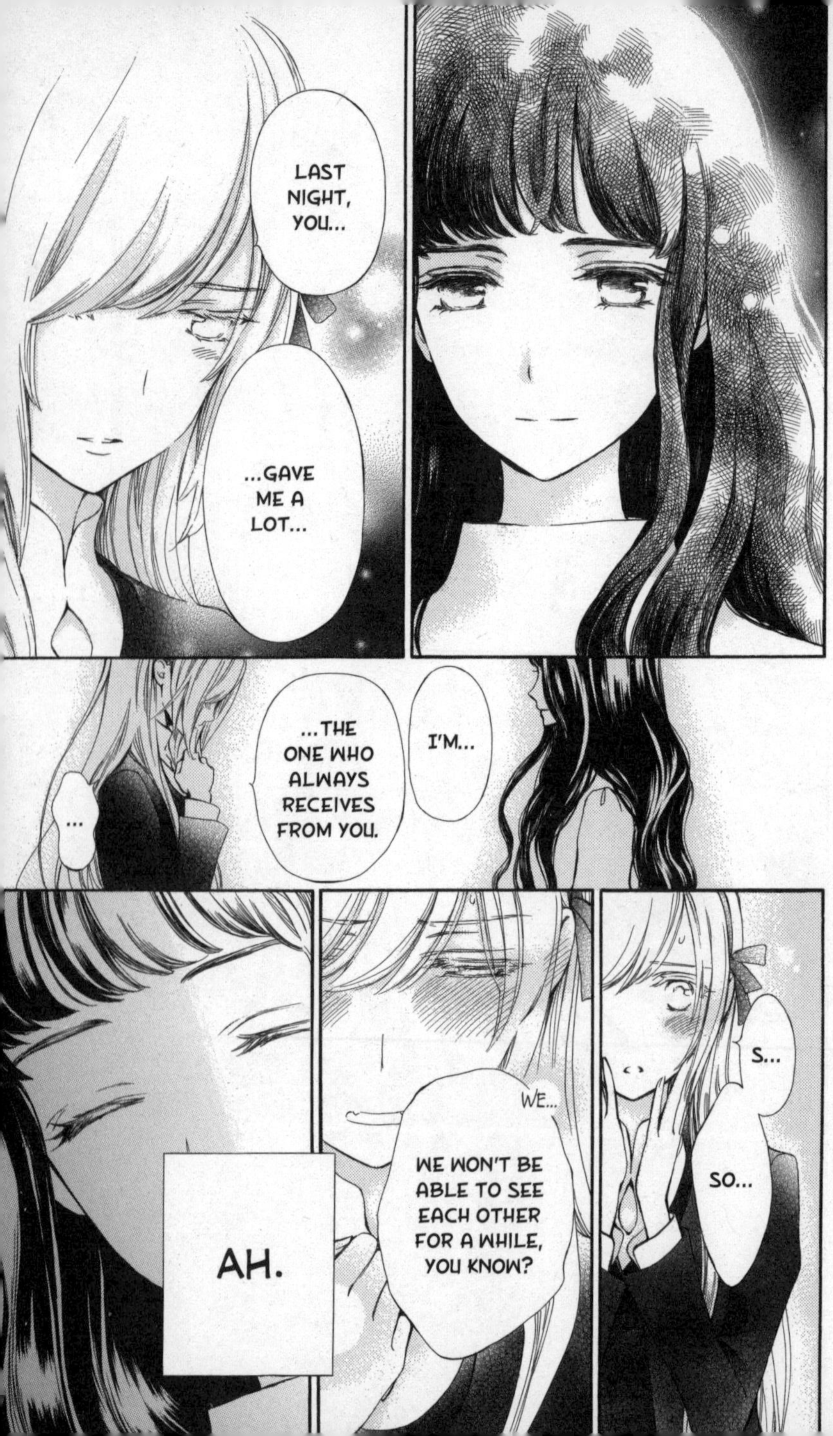
LAST NIGHT, YOU...
...GAVE ME A LOT...
I'M...
...THE ONE WHO ALWAYS RECEIVES FROM YOU.
...
S...
SO...
WE...
WE WON'T BE ABLE TO SEE EACH OTHER FOR A WHILE, YOU KNOW?
AH.

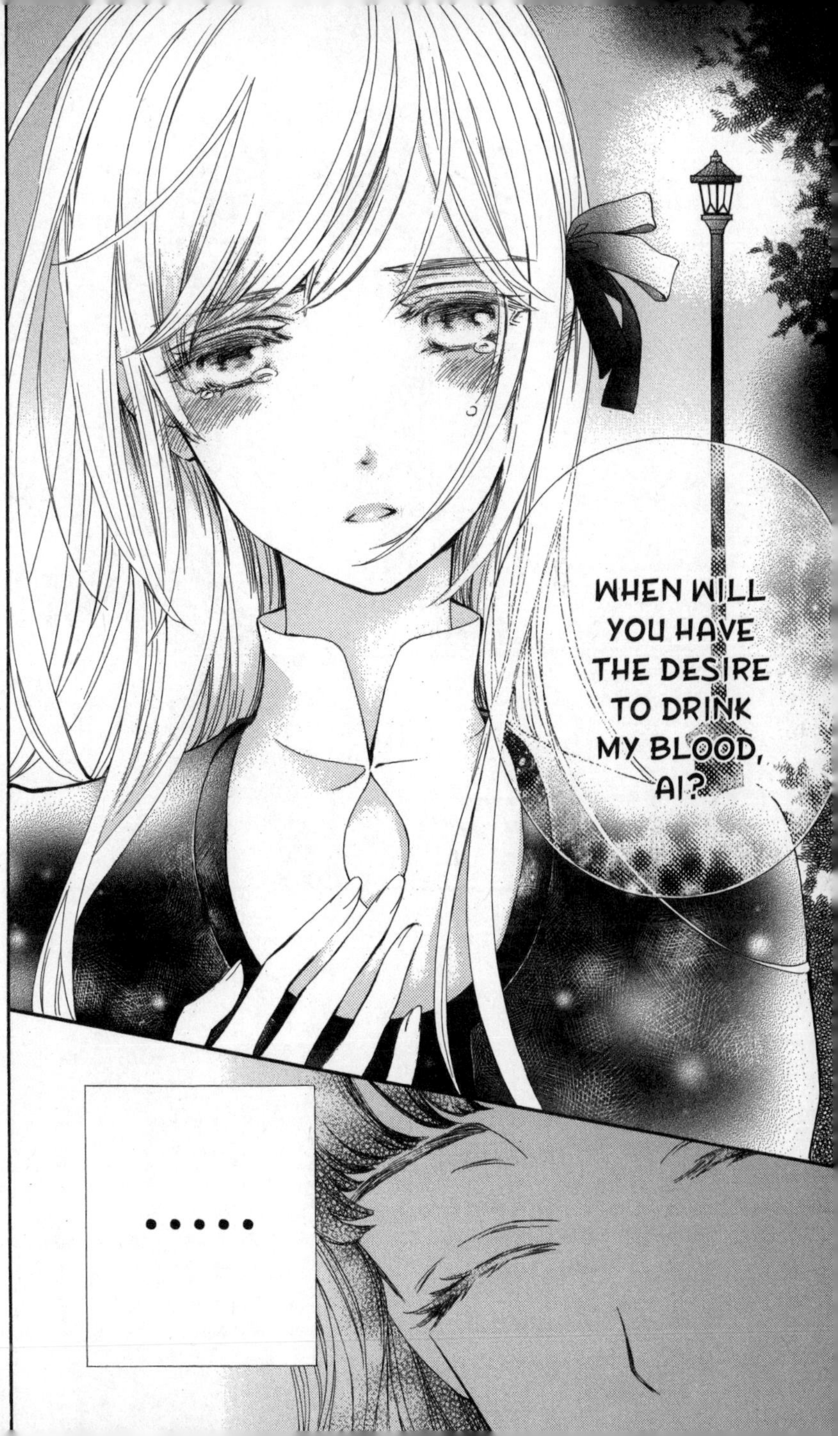
WHEN WILL YOU HAVE THE DESIRE TO DRINK MY BLOOD, AI?
.....

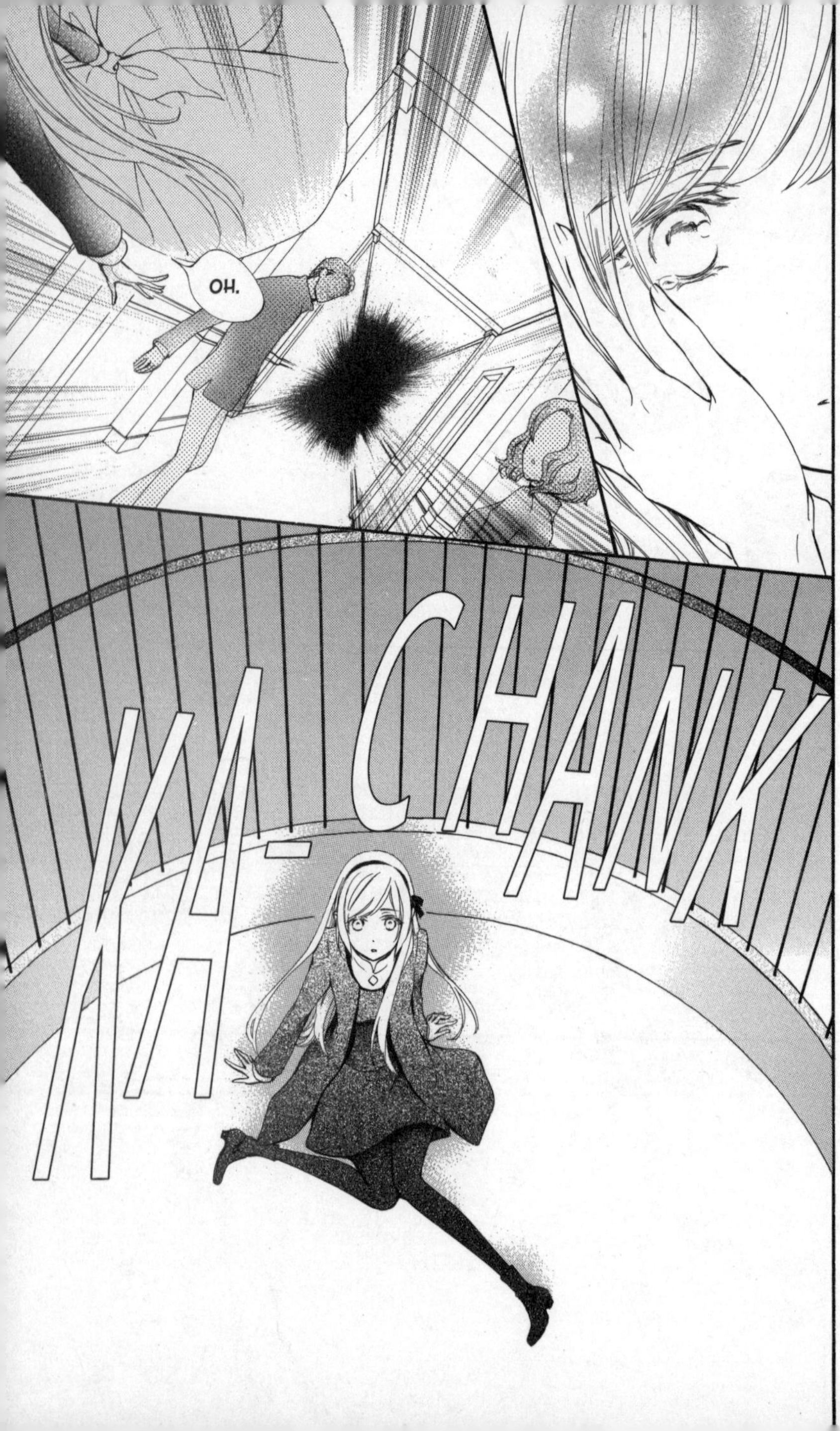
OH.
KA-CHANK

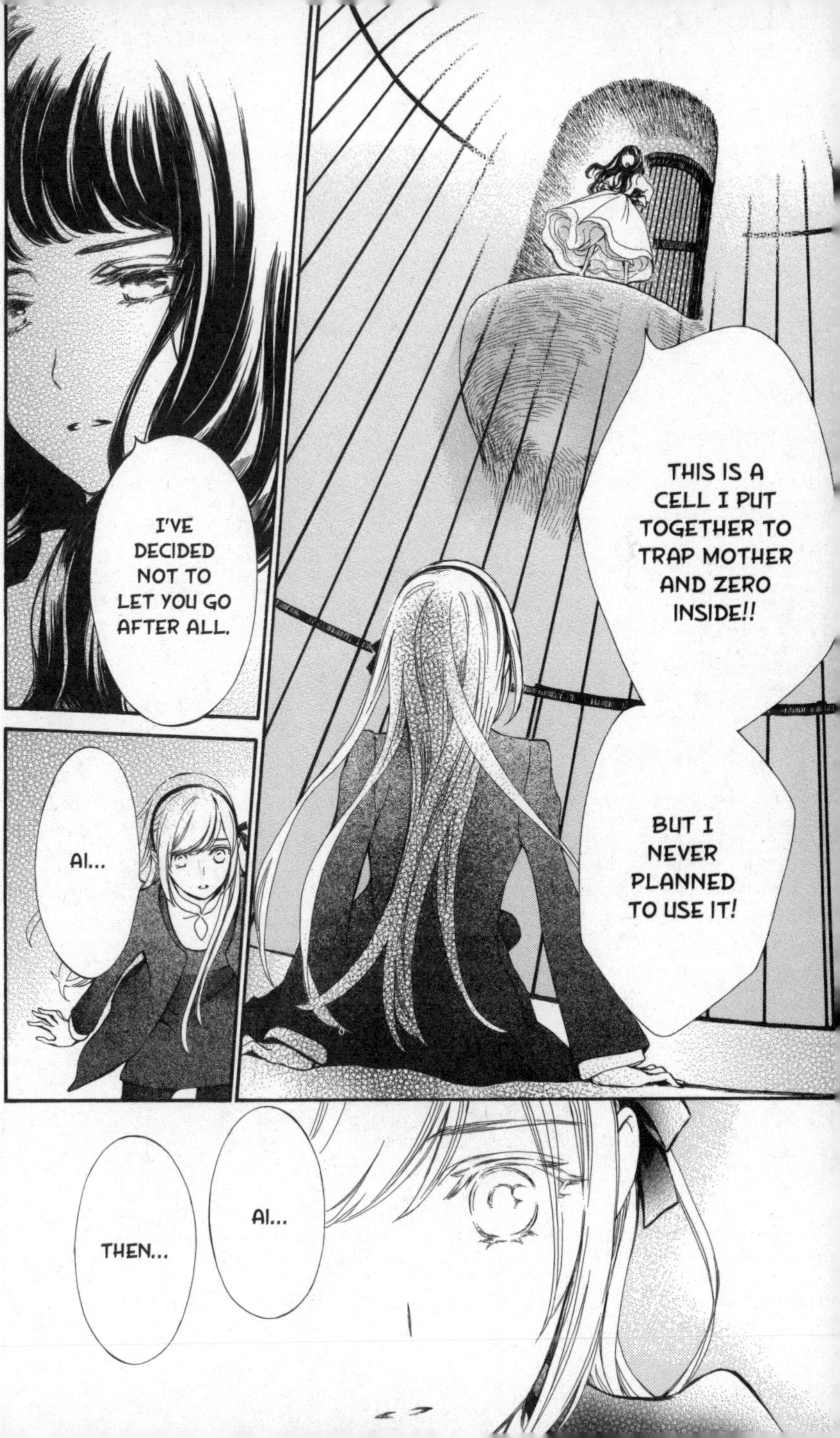
THIS IS A CELL I PUT TOGETHER TO TRAP MOTHER AND ZERO INSIDE!!
BUT I NEVER PLANNED TO USE IT!
I'VE DECIDED NOT TO LET YOU GO AFTER ALL.
AI...
AI...
THEN...

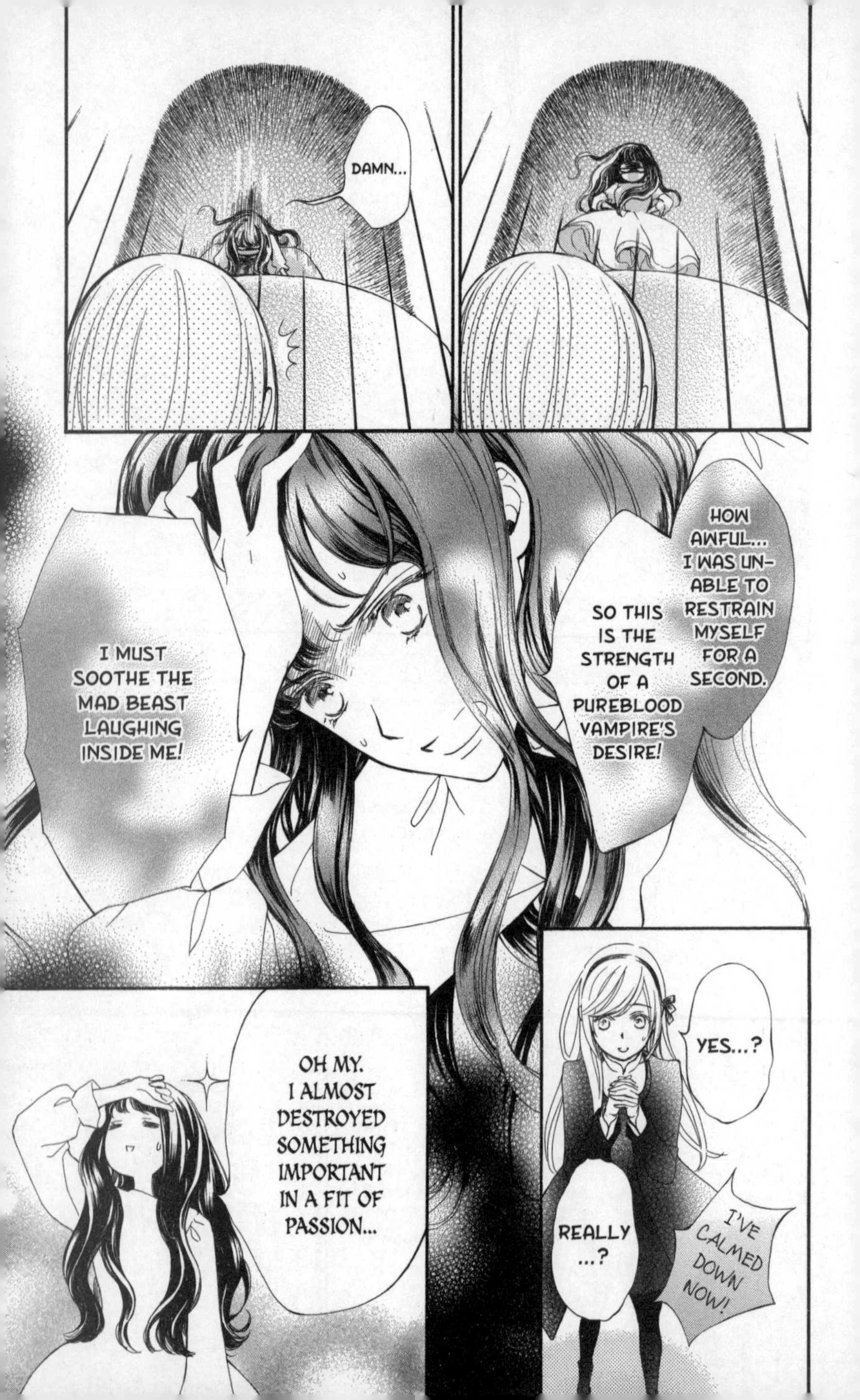
DAMN...
HOW AWFUL... I WAS UN-ABLE TO RESTRAIN MYSELF FOR A SECOND.
SO THIS IS THE STRENGTH OF A PUREBLOOD VAMPIRE'S DESIRE!
I MUST SOOTHE THE MAD BEAST LAUGHING INSIDE ME!
OH MY. I ALMOST DESTROYED SOMETHING IMPORTANT IN A FIT OF PASSION...
YES...?
I'VE CALMED DOWN NOW!
REALLY ...?

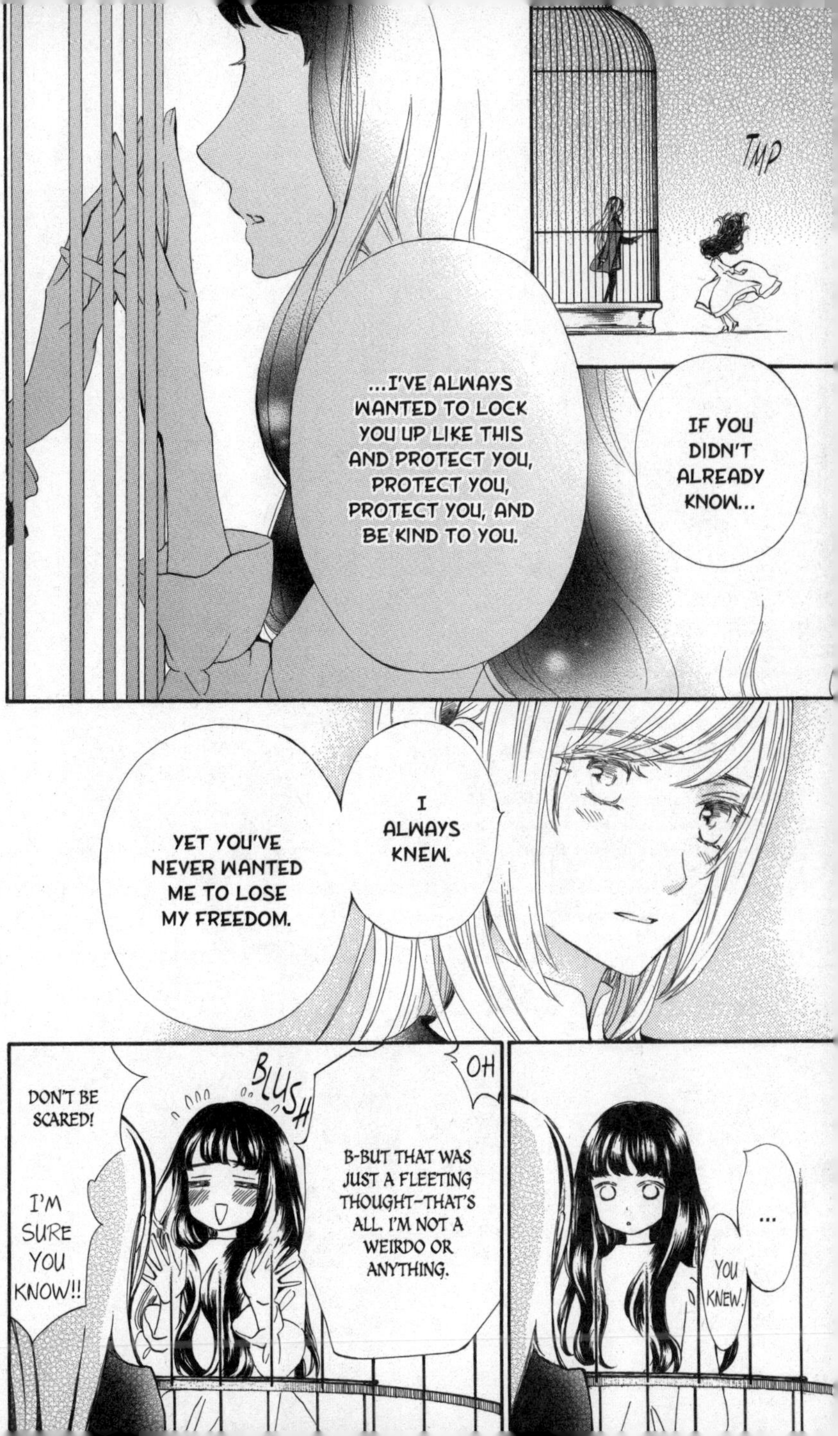
TMP
IF YOU DIDN'T ALREADY KNOW...
...I'VE ALWAYS WANTED TO LOCK YOU UP LIKE THIS AND PROTECT YOU, PROTECT YOU, PROTECT YOU, AND BE KIND TO YOU.
I ALWAYS KNEW.
YET YOU'VE NEVER WANTED ME TO LOSE MY FREEDOM.
...
YOU KNEW.
OH
BLUSH
B-BUT THAT WAS JUST A FLEETING THOUGHT—THAT'S ALL. I'M NOT A WEIRDO OR ANYTHING.
DON'T BE SCARED!
I'M SURE YOU KNOW!!

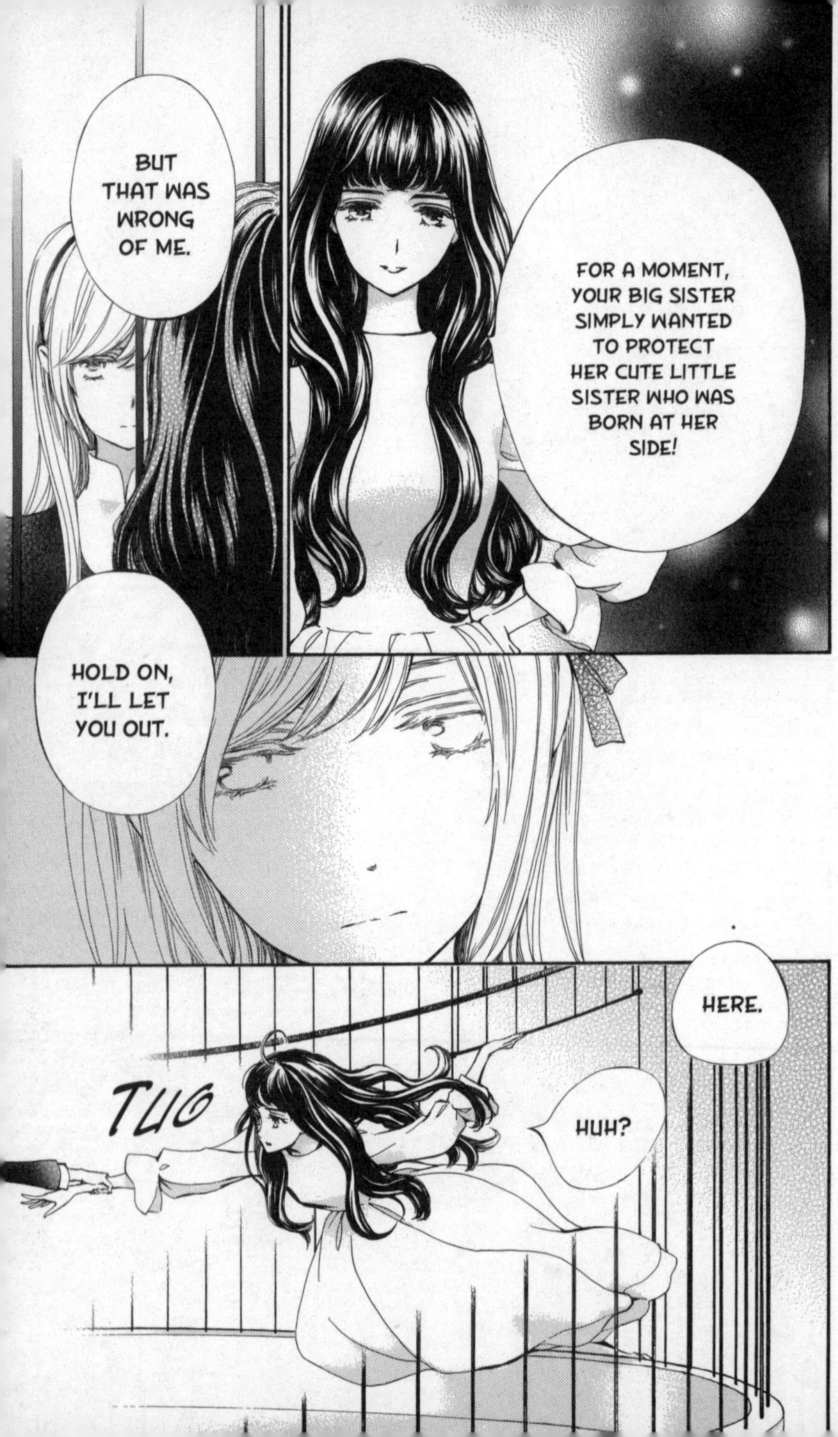
FOR A MOMENT, YOUR BIG SISTER SIMPLY WANTED TO PROTECT HER CUTE LITTLE SISTER WHO WAS BORN AT HER SIDE!
BUT THAT WAS WRONG OF ME.
HOLD ON, I'LL LET YOU OUT.
HERE.
HUH?
TUG

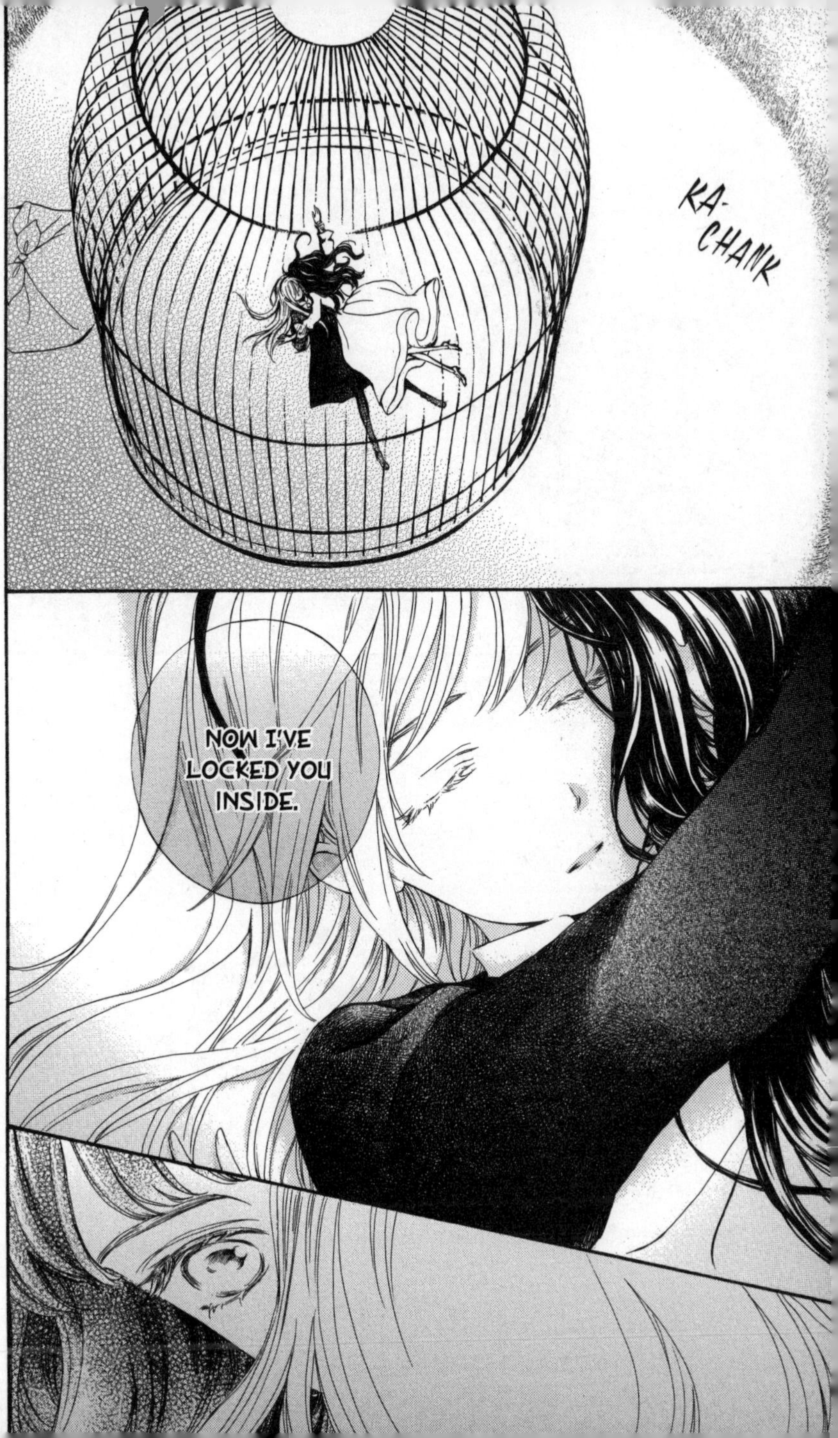
KA-CHANK
NOW I'VE LOCKED YOU INSIDE.

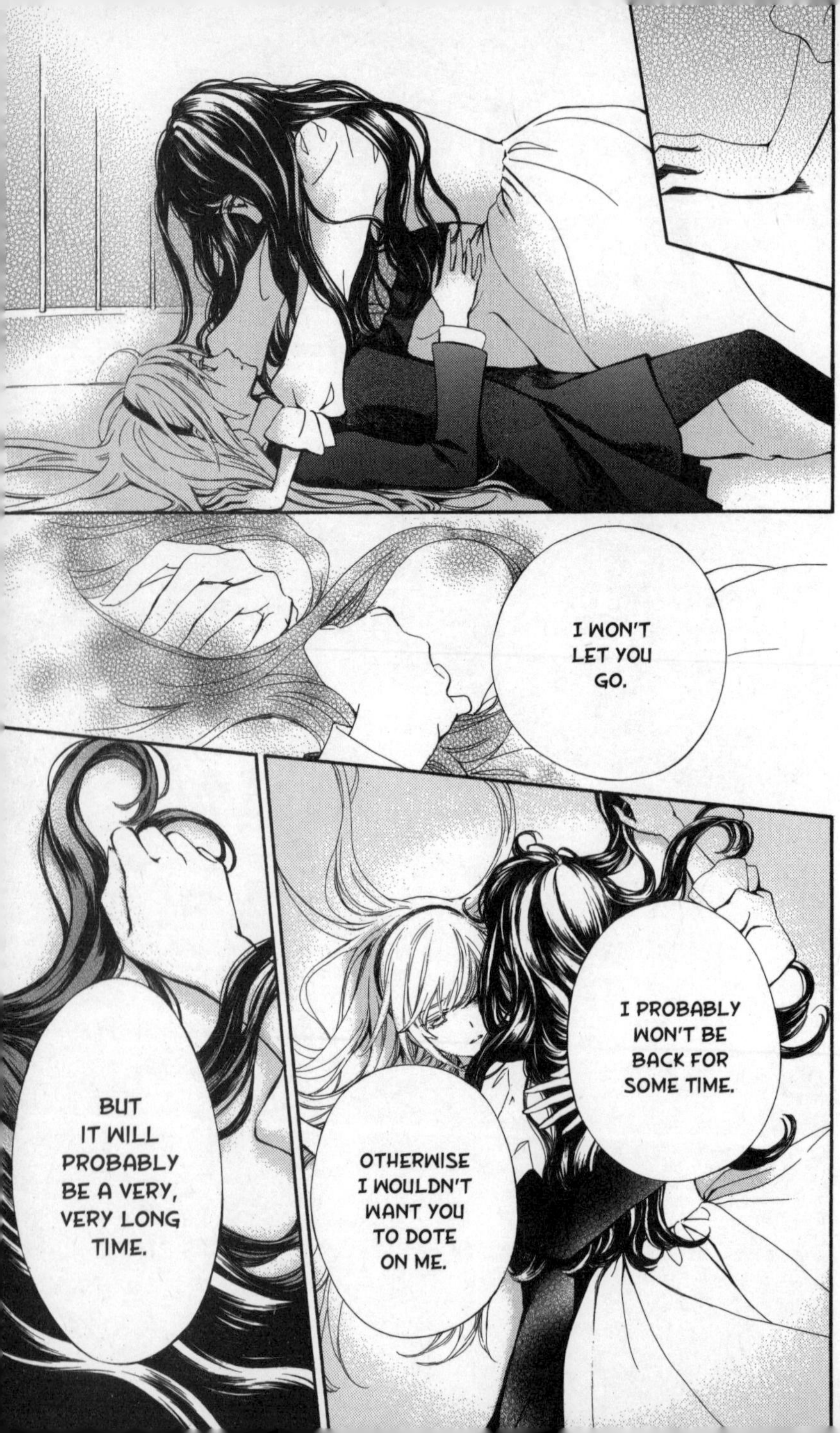
I WON'T LET YOU GO.
I PROBABLY WON'T BE BACK FOR SOME TIME.
OTHERWISE I WOULDN'T WANT YOU TO DOTE ON ME.
BUT IT WILL PROBABLY BE A VERY, VERY LONG TIME.

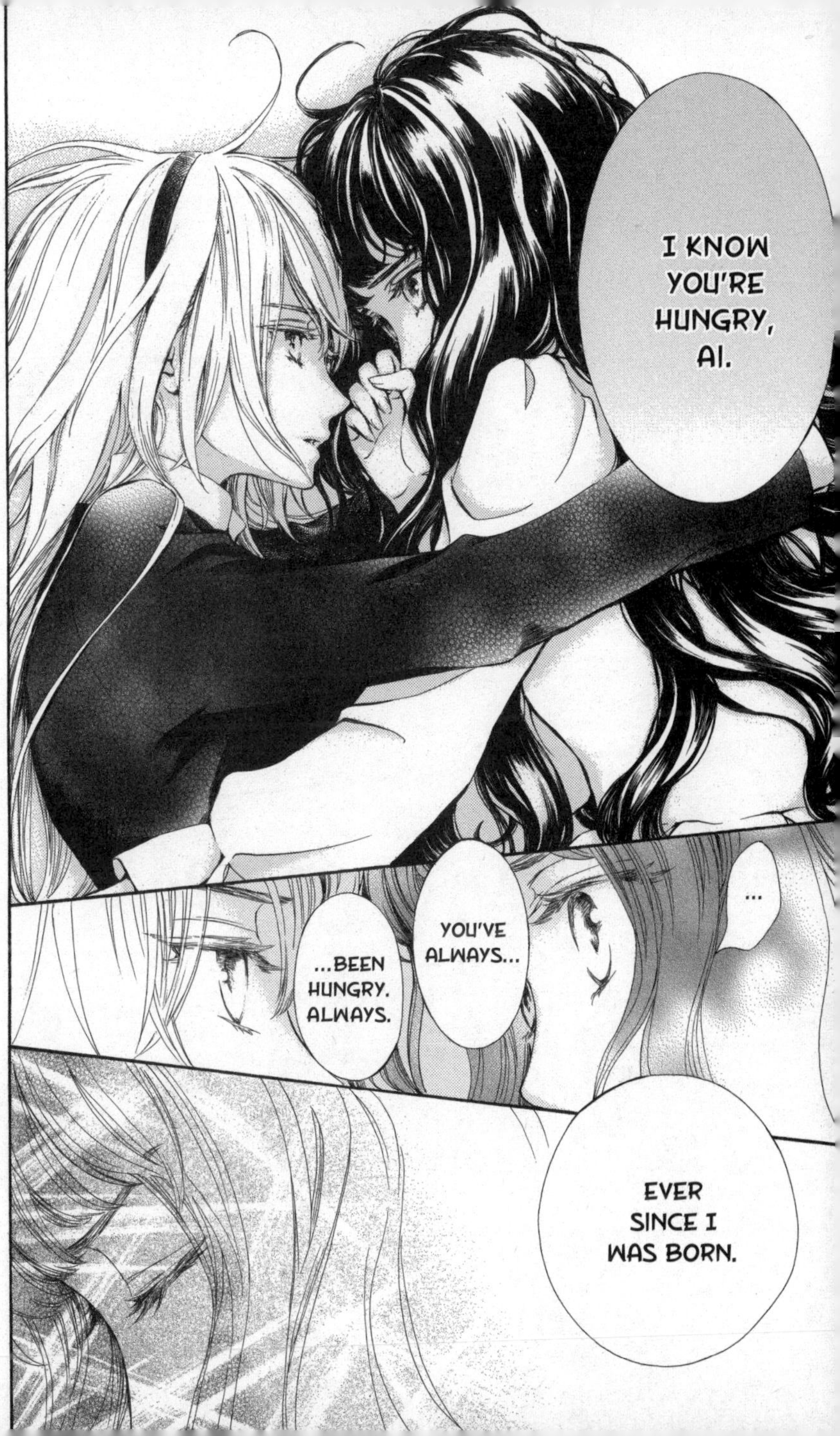
I KNOW YOU'RE HUNGRY, AI.
...
YOU'VE ALWAYS...
...BEEN HUNGRY. ALWAYS.
EVER SINCE I WAS BORN.

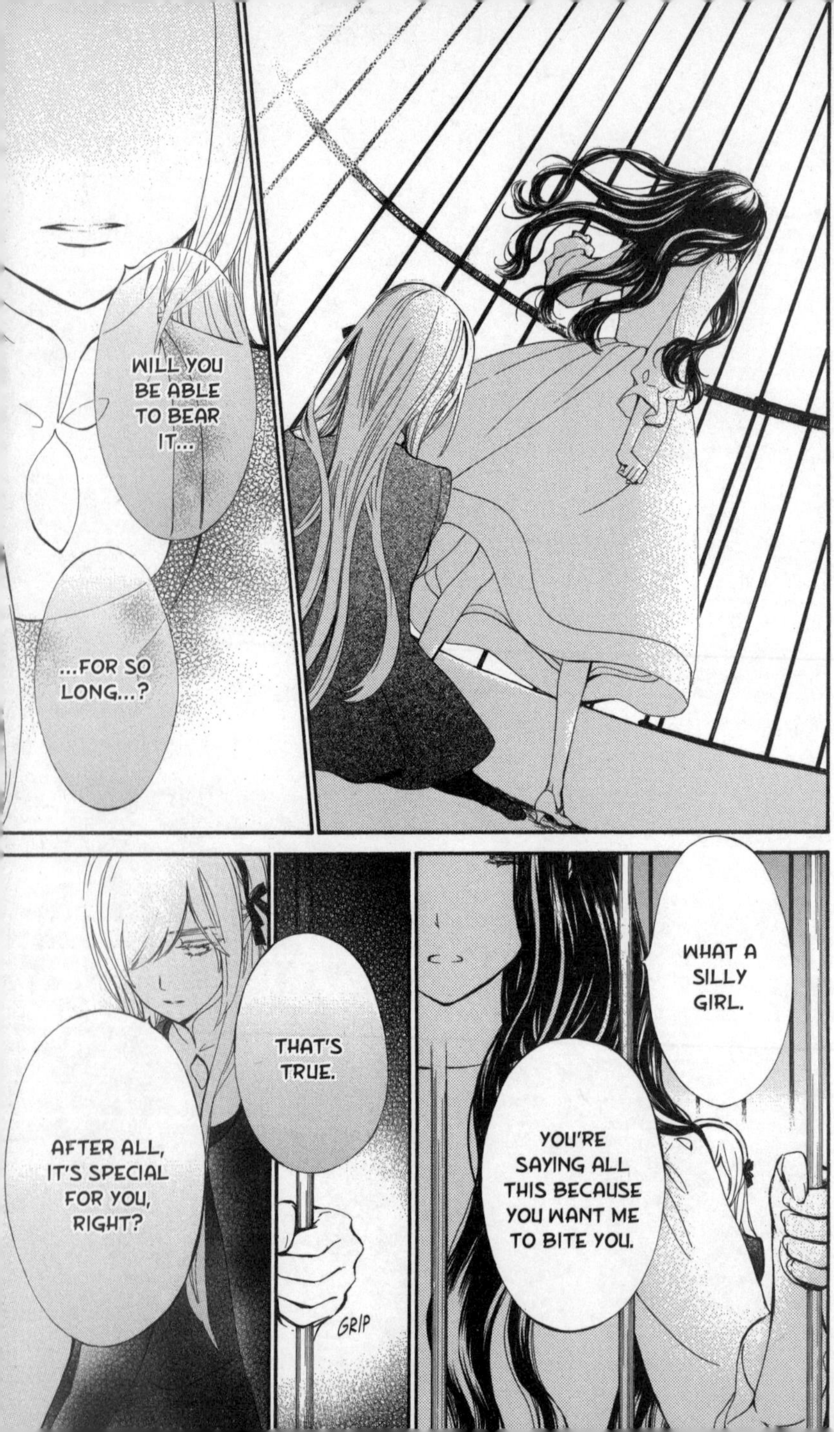
WILL YOU BE ABLE TO BEAR IT...
...FOR SO LONG...?
WHAT A SILLY GIRL.
YOU'RE SAYING ALL THIS BECAUSE YOU WANT ME TO BITE YOU.
THAT'S TRUE.
GRIP
AFTER ALL, IT'S SPECIAL FOR YOU, RIGHT?

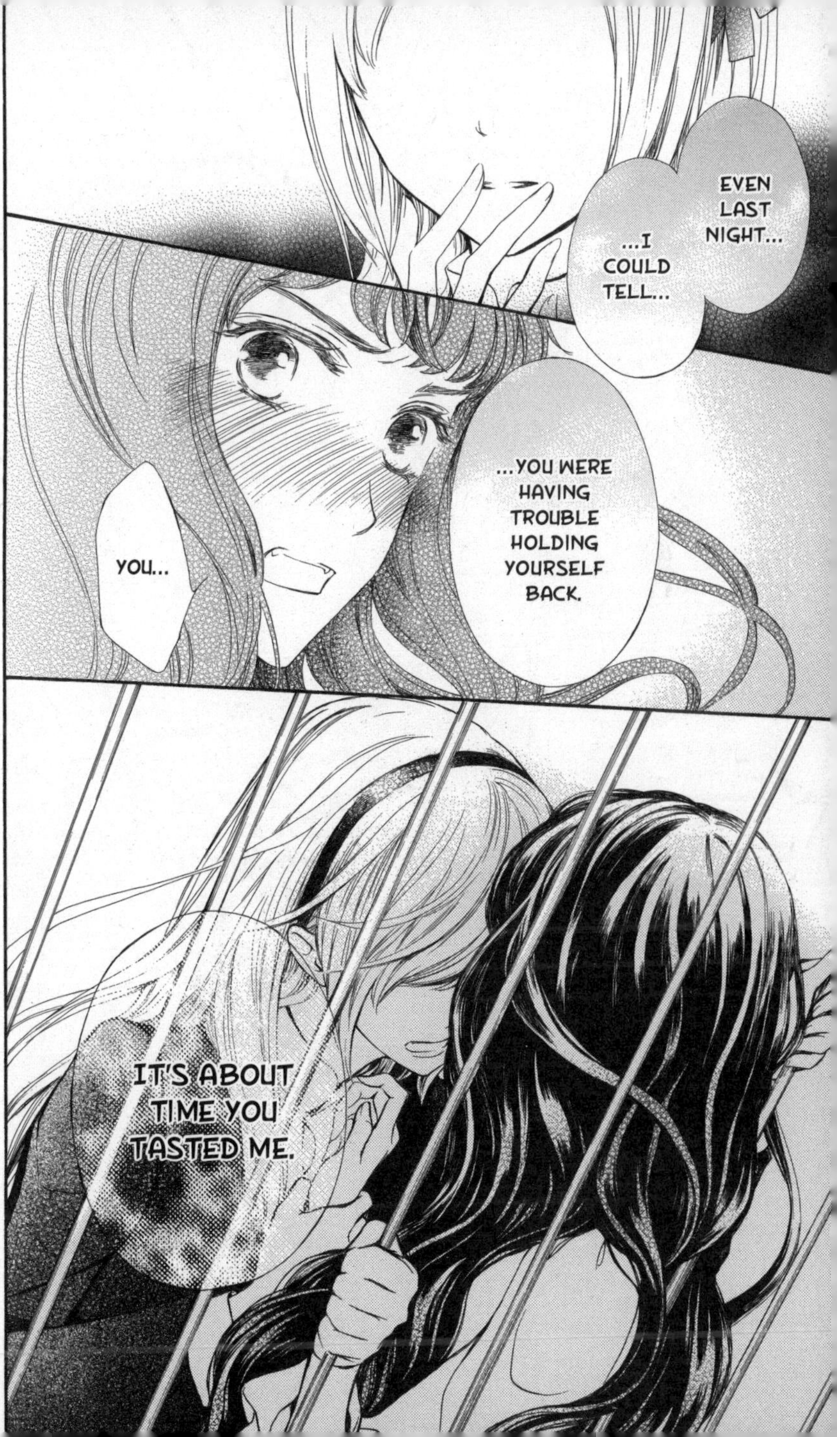
EVEN LAST NIGHT...
...I COULD TELL...
...YOU WERE HAVING TROUBLE HOLDING YOURSELF BACK.
YOU...
IT'S ABOUT TIME YOU TASTED ME.

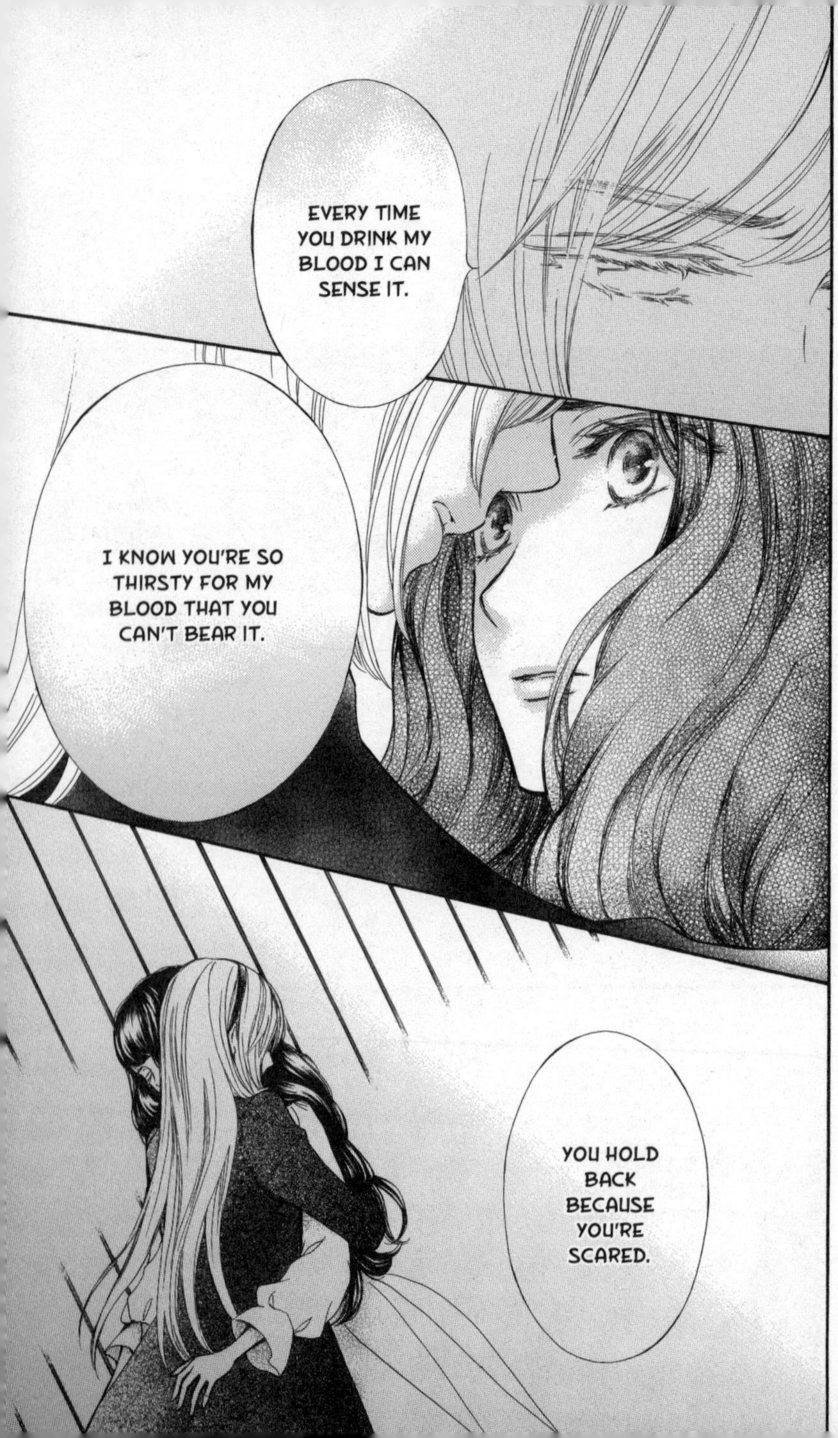

EVERY TIME YOU DRINK MY BLOOD I CAN SENSE IT.
I KNOW YOU'RE SO THIRSTY FOR MY BLOOD THAT YOU CAN'T BEAR IT.
YOU HOLD BACK BECAUSE YOU'RE SCARED.

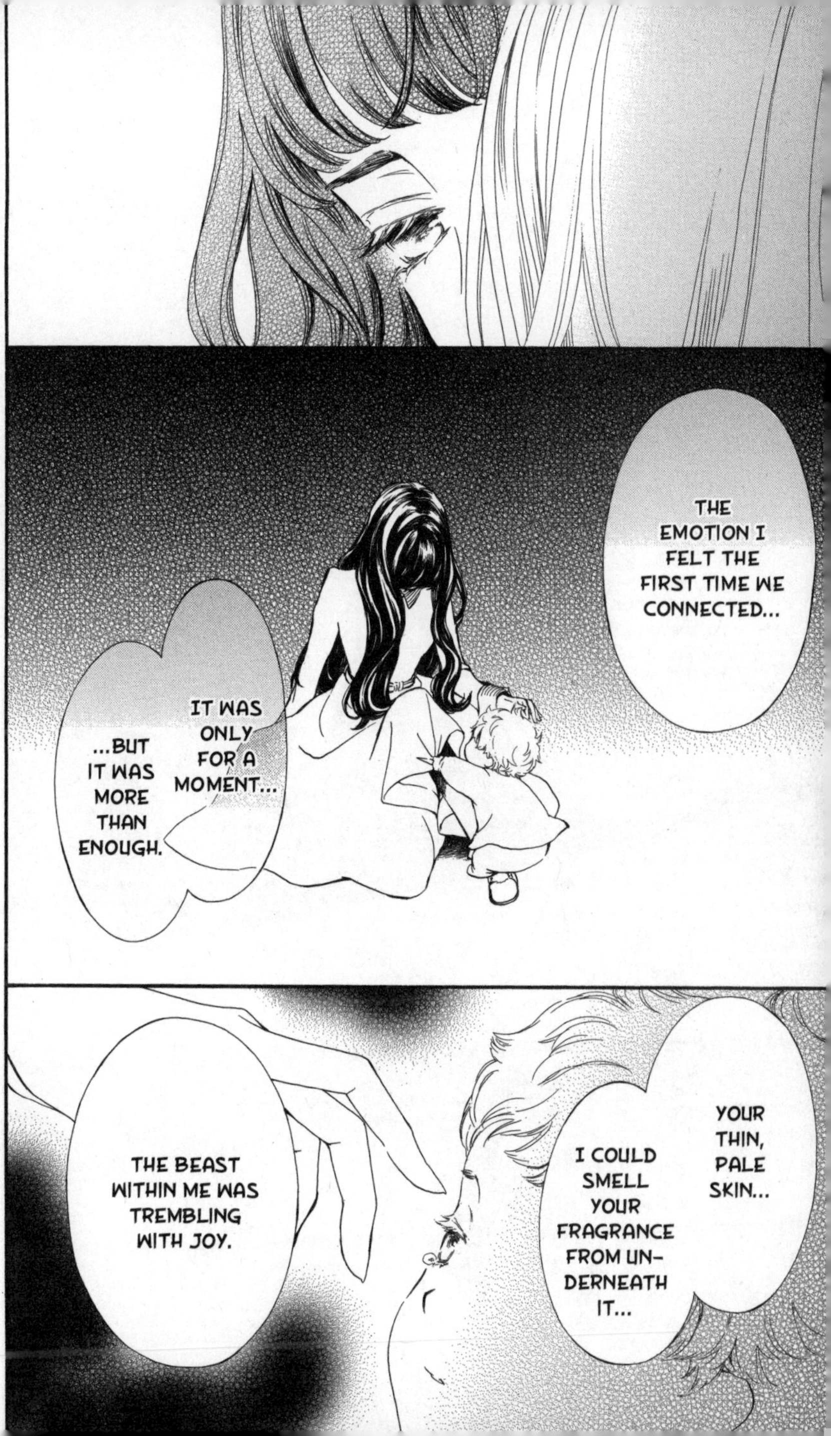
THE EMOTION I FELT THE FIRST TIME WE CONNECTED...
IT WAS ONLY FOR A MOMENT...
...BUT IT WAS MORE THAN ENOUGH.
YOUR THIN, PALE SKIN...
I COULD SMELL YOUR FRAGRANCE FROM UN-DERNEATH IT...
THE BEAST WITHIN ME WAS TREMBLING WITH JOY.

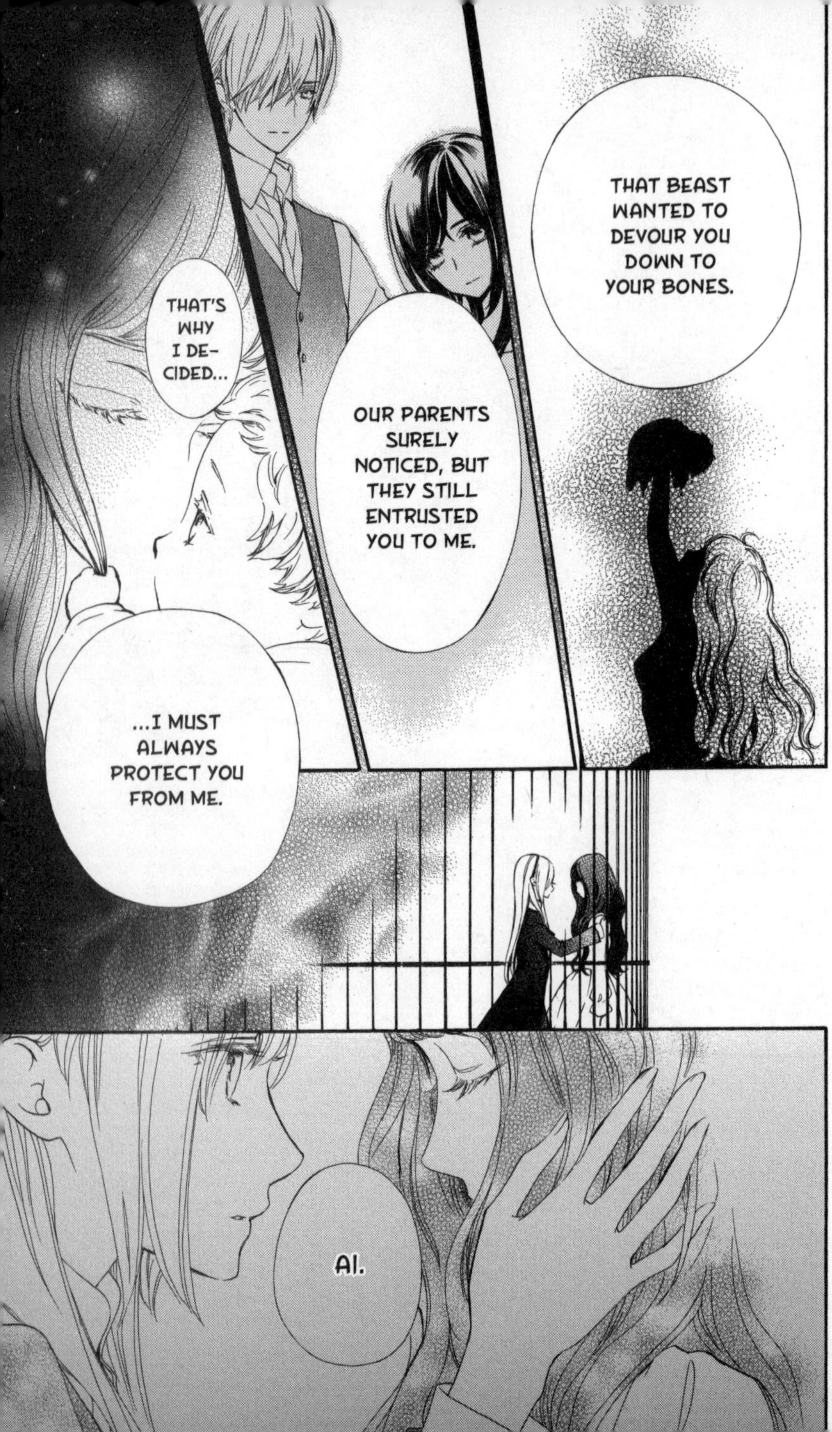
THAT BEAST WANTED TO DEVOUR YOU DOWN TO YOUR BONES.
OUR PARENTS SURELY NOTICED, BUT THEY STILL ENTRUSTED YOU TO ME.
THAT'S WHY I DE-CIDED...
...I MUST ALWAYS PROTECT YOU FROM ME.
AI.

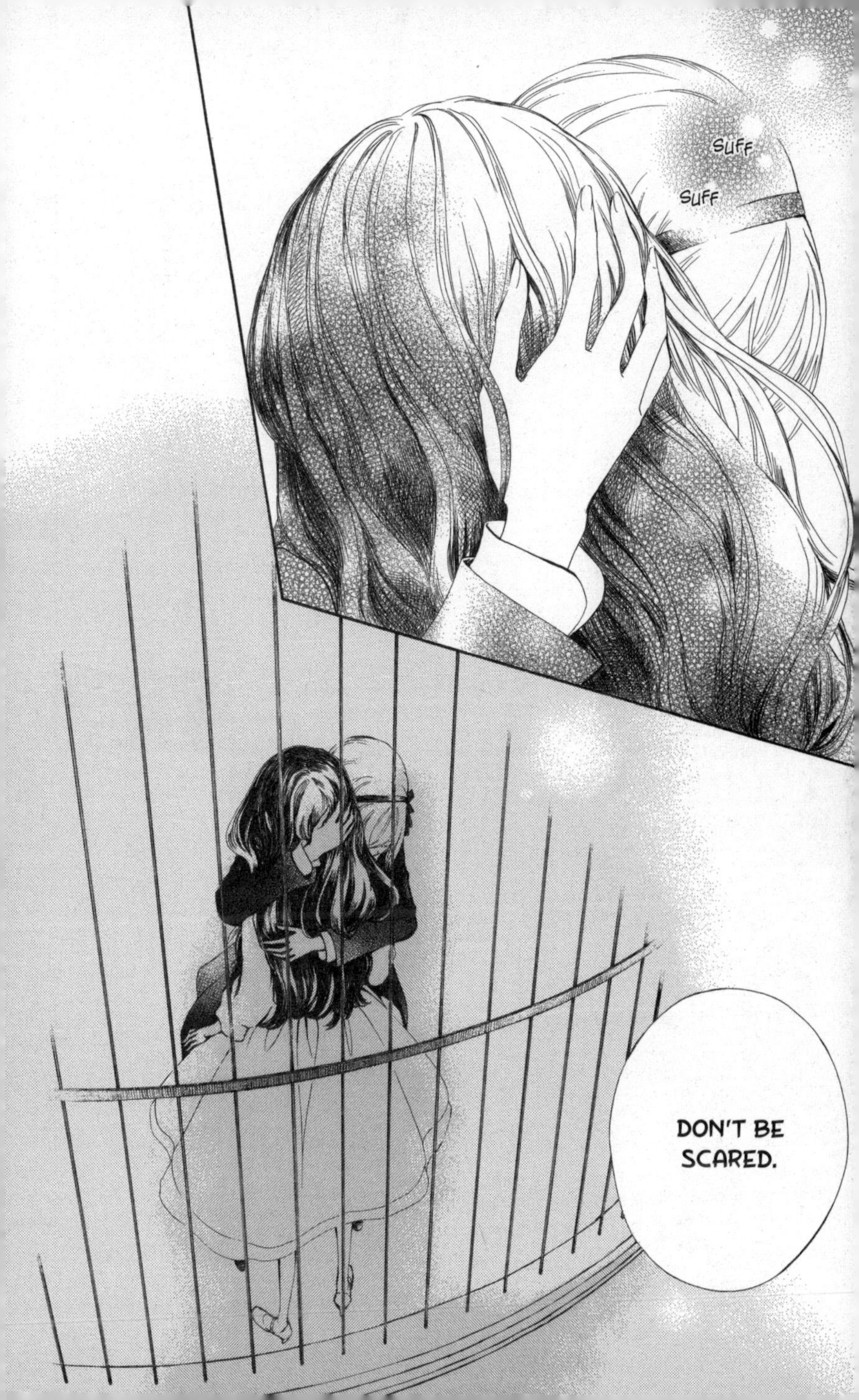
SUFF
SUFF
DON'T BE SCARED.

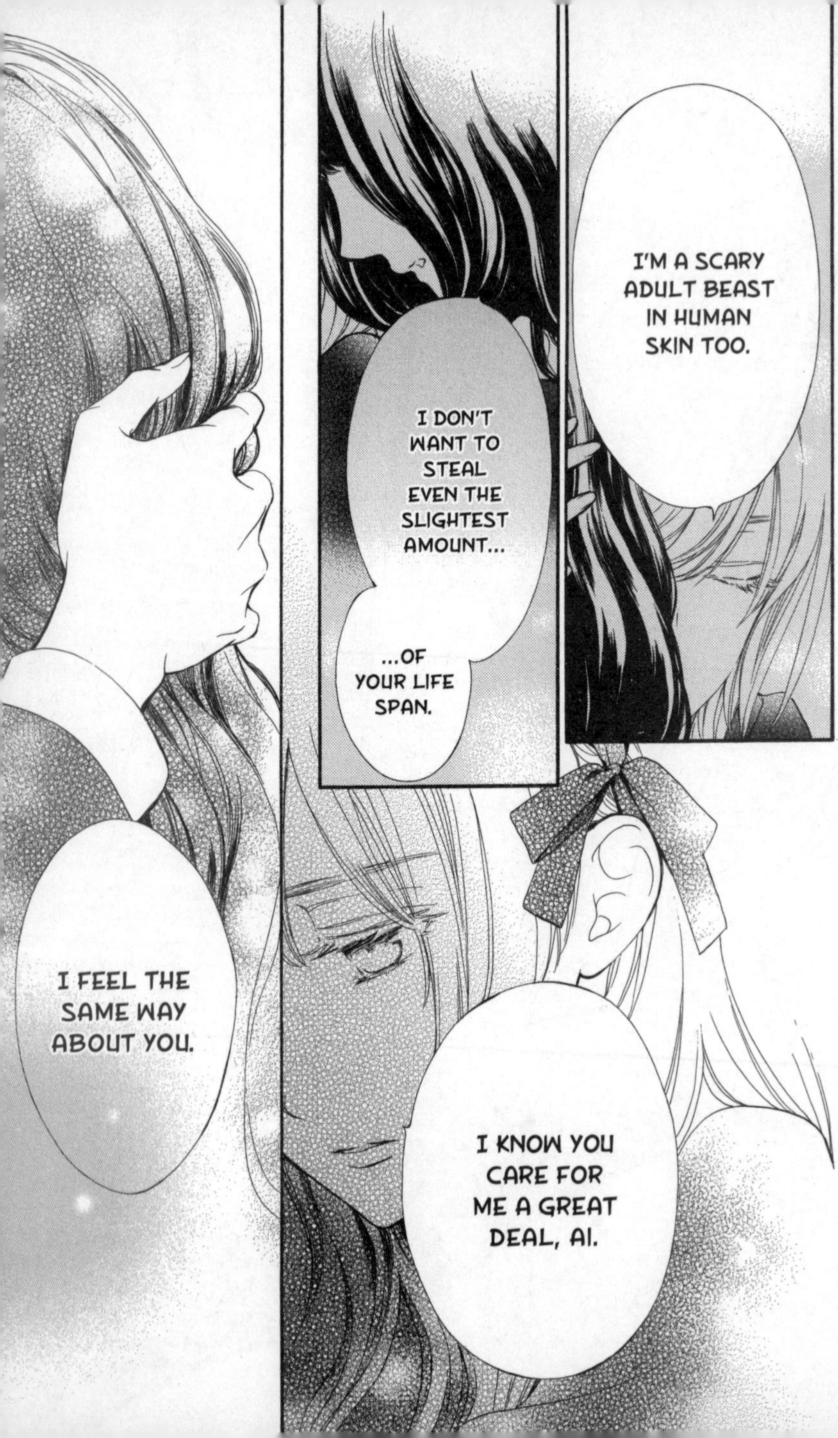
I'M A SCARY ADULT BEAST IN HUMAN SKIN TOO.
I DON'T WANT TO STEAL EVEN THE SLIGHTEST AMOUNT...
...OF YOUR LIFE SPAN.
I KNOW YOU CARE FOR ME A GREAT DEAL, AI.
I FEEL THE SAME WAY ABOUT YOU.

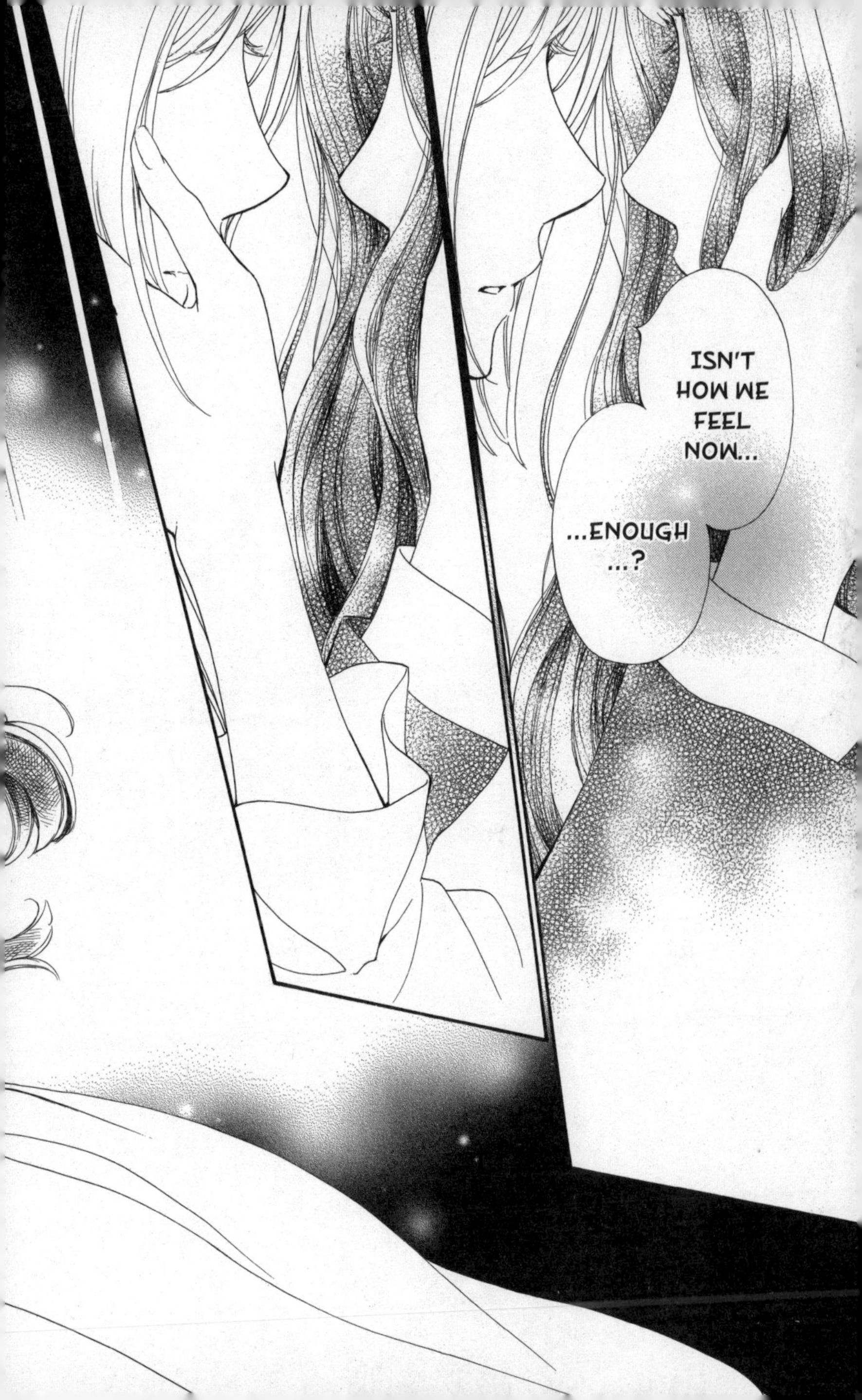
ISN'T HOW WE FEEL NOW...
...ENOUGH ...?

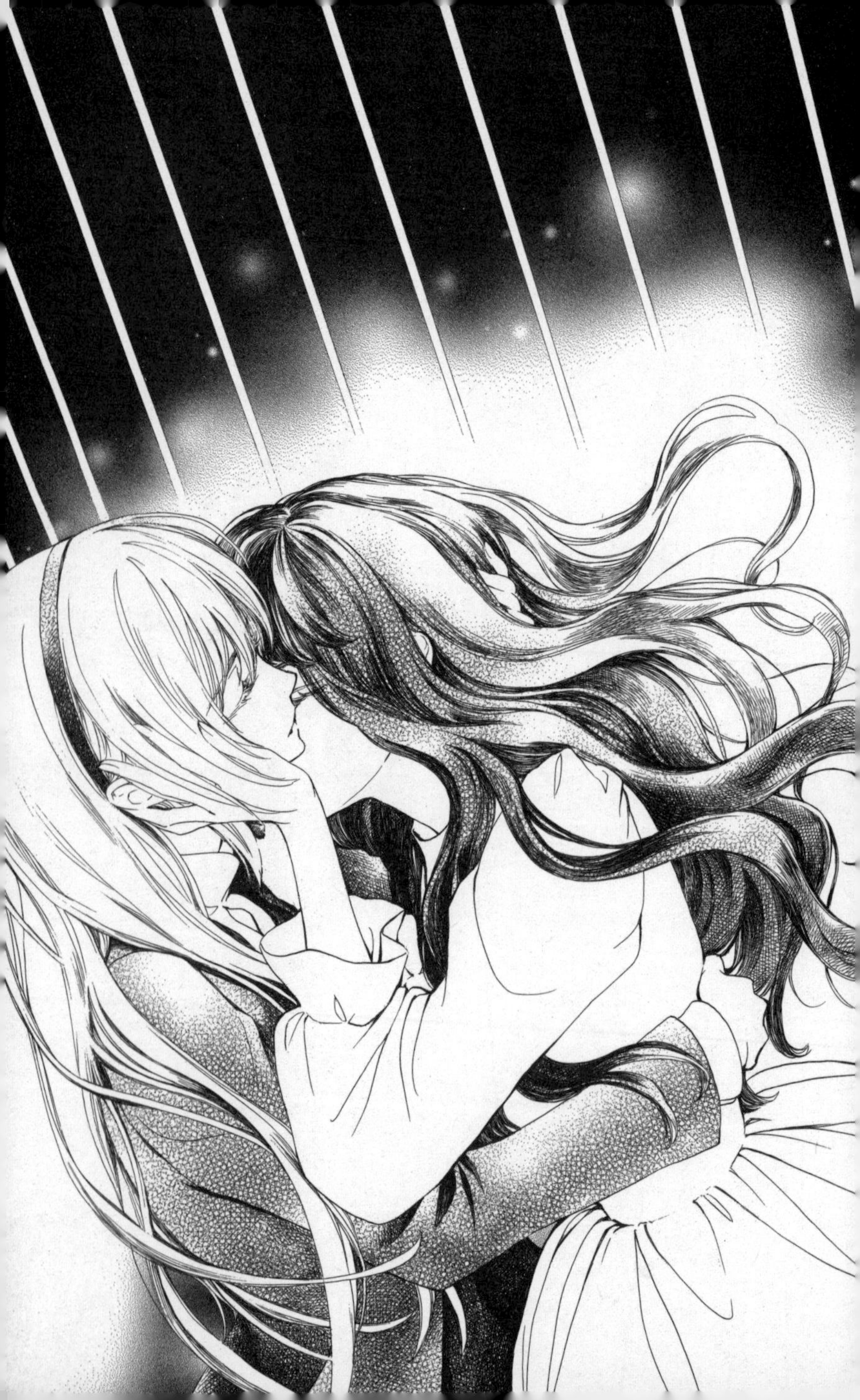

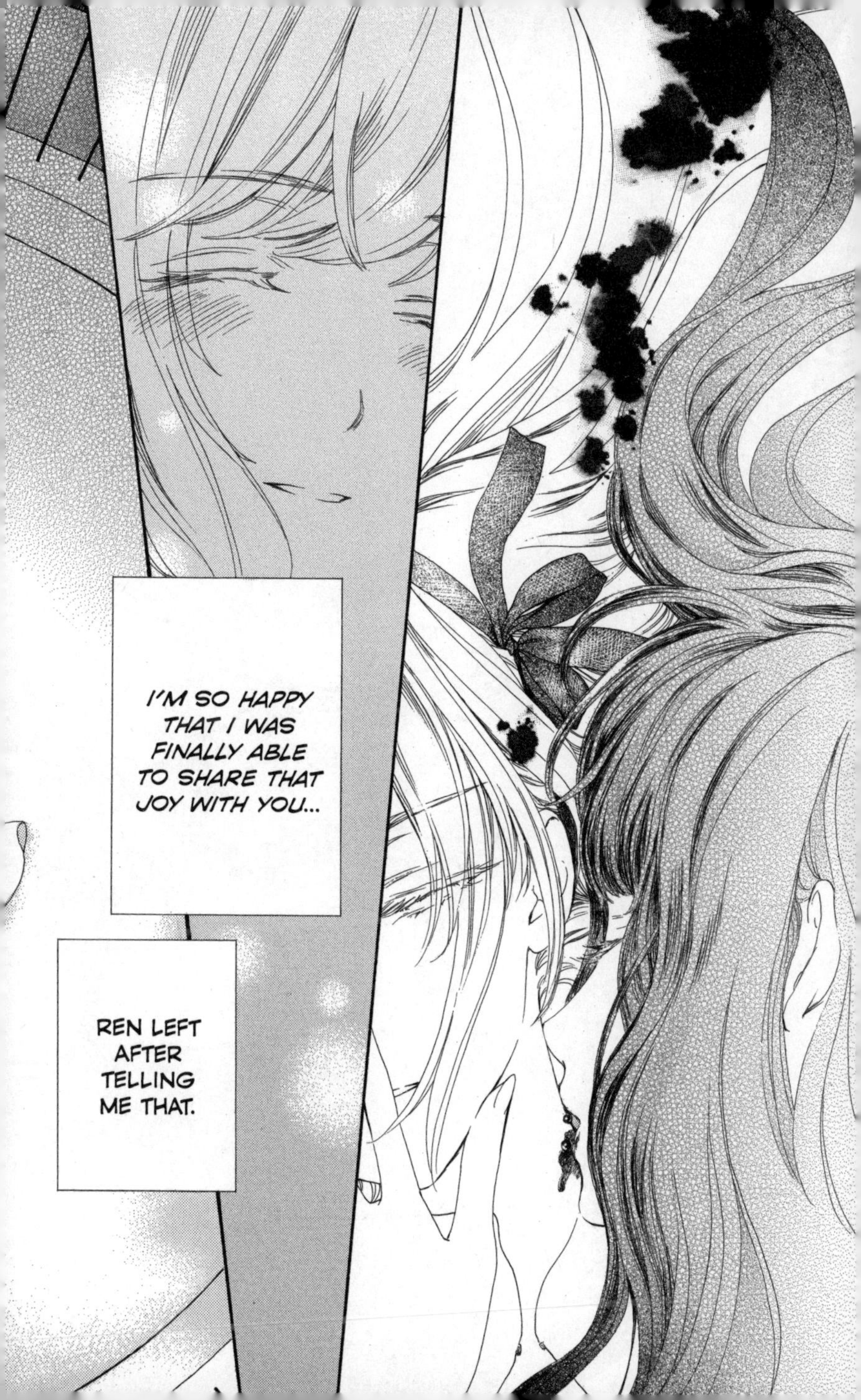
I'M SO HAPPY THAT I WAS FINALLY ABLE TO SHARE THAT JOY WITH YOU...
REN LEFT AFTER TELLING ME THAT.

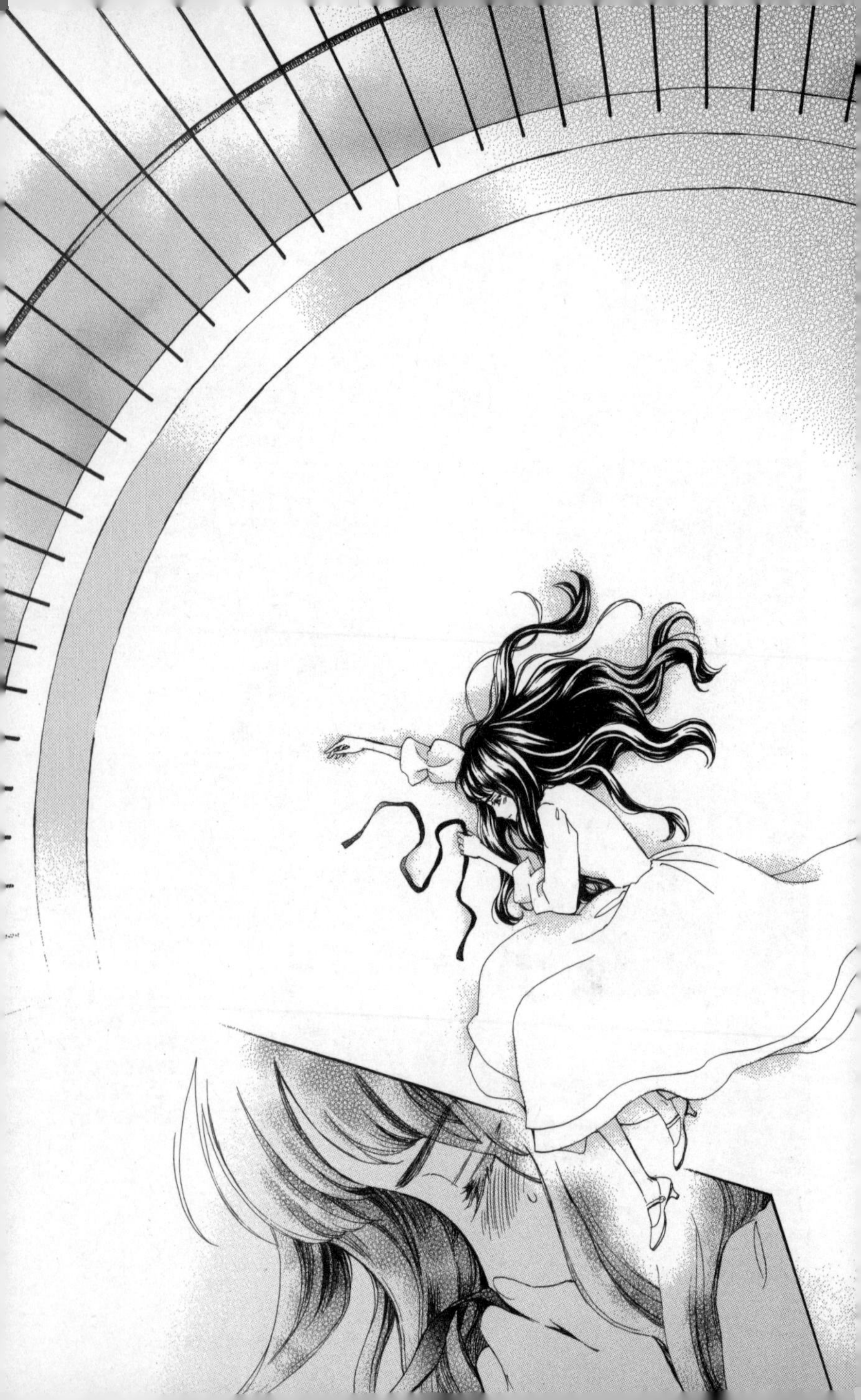

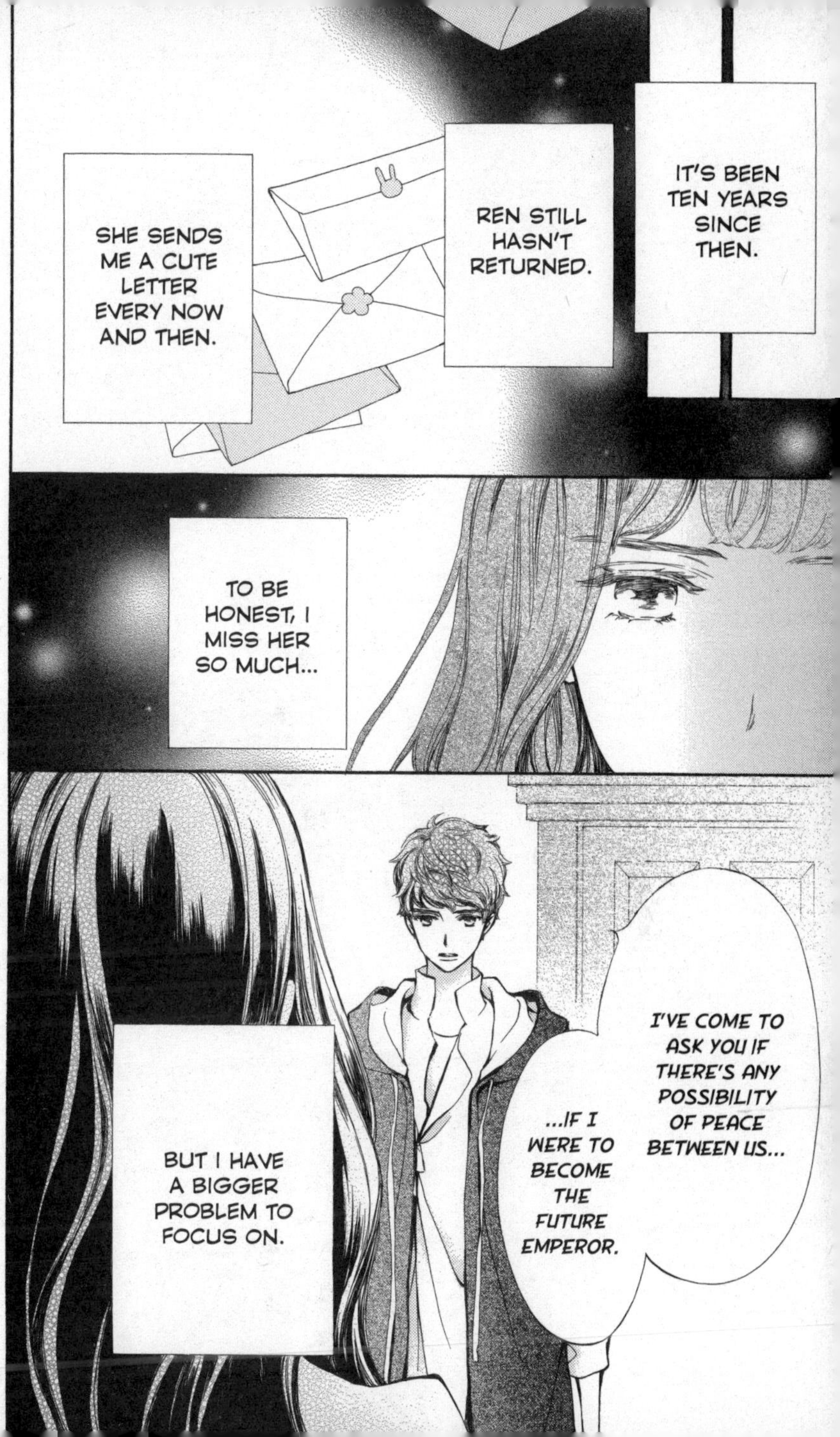
IT'S BEEN TEN YEARS SINCE THEN.
REN STILL HASN'T RETURNED.
SHE SENDS ME A CUTE LETTER EVERY NOW AND THEN.
TO BE HONEST, I MISS HER SO MUCH...
I'VE COME TO ASK YOU IF THERE'S ANY POSSIBILITY OF PEACE BETWEEN US...
...IF I WERE TO BECOME THE FUTURE EMPEROR.
BUT I HAVE A BIGGER PROBLEM TO FOCUS ON.

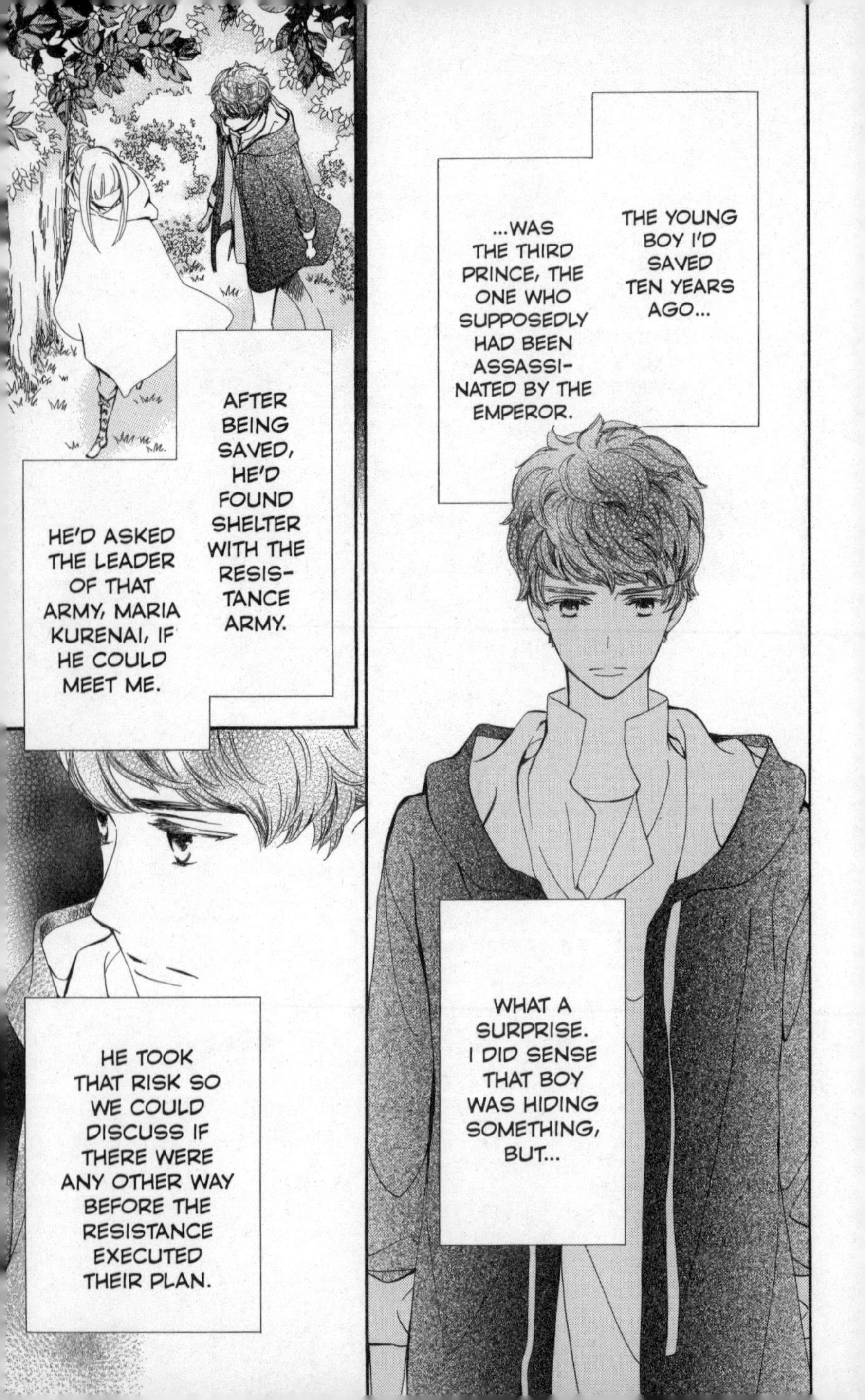
THE YOUNG BOY I'D SAVED TEN YEARS AGO...
...WAS THE THIRD PRINCE, THE ONE WHO SUPPOSEDLY HAD BEEN ASSASSI-NATED BY THE EMPEROR.
WHAT A SURPRISE. I DID SENSE THAT BOY WAS HIDING SOMETHING, BUT...
AFTER BEING SAVED, HE'D FOUND SHELTER WITH THE RESIS-TANCE ARMY.
HE'D ASKED THE LEADER OF THAT ARMY, MARIA KURENAI, IF HE COULD MEET ME.
HE TOOK THAT RISK SO WE COULD DISCUSS IF THERE WERE ANY OTHER WAY BEFORE THE RESISTANCE EXECUTED THEIR PLAN.

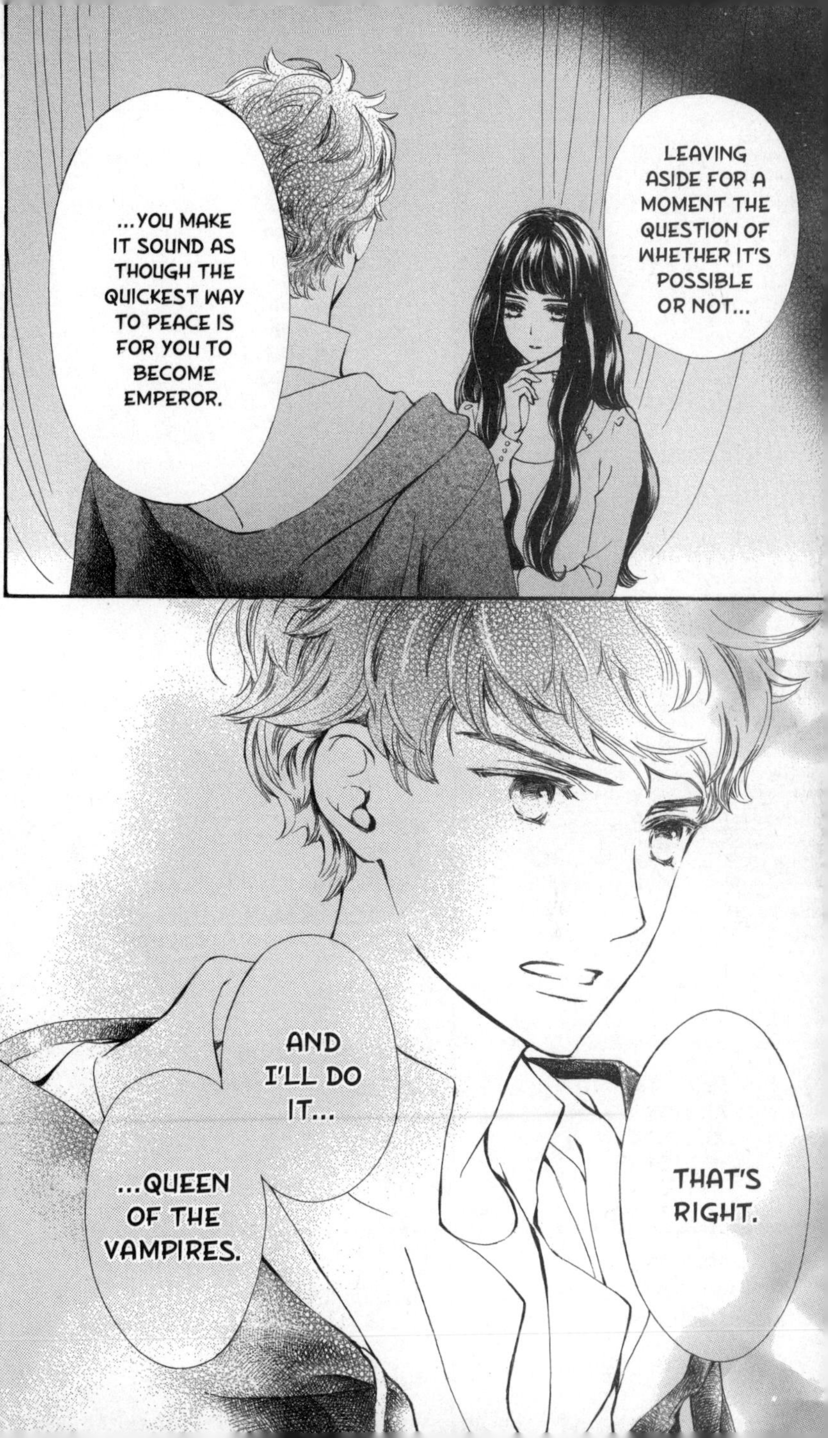
LEAVING ASIDE FOR A MOMENT THE QUESTION OF WHETHER IT'S POSSIBLE OR NOT...
...YOU MAKE IT SOUND AS THOUGH THE QUICKEST WAY TO PEACE IS FOR YOU TO BECOME EMPEROR.
THAT'S RIGHT.
AND I'LL DO IT...
...QUEEN OF THE VAMPIRES.

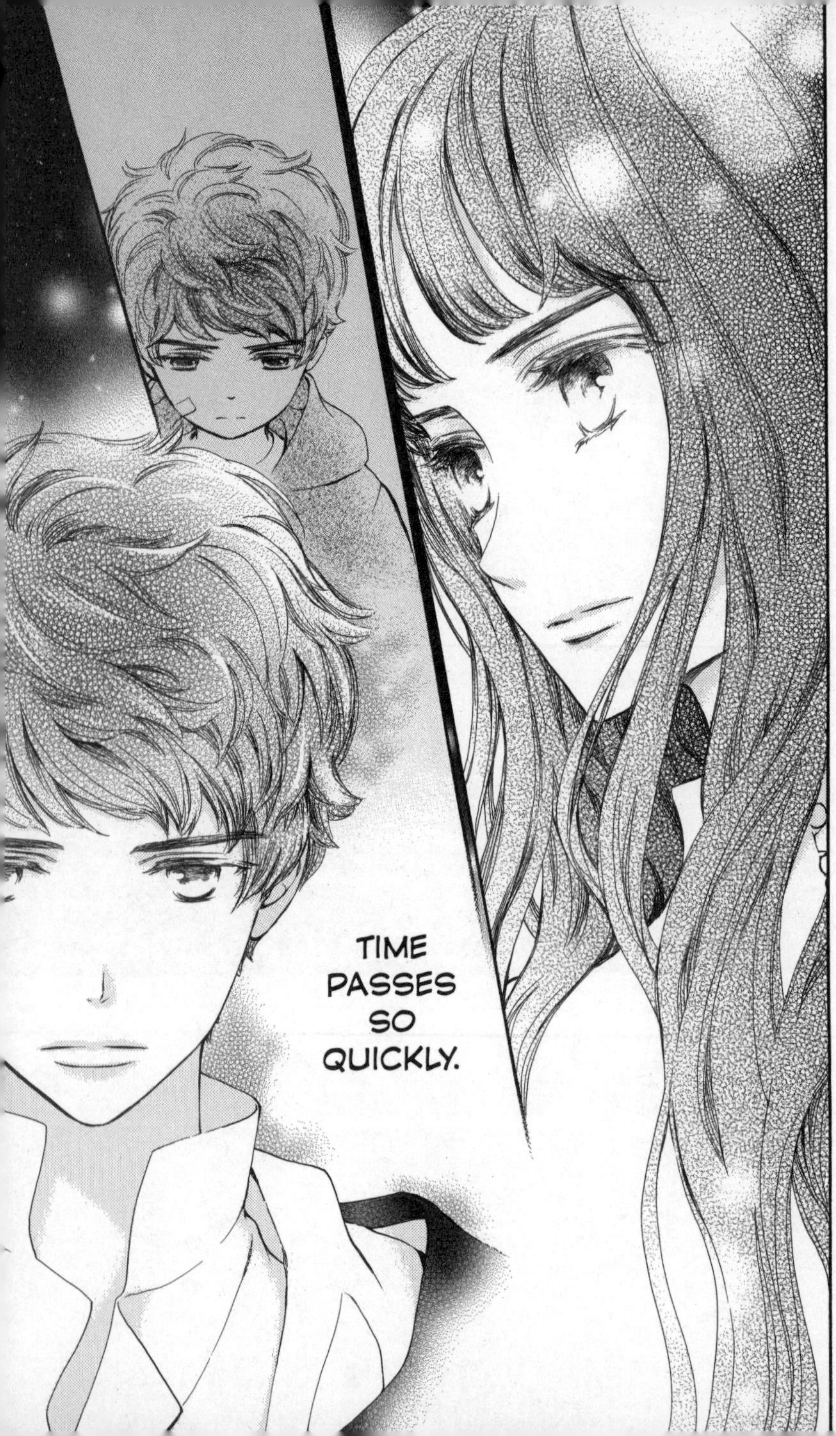
TIME PASSES SO QUICKLY.

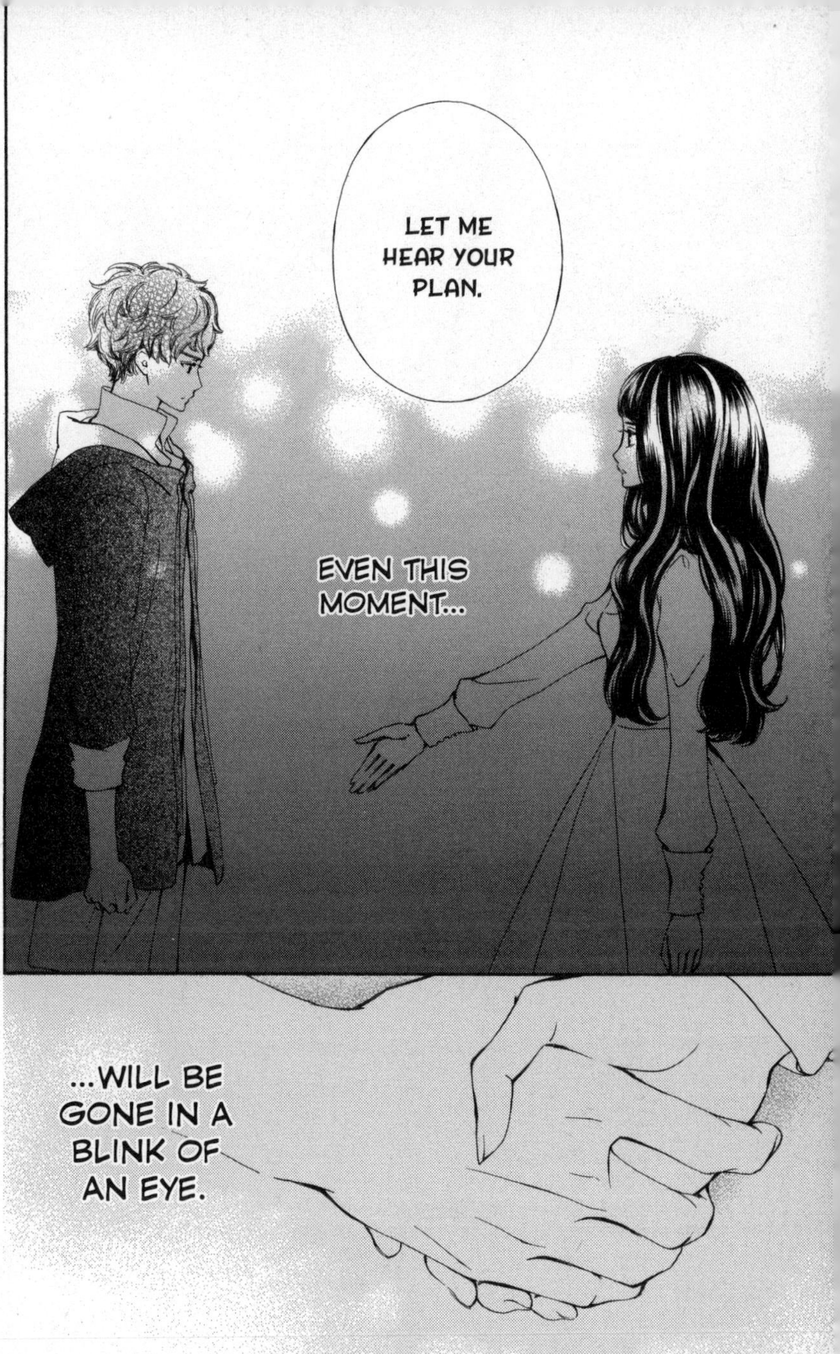
LET ME HEAR YOUR PLAN.
EVEN THIS MOMENT...
...WILL BE GONE IN A BLINK OF AN EYE.

REN'S HONEY/END

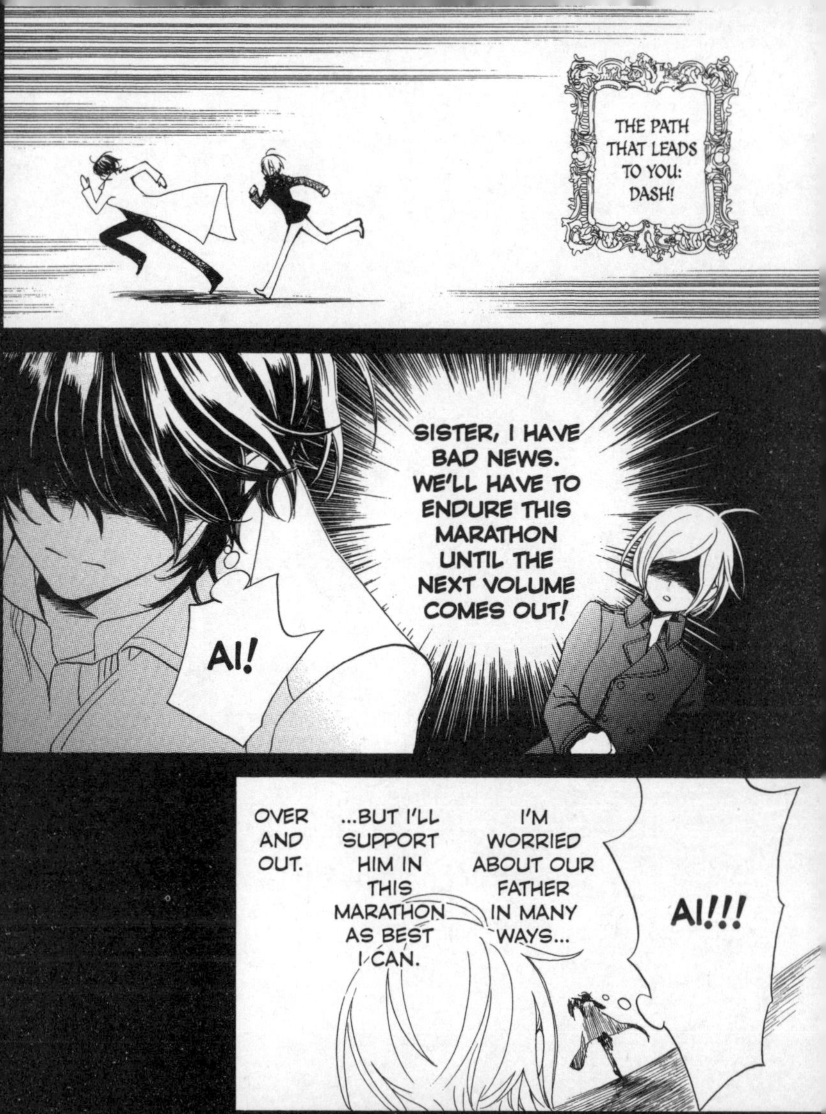
THE PATH THAT LEADS TO YOU: DASH!
SISTER, I HAVE BAD NEWS. WE'LL HAVE TO ENDURE THIS MARATHON UNTIL THE NEXT VOLUME COMES OUT!
AI!
AI!!!
I'M WORRIED ABOUT OUR FATHER IN MANY WAYS...
...BUT I'LL SUPPORT HIM IN THIS MARATHON AS BEST I CAN.
OVER AND OUT.

Thank you to my assistants and everyone who helped make volume 7 possible: O. Mio-sama, A. Ichiya-sama. And to all you readers, thank you very much from the bottom of my heart!

Hino

EDITOR'S NOTES

CHARACTERS

Matsuri Hino puts careful thought into the names of her characters in *Vampire Knight*. Below is the collection of characters throughout the manga. Each character's name is presented family name first, per the kanji reading.

黒主優姫

Cross Yuki

Yuki's last name, *Kurosu*, is the Japanese pronunciation of the English word "cross." However, the kanji has a different meaning—*kuro* means "black" and *su* means "master." Her first name is a combination of *yuu*, meaning "tender" or "kind," and *ki*, meaning "princess."

錐生零

Kiryu Zero

Zero's first name is the kanji for *rei*, meaning "zero." In his last name, *Kiryu*, the *ki* means "auger" or "drill" and the *ryu* means "life."

玖蘭枢

Kuran Kaname

Kaname means "hinge" or "door." The kanji for his last name is a combination of the old-fashioned way of writing *ku*, meaning "nine," and *ran*, meaning "orchid": "nine orchids."

藍堂英

Aido Hanabusa

Hanabusa means "petals of a flower." *Aido* means "indigo temple." In Japanese, the pronunciation of *Aido* is very close to the pronunciation of the English word *idol*.

架院暁

Kain Akatsuki

Akatsuki means "dawn" or "day-break." In *Kain*, *ka* is a base or support, while *in* denotes a building that has high fences around it, such as a temple or school.

早園瑠佳

Souen Ruka

In *Ruka*, the *ru* means "lapis lazuli"
while the *ka* means "good-looking"
or "beautiful." The *sou* in Ruka's
surname, *Souen*, means "early,"
but this kanji also has an obscure
meaning of "strong fragrance." The
en means "garden."

一条拓麻

Ichijo Takuma

Ichijo can mean a "ray" or
"streak." The kanji for *Takuma* is a
combination of *taku*, meaning "to
cultivate," and *ma*, which is the
kanji for *asa*, meaning "hemp" or
"flax," a plant with blue flowers.

支葵千里

Shiki Senri

Shiki's last name is a combination
of *shi*, meaning "to support," and *ki*,
meaning "mallow"—a flowering plant
with pink or white blossoms. The *ri* in
Senri is a traditional Japanese unit of
measure for distance, and one *ri* is
about 2.44 miles. *Senri* means "1,000 *ri*."

夜刈十牙

Yagari Toga

Yagari is a combination of *ya*, meaning "night," and *gari*, meaning "to harvest." *Toga* means "ten fangs."

一条麻遠, 一翁

Ichijo Asato, a.k.a. "Ichio"

Ichijo can mean a "ray" or "streak." Asato's first name is comprised of *asa*, meaning "hemp" or "flax," and *tou*, meaning "far-off." His nickname is *ichi*, or "one," combined with *ou*, which can be used as an honorific when referring to an older man.

若葉沙頼

Wakaba Sayori

Yori's full name is Sayori Wakaba. *Wakaba* means "young leaves." Her given name, *Sayori*, is a combination of *sa*, meaning "sand," and *yori*, meaning "trust."

星煉

Seiren

Sei means "star" and *ren* means "to smelt" or "to refine." *Ren* is also the same kanji used in *rengoku*, or "purgatory." Her previous name, *Hoshino*, uses the same kanji for "star" (*hoshi*) and *no*, which can mean "from" and is often used at the end of traditional female names.

遠矢莉磨

Toya Rima

Toya means a "far-reaching arrow." Rima's first name is a combination of *ri*, or "jasmine," and *ma*, which signifies enhancement by wearing away, such as by polishing or scouring.

紅まり亜

Kurenai Maria

Kurenai means "crimson." The kanji for the last *a* in Maria's first name is the same that is used in "Asia."

錐生壱縷

Kiryu Ichiru

Ichi is the old-fashioned way of writing "one," and *ru* means "thread." In *Kiryu*, the *ki* means "auger" or "drill" and the *ryu* means "life."

緋桜閑, 狂咲姫

Hio Shizuka, Kuruizaki-hime

Shizuka means "calm and quiet." In Shizuka's family name, *hi* is "scarlet" and *ou* is "cherry blossoms." Shizuka Hio is also referred to as the "Kuruizaki-hime." *Kuruizaki* means "flowers blooming out of season" and *hime* means "princess."

藍堂月子

Aido Tsukiko

Aido means "indigo temple." *Tsukiko* means "moon child."

白蔟更

Shirabuki Sara

Shira is "white" and *buki* is "butterbur," a plant with white flowers. *Sara* means "to renew."

黒主灰闇

Cross Kaien

Cross, or *Kurosu*, means "black master." *Kaien* is a combination of *kai*, meaning "ashes," and *en*, meaning "village gate." The kanji for *en* is also used for Enma, the ruler of the underworld in Buddhist mythology.

玖蘭李土

Kuran Rido

Kuran means "nine orchids." In *Rido*, *ri* means "plum" and *do* means "earth."

玖蘭樹里

Kuran Juri

Kuran means "nine orchids." In her first name, *ju* means "tree" and a *ri* is a traditional Japanese unit of measure for distance. The kanji for *ri* is the same as in Senri's name.

玖蘭悠

Kuran Haruka

Kuran means "nine orchids." *Haruka* means "distant" or "remote."

鷹宮海斗

Takamiya Kaito

Taka means "hawk" and *miya* means "imperial palace" or "shrine." *Kai* is "sea" and *to* means "to measure" or "grid."

菖藤依砂也

Shoto Isaya

Sho means "Siberian iris" and *to* is "wisteria." The *I* in *Isaya* means "to rely on" while the *sa* means "sand." *Ya* is a suffix used for emphasis.

橙茉

Toma

In the family name *Toma*, *to* means "Seville orange" and *ma* means "jasmine flower."

藍堂永路

Aido Nagamichi

The name *Nagamichi* is a combination of *naga*, which means "long" or "eternal," and *michi*, which is the kanji for "road" or "path." *Aido* means "indigo temple."

縹木

Hanadagi

In this family name, *hanada* means "bright light blue" and *gi* means "tree."

影山霞

Kageyama Kasumi

In the Class Rep's family name, *kage* means "shadow" and *yama* means "mountain." His first name, *Kasumi*, means "haze" or "mist."

愛

Ai

Ai means "love." It is used in terms of unconditional, unending love and affection.

恋

Ren

Ren means "love." It is used in terms of a romantic love or crush.

藍堂星夜

Aido Seiya

Aido means "indigo temple." *Sei* means "star" and *ya* means "night": "starry night."

Terms

-sama: The suffix *-sama* is used in formal address for someone who ranks higher in the social hierarchy. The vampires call their leader "Kaname-sama" only when they are among their own kind.

Matsuri Hino burst onto the manga scene with her title *Kono Yume ga Sametara* (When This Dream Is Over), which was published in *LaLa DX* magazine. Hino was a manga artist a mere nine months after she decided to become one.

With the success of her popular series *Captive Hearts*, *MeruPuri*, and *Vampire Knight*, Hino is a major player in the world of shojo manga.

Hino enjoys creative activities and has commented that she would have been either an architect or an apprentice to traditional Japanese craftsmasters if she had not become a manga artist.

VAMPIRE KNIGHT: MEMORIES
Vol. 7
Shojo Beat Edition

STORY AND ART BY
MATSURI HINO

Adaptation/Nancy Thistlethwaite
Translation/Tetsuichiro Miyaki
Touch-Up Art & Lettering/Inori Fukuda Trant
Graphic Design/Alice Lewis
Editor/Nancy Thistlethwaite

Vampire Knight memories by Matsuri Hino © Matsuri Hino 2021
All rights reserved. First published in Japan in 2021 by HAKUSENSHA,
Inc., Tokyo. English language translation rights arranged with
HAKUSENSHA, Inc., Tokyo.

The stories, characters, and incidents mentioned in this publication are
entirely fictional.

Printed in the U.S.A.

Published by VIZ Media, LLC
P.O. Box 77010
San Francisco, CA 94107

10 9 8 7 6 5 4 3 2 1
First printing, July 2022

viz.com

shojobeat.com

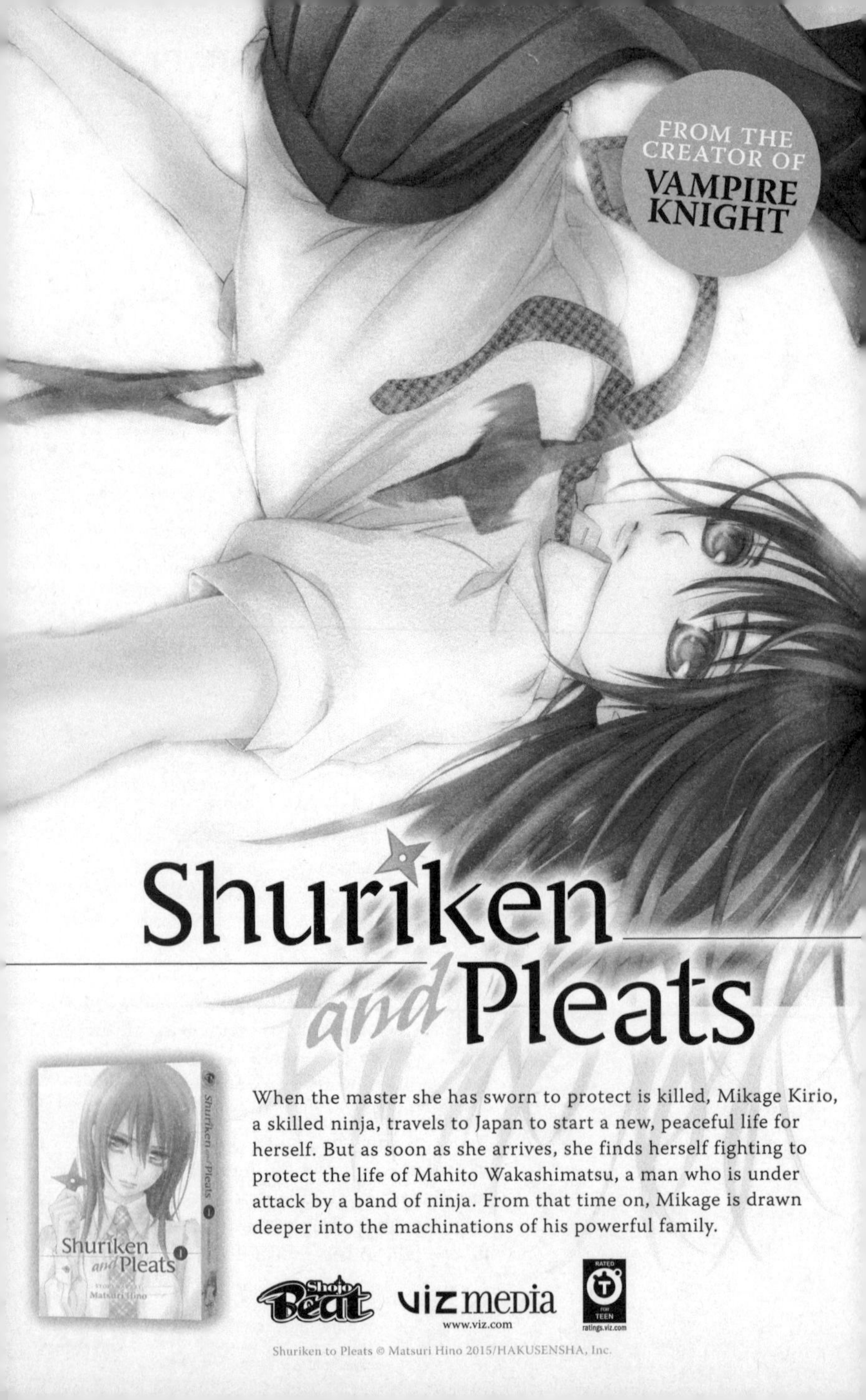
FROM THE CREATOR OF VAMPIRE KNIGHT
Shuriken and Pleats
When the master she has sworn to protect is killed, Mikage Kirio, a skilled ninja, travels to Japan to start a new, peaceful life for herself. But as soon as she arrives, she finds herself fighting to protect the life of Mahito Wakashimatsu, a man who is under attack by a band of ninja. From that time on, Mikage is drawn deeper into the machinations of his powerful family.
Shuriken and Pleats 1
Matsuri Hino
Shojo Beat
viz media
www.viz.com
RATED T FOR TEEN
ratings.viz.com
Shuriken to Pleats © Matsuri Hino 2015/HAKUSENSHA, Inc.

TO SAVE HER KINGDOM, A SIMPLE VILLAGE GIRL MUST LIVE A ROYAL LIE.

PRINCE Freya

Story and Art by KEIKO ISHIHARA

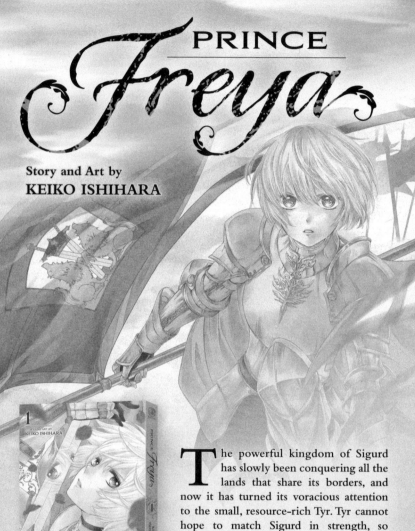

The powerful kingdom of Sigurd has slowly been conquering all the lands that share its borders, and now it has turned its voracious attention to the small, resource-rich Tyr. Tyr cannot hope to match Sigurd in strength, so in order to survive, it must rely on the intelligence, skill and cunning of its prince and his loyal knights. But should their prince fall, so too shall Tyr...

RATED T+ OLDER TEEN VIZ

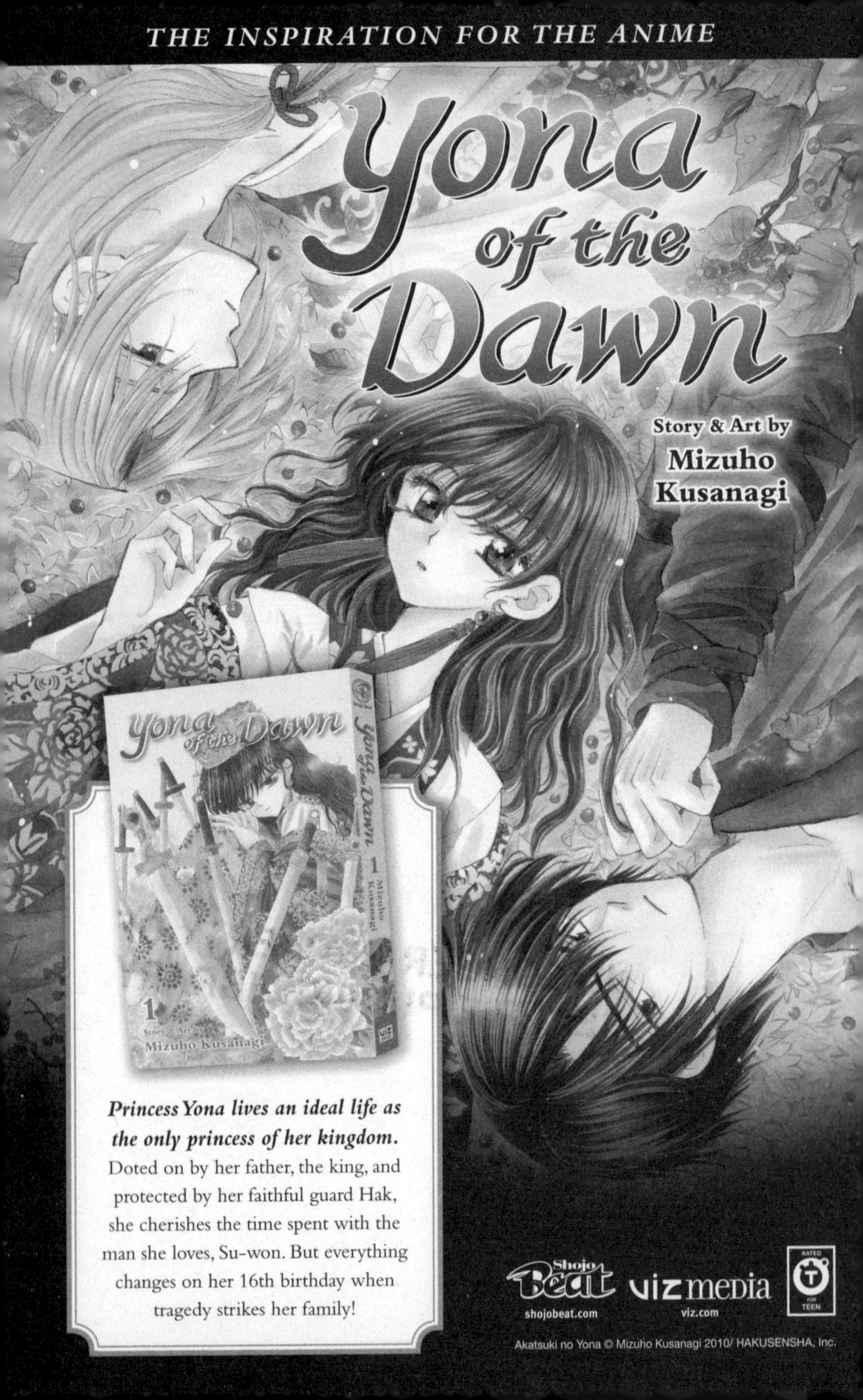
THE INSPIRATION FOR THE ANIME
Yona of the Dawn
Story & Art by Mizuho Kusanagi
Yona of the Dawn 1 Story & Art by Mizuho Kusanagi
Princess Yona lives an ideal life as the only princess of her kingdom.
Doted on by her father, the king, and protected by her faithful guard Hak, she cherishes the time spent with the man she loves, Su-won. But everything changes on her 16th birthday when tragedy strikes her family!
Shojo Beat
shojobeat.com
viz media
viz.com
RATED T FOR TEEN
Akatsuki no Yona © Mizuho Kusanagi 2010/ HAKUSENSHA, Inc.

SO-ATY-771

RECEIVED

OCT 0 8 2022

NO LONGER PROPERTY OF
SEATTLE PUBLIC LIBRARY

STOP!

You may be reading
the wrong way!

In keeping with the original Japanese comic format, this book reads from right to left—so word balloons, action, and sound effects and are reversed to preserve the orientation of the original artwork.

Check out the diagram shown here to get the hang of things, and then turn to the other side of the book to get started!

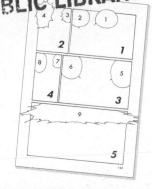